Michael Maukkelow
Stockholm
December 1995

Churches of Northern Europe in Profile

A Thousand years of Anglo-Nordic relations

LARS ÖSTERLIN

THE CANTERBURY PRESS
NORWICH

Cover Picture: Detail from Jacob Ulfsson's chasuble in Uppsala Cathedral; late 15th century embroidery by the school of Albertus 'Pictor', the famous painter of murals in chalk in the Churches of Härkeberga and Täby, not far from Stockholm. At the bottom of the picture Jacob Ulfsson, Archbishop of Uppsala, is seen kneeling before the picture of his predecessor, the English missionary, St Sigfrid (See Chapter 1).

Lars Österlin 1995

First published 1995 by The Canterbury Press Norwich
(a publishing imprint of Hymns Ancient & Modern Limited,
a registered charity)
St Mary's Works, St Mary's Plain,
Norwich, Norfolk, NR3 3RW

Swedish Original: Svenska Kyrkan i Profil. Ur engelskt och nordiskt perspektiv, Verbum, Stockholm, 1994.

The English edition of this book has been subsidised by the Thora Ohlsson Trust, Lund.

British Library Cataloguing in Publication Data

A catalogue record for this book is available from the British Library

ISBN 1-85311-128-7

*Typeset by Rowland Phototypesetting Limited,
Bury St Edmunds, Suffolk
and printed in Great Britain by
St Edmundsbury Press Limited,
Bury St Edmunds, Suffolk*

Contents

Foreword

by Rt Revd Stephen Sykes,
Bishop of Ely

One could not wish for a clearer or more skilful guide to the bewildering combination of similarities and differences between Anglican and Nordic Lutheran traditions. Professor Österlin, a major participant in recent Anglo–Scandinavian relationships, tells the fascinating story of contacts between the Churches going back more than a thousand years. This book will be essential reading for all who will now want to enter more wholeheartedly into the opportunities opened up by the Porvoo Common Declaration.

✠ Stephen Ely

CHAPTER 1

Mission from the West

IN THE BEGINNING

The earliest known description of a bishop celebrating mass in Sweden is to be found in the legend of St Sigfrid. It tells of an English bishop by that name who, around the year 1000, was working as a missionary in what is now known as Scandinavia.

The legend refers to a Swedish king, Olov. Still a heathen, and having heard of the arrival of an English missionary, he sent one of his men to observe the newcomer's conduct. The king's man thus came to witness a Christian service. The place was somewhere on the coast of southern Sweden, where the missionary and his retinue had just gone ashore. King Olov received the following report:

'First the man who led the service was bedecked in a purple cloak; and placed upon his head was a cap, adorned with gold and precious stones and crowned by two horns, bowing towards one other. He carried a staff of rare beauty. His assistants, too, were dressed in splendid garments. Then they began to sing a song, the like of which has never been heard. Then something happened, as everyone fell to their knees. Soon thereafter, I saw in the old man's hands a little boy-child who smiled up at him, and whom he placed upon the table and kissed upon the mouth.'

The report contains several details which prove that the St Sigfrid legend cannot have been written at the time in which it is set. For instance, the legend exists in several versions, and the description of St Sigfrid's mass appears in versions originating at Uppsala Cathedral, which points to a far later date – close to the end of the 13th century. Again, around the year 1000, when St Sigfrid was carrying

1

out his mission, bishops were not mitred in the way described here, and the concept of the miraculous transformation – the bread suddenly turning into a boy-child – is characteristic of the time after the Lateran Council of 1215.

And yet the story is remarkable, not only because it constitutes the first Swedish record – albeit written in the 13th century – of a bishop's vestments, the liturgical song and the central feature of the mass. It is no less interesting in that it presents us with an English missionary in this pioneer role – an Englishman who in the legend takes on truly great dimensions. In one version, clearly lacking historical accuracy, he is called the Archbishop of York. If one were to add up his activities in Sweden by taking all the versions into account, then they would appear to have been widespread indeed. The earlier versions locate his missionary centre in southern Småland, where he is said to have had as his assistants three 'nephews' – all of whom died as martyrs. It is in that area that the Diocese of Växjö, which he is said to have founded, lies. It is frequently referred to as 'the Diocese of St Sigfrid', and the diocesan arms still show the English missionary bishop, carrying the heads of his three murdered 'nephews'. The later versions of the legend extend his role to cover the whole nation, but he is above all associated with Sigtuna, a place which, before the establishment of an episcopal see at Uppsala, was a most important church centre. On those grounds he could be viewed as the first Archbishop of Uppsala, albeit prior to there being any corresponding see. According to these versions of the legend, King Olov summoned Sigfrid, and was subsequently christened by him. But this is supposed to have taken place in Husaby, in Västergötland – to which King Olov would have fled, away from the rather more heathen areas around Sigtuna. It would then be to Husaby, to what was to become the Diocese of Skara, that Sweden could trace its first king to convert to the Christian faith – thanks to an English bishop.

The historical kernel of these various stories is a little less comprehensive and glamorous. Once the successive

2

layers of legend have been peeled away, we are left with a few plain facts. At the beginning of the eleventh century, a bishop arrived in Sweden via Norway; his name was Sigfrid and his country England; he worked as a missionary in Västergötland and in Värend, southern Småland. To this much the contemporary German historian, Adam of Bremen, has testified. But the historical truth, however plain, is interesting in itself – as is, of course, the fact that it was an English missionary – Sigfrid – who came to be perceived as such an impressive figure. This could hardly have happened had there not been an underlying awareness of the importance of the Anglo-Saxon Church in the Christianization of Sweden, indeed of all the Nordic countries.

The later versions of St Sigfrid's legend present this English missionary as the 'national' Bishop of Sweden, a claim for which we have more than legendary proof: Among the medieval vestments of Uppsala Cathedral is a chasuble, which was probably made for one of the late medieval Archbishops, Jacob Ulfsson. Its embroidery shows the Archbishop kneeling in front of a picture of St Sigfrid, who is dressed in full episcopal vestments, holding his characteristic attributes. The Archbishop of Uppsala, in the late Middle Ages, considered himself the successor of St Sigfrid's Chair, and the Feast of St Sigfrid was kept as a major 'red-letter-day' in the diocesan calender.

As the Nordic countries were united at this time in a more or less continuous personal union under one monarch, so the Sigfrid legend had ample room to expand. A chapel was dedicated to Sigfrid in Roskilde Cathedral, the prestigious royal shrine of the Danes. In Norway, St Sigfrid was associated with King Olav Tryggvason. In our own century a statue of St Sigfrid by Gustav Vigeland has been added to the west front of Trondheim Cathedral. St Sigfrid's name is also associated with Turku Cathedral, Finland.

The Englishman Sigfrid came to exert a unifying power over these Nordic countries. It is clear that he was given

St Sigfrid. 15th century wall painting in Vendel church in the county of Uppland, Sweden. Sigfrid, in pontificals with, as his attributes, the heads of three 'nephews'. *Photograph: ATA*

symbolic status. That this should have been bestowed upon a missionary of the Anglo-Saxon Church is significant. Over the centuries – together with others whom we know by name and yet others who remain anonymous – Sigfrid came to personify the important initial stage of Anglo-Scandinavian ecclesiastical connections.

ST ANSGAR'S MISSION IN THE NORTH

It is a well-known fact that the Christian mission reached the Nordic countries along a variety of routes. One followed the sea passage from the West, i.e. from the British Isles; another from the East had its starting point in Byzantium. But the shortest route was from the South – from the European mainland – and the written sources tell us that the earliest missionaries came from there. Ansgar, a Benedictine monk, is mentioned as the very first, and is known to us as 'The Apostle of the North'.

To begin with, Ansgar worked in the kingdom of the Danes in southern Jutland, in the area that now forms the border between present-day Denmark and Germany. This was an area of strategic settlements, serving the trade-routes between West and East. From here, Ansgar set off by sea to the land of the Swedes. In the trading city of Birka, he founded the first Christian community in what is now Sweden. Following the archaeological discovery of an island settlement in Lake Mälaren, Birka is thought to have been located on the island of Björkö.

Ansgar's earliest missionary travels in Scandinavia took place in the 820s. He was later appointed Archbishop of Hamburg, with continued responsibilities for the Northern mission. Following the sack of Hamburg by the Vikings, the archiepiscopal see was moved to Bremen. In the year of 852, Ansgar again visited Birka, where the young church was showing signs of faltering. The not very significant results of his missionary activities in the North did not survive him long, except in Ribe, on the western coast of

5

Jutland – now an idyllic little town with a dignified Romanesque cathedral, built long after his death. Ansgar's lasting achievement was the foundation of the Archbishopric of Hamburg-Bremen, with its responsibility for continued missionary work in the Nordic countries – a responsibility not to be shirked by his successors of later centuries.

Ansgar's place in Nordic church-history is well documented, not least in a remarkable wealth of written source-material – unique in the history of this period – acquainting readers both with the man and his successors. Not only do we have a special biography of St Ansgar, the *Vita Ansgarii*, written by his successor, Archbishop Rimbert, but there is also the extensive survey of the Archbishops of Hamburg-Bremen and their work, the so-called *Gesta*, written in the 1060s by Master Adam, a tutor at the Cathedral School of Bremen. Adam was well versed in his subject, having, for example, had a personal audience with the Danish King, Sven Estridsen, the nephew of Canute the Great. In addition, official documents written by Ansgar in his archiepiscopal capacity survive. The picture of 'the Apostle of the North' that these sources combine to produce is quite impressive. He appears to have been an important man, and most tenacious of purpose in the area of church politics, who at the same time displayed the ascetic and pious ideals of his time.

Ansgar undertook his Nordic mission as an envoy of the Frankish Imperial Court. One of the motives behind the expansion of the Church was, of course, political. Charlemagne's empire had been successively enlarged eastwards, and the extension of ecclesiastical and of secular-political power had proceeded hand in hand. With regard to the Nordic peoples, however, this twofold end was never achieved; the Nordic countries were never incorporated into the Holy Roman Empire. The original Roman Empire had also failed in this respect – a fact which distinguishes the Nordic countries from England. It was of decisive importance to the history of the Nordic peoples that the Holy Roman Empire was halted on the shores of the Baltic.

As the Nordic peoples were never integrated with their neighbours on the European mainland, so their development has in many respects remained independent.

The relationship between the Frankish realm and the peoples of the North, initiated by St Ansgar, was not, however, without consequences. From it important features of Nordic church life can be traced in subsequent centuries – features originating in the rich spiritual culture of the Carolingian lands. We can see this influence in literary church tradition, as well as in ecclesiastical organization. The power exercised by the Carolingian Emperor was exercised over completely integrated secular and spiritual authorities. On this ground a uniform church culture would develop throughout the Middle Ages.

Ansgar belonged to a monastery at Corbie, in what is now Picardy, France, but was transferred from there to Corvey, by the river Weser – to a newly founded monastery which also served as an eastern Frankish outpost. Charlemagne had now been succeeded by his son, Louis, called 'the Pious' in recognition of his contribution to church life. The monastic buildings at Corvey are preserved, though transformed into a vast baroque palace. The abbey church itself is typically Carolingian, and remains intact from Ansgar's days. Its western part is a majestic 'west-work', with an entrance hall (*nartex*) and, above it, a gallery reserved for the imperial throne. In this respect the church at Corvey and the famous imperial church at Aachen, where Charlemagne's own gallery and throne face the altar, are companion pieces. It is symptomatic of the Carolingian mission to the Nordic countries that it came from Corvey, where theocratic thinking had so conspicuously found expression in the very architecture of its churches. Once the kings of the Nordic countries had been won over to Christianity, it did not take them long to assimilate mainland fashion. A 'national church' tradition has existed in the Nordic churches from their very beginnings – and its expression in church architecture came to include the royal gallery (in the manner of the imperial court churches) to

7

the west, in symmetry with the altar to the east. The oldest surviving Nordic cathedral, in Dalby, not far from Lund – nowadays reduced in size and serving as the parish church – still contains the Carolingian entrance hall and royal gallery, and there are further such examples in other parts of Scandinavia. One of the most beautiful churches of this kind stands in Fjennesløv, Zealand. It was erected not by a king, but by one of the Danish kingdom's most distinguished aristocratic families.

The history of the Christianization of the Nordic peoples begins, then, against the background of the Frankish realm, the Carolingian renaissance and Ansgar's see at Bremen. But St Ansgar's missionary work in the North amounts to no more than an isolated episode, however much the archbishops, his successors, deemed it fundamental and binding. Even before Ansgar's death, political reality had made it impossible for his North German church to continue his Nordic work.

Ansgar died in the year 865. Louis the Pious, his employer as a missionary, was long since dead, his kingdom divided and in increasingly serious disarray. During the second half of the ninth century the initiative with regard to the peoples of the North did not lie with the mainland powers. On the contrary, it was now the turn of the Vikings to have the political upper hand. They ruled the waves, they laid siege to Paris, and to their chieftains was surrendered the earldom of Normandy. Towards the end of the 900s, Otto the Great and his sons were to emerge – but by then a century had passed since Ansgar's days.

Around the Middle of the eleventh century, hardly sooner, came a period of purposeful missionary strategy, instigated by Adalbert, a great prince of the Church and Ansgar's then successor as Archbishop of Bremen. It was during his time that Master Adam wrote the *Gesta* of the archbishops. Adalbert was keenly interested in relations with the Nordic countries, but he was also involved in the power struggles between Emperor and Pope which eventu-

ally resulted in his own downfall. This occurred in 1066 –
an easily remembered date, especially by the English, as
the year of William the Conqueror's victory at the Battle
of Hastings.

THE WORLD OF THE VIKINGS –
THE WORLD OF MISSION

A great deal of what occurred during the span covering the
Christianization of the Nordic peoples is lost in the mists
of time, and will most likely so remain. As is the case with
large slices of history, including that of our own Continent,
there is much that we may never know with any certainty.
This is especially frustrating in matters as fundamental as
the origin of nations and the transformation of national
culture through the thinking and organization of the
Church. Still, the general picture of this massive chain of
events is reasonably clear, and research and analysis over
the last decades have made it considerably more distinct
and credible.

It should be stressed, right at the start, that the events
leading to the Christianization of the North unfolded over
a very long span of time. The Nordic peoples were in truth
slow to convert – the Swedes and the Finns even more so
than the Danes and the Norwegians. In order to understand
this process which took several hundred years, we need first
to understand the situation in contemporary Europe and
the part played by the North in its political manoeuvres
and communications.

The period in question is pretty much the one we Scandinavians refer to as the age of the Vikings. Their story has
always held a certain fascination – well beyond our own
borders and not least in Great Britain – which shows no sign
of diminishing. Feelings of admiration mixed with terror
have found their expression in literature and other art forms,
frequently in a highly romanticized way. The year of 793 is
the one generally chosen to mark the beginning of this era –

9

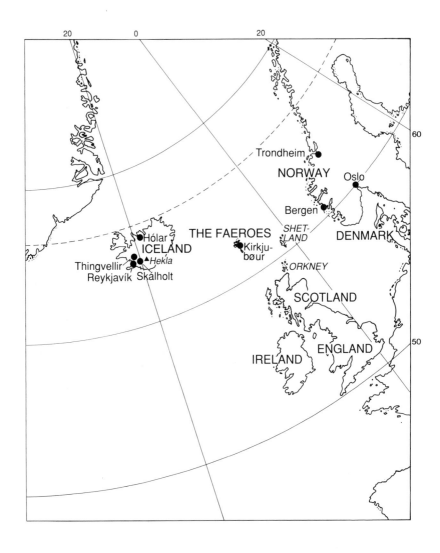

Map of North-Western Europe, showing Ireland and Great Britain, the North Atlantic Islands and Western Scandinavia, which form a single geographic area. From the catalogue to the exhibition 'From Viking to Crusader', published by the Nordic Council of Ministers in collaboration with the Council of Europe. *Cartographer: Jörgen Myrman-Lund.*

10

this being the date of a merciless attack by the Vikings on the monastery on Lindisfarne, an island off the Northumberland coast. Shortly thereafter they sacked Iona, the venerable centre of the Celtic Church off the west coast of Scotland. As is well known, the time that followed was to be marked by the Vikings' brutal raids in Western Europe. These appalling acts of violence continued during the Carolingian epoch and prompted various efforts to defuse Viking aggression through, for example, the work of the missionaries.

These numerous events, infamous though they are, should not be allowed to darken totally our view of the early Viking age. This era in Nordic history has to be seen as a part of the overall European picture, not least when it comes to tracing the sequences of steps that led to the Christianization of the Nordic peoples. We must not think that their countries were at this time isolated from the rest of the known world, or were poorer, or of a more primitive culture than that of their neighbours. As early as Roman times, links between the Romans and the Germanic peoples were extensive. As we move on to the eighth and ninth centuries, i.e. to the early Viking age, an interesting picture develops – of trade connections, exchange of capital, and cultural exchange – in all of which the Nordic countries played a large part. The Vikings harvested great riches from the East: in exchange for costly furs, a wealth of silver and silk was brought home from the Islamic world via Russia, to be used in trade with Western Europe. The blocking, after the Islamic conquests, of East-West links serving the Mediterranean ports explains why European trade took the otherwise roundabout route via the North. The Nordic countries were certainly not isolated, and can hardly be considered poor. They made up a central part of a cohesive Northern European region, with the British and North Atlantic Isles to the West and the Russian rivers to the East, held together by the nautical trade routes. One might compare it to *Græcia Magna* of antiquity, similarly united by much-used maritime links.

*　　*　　*

The Nordic seafarers are commonly thought to have been pirates – primitive and wild. That is how they have been portrayed, not without justification, by monastic chroniclers keeping track of those rampageous forays. It has to be said, however, that such expeditions far and wide presupposed considerable economic resources and notable organizational talent, as well as a substantial knowledge of ship-building and navigation. It does not, of course, follow from the well documented Viking ruthlessness on a great number of occasions that they could not, on other occasions, have travelled in peaceful pursuit of trade – or, as the results of modern research show, in search of pastures new, there to settle for generations to come. It is against this background, that we must understand the Christianization of the Nordic peoples.

Vikings arriving in the East had the opportunity of experiencing the Christian religion as practised in Byzantium. This had its consequences, though not especially extensive ones, in their homelands. A fascinating thought: did the Swedes and Finns of the Viking age behold and marvel at the holy magnificence of Byzantine liturgy, as did the Grand Duke Vladimir's envoys to Constantinople, where one of them, according to the Nestor Chronicles, exclaimed 'We did not know whether we were in heaven or on the earth. It would be impossible to find on earth any splendour greater than this.' Did the Nordic Vikings once use similar terms to describe their experience of the Orthodox liturgy? And did Byzantine monks and priests accompany them on their way home to Finland and Sweden? There is very little concrete evidence for this – but there is some, and more will most likely be unearthed. The archaeological excavations at Sigtuna in 1988–1990 yielded a rich collection of ecclesiastical objects from approximately the year 1000, such as a crucifix and cross-shaped pendants, of a kind indicating established dealings with the Eastern Church and Byzantium. Recent excavations in the centre of Lund have further uncovered a magnificent eleventh century processional cross, identified as crafted in Byzantium.

However, the overwhelming influence of the Christian Church on the Vikings of the North came from the islands to the West. It spread most widely among the Danes and Norwegians and, as time went by, reached the peoples who, a little further eastwards, were beginning to form themselves into the Swedish-Finnish realm. In the tenth and eleventh centuries, the strongest Christian influence on all the Nordic countries came, then, from the West – and not only by isolated contributions from visiting missionaries, but by continuous and widespread influence. Generations of peoples were in constant touch with one another through commerce and shipping – indeed, lived as neighbours in the same areas and the same towns in the British Isles and Ireland and on other islands in the North Atlantic.

It is not primarily from narrative sources that we know the extent of the Nordic settlements in the West, but rather from archaeology and the study of linguistics and place-names. The foundations for work in this area were laid by Eilert Ekvall, professor at Lund University and author of *The Concise Oxford Dictionary of English Place-Names* (1936, and several subsequent editions). It is above all the very large number of place-names ending in *-by* or *-thorp* that testifies to the existence of Nordic settlements.There were such settlements in England as early as the 870s. In subsequent centuries, Norwegians and Danes arrived in ever greater numbers – taking over established arable land, or cultivating previously barren ground. It is, of course, difficult to gauge the proportion of immigrants to already established residents, but the Viking stamp on so many place-names speaks clearly of their influence. Archaeological findings and land surveys – especially the *Domesday Book* – complement the research into place-names. The most intensive occupation was that of the Danes, covering almost all of the area north of a line between London and Chester – an area known as 'the Danelaw'. The Nordic

13

immigrants did not restrict themselves to rural areas. Important cities, founded in Roman times, became considerable trading centres for the Vikings too. The archiepiscopal city of York was certainly no exception. Recently, archaeologists have been able to identify a large area of this city as the town the Vikings called Jorvik, a lively impression of which can be gained from a visit to the Viking Museum there.

Living in England soon brought generations of Vikings into contact with the Anglo-Saxon Church, and many were converted to Christianity. Christian stone crosses of Celtic-Nordic design within the Danelaw bear witness to this. There is also clear evidence that the Christian form of burial was rapidly adopted, and Old English (ie not Old German) ecclesiastical terms were brought back home by returning Northerners. These remain in use in Danish, Norwegian and Swedish. (Naturally, their root is frequently a Latin loan-word.) The Swedish word for chalice is *kalk*, from the Old English word *calic* or the middle English word *calc*, and the word for confession is *skriftermål* or *skrift*, from the Old English word *scrift*. It is clear that it was in England that the Vikings became acquainted with the Christian practices denoted by these terms, and that both words and practices came to the Nordic countries from the Anglo-Saxon Christian world.

It is impossible, today, to trace this movement in any detail. We are unlikely to find the right answers to very many of the questions that present themselves. Was there constant traffic in both directions between the British Isles and the Nordic countries – within families, maybe, with some members living in England, Scotland or Ireland and others having remained in the old country? Were missionaries to the North chosen from among people originating from those parts? Were language barriers between Old English and the North-Germanic dialects relatively easy to overcome, and might some of the missionaries have been Anglo-Saxons? Imagination can suggest some answers. When legend names St Sigfrid as the first Archbishop of York, we must of course

14

on his behalf decline that title – but he may still have come from York. Would he then have belonged to the community of Jorvik, and would this have been where he received his missionary calling and consecration?

The huge numbers of archaeological finds in Scandinavia, dating from the age of the Vikings, have yielded many artefacts in precious metals – pointing to frequent traffic with the western islands. These objects reveal how inspiration from Ireland and the North of England carried over to the Nordic countries. There it was successfully transformed into a Nordic style in its own right – as witness many objects with Christian motifs from the eighth century and onwards, found in excavations in Scandinavia.

There are places where the archaeological material points especially clearly to international connections and Christian influence. Such a place is Sigtuna. By about the year 1000, Sigtuna had become a centre in the lands of the Swedes. (As yet, there was no united kingdom of Sweden.) The latest excavations have pin-pointed the location, at the very heart of this city, of a royal homestead. Here resided a king named Olov. In other sources we find this same Olov as King of Västergötland, where he is said to have been christened by the English missionary, Sigfrid (see above, p 2). This would appear rather less than certain. On the other hand, there is definite archaeological proof that King Olov had a Royal Mint at Sigtuna, and that the pattern used for his coins came from two sources: England and Byzantium. The Byzantine coins, copied by King Olov and found – though only in very small numbers – in Sigtuna, were minted for the two co-regents, the Emperors Basileios II and Konstantinos VIII. The English, or English-inspired, coins – of which a great many have come to light – were minted for (or meant to resemble coins minted for) Ethelred II, 'the Unready', Regent (978–1016). Ethelred was the king most exposed to Viking attacks, and his widow, Emma, was to become the Queen of King Canute. Large numbers of Ethelred coins have been found in the Nordic countries – to date close on three thousand. All bear the Christian cross. Of those minted in Sigtuna, some carry the inscription *Si Dei*, assumed to mean 'God's Sigtuna'.

Sigtuna was strategically well placed to keep secure the rich lands around Lake Mälaren, including the seat of a king and, without a doubt, also the seat of a bishop under the king's protection. (Uppsala, situated a little further north, was still a heathen cult centre.) Excavations have been able to map a large part of eleventh century Sigtuna. The town is laid out in many ways like York and Dublin or, in Scandinavia, Trondheim and Oslo. The ruins of several of Sigtuna's early churches still remain to fascinate us. Interpretations of their architectural origins are not uniform. But it seems possible to establish, firstly, that they were founded soon after the middle of the eleventh century; secondly, that they were built in a style combining Anglo-Saxon and Norman features. This would correspond with the evidence of church buildings of the same period in other places in Scandinavia, e.g. in Lund, a city which at that time belonged to Denmark.

The Anglo-Saxon influence on the earliest Nordic church history was to dominate until the beginning of the eleventh century, but by no means ended there. By the middle of that century, the ambitions of the Archbishop of Bremen to incorporate more firmly the growing church life in the Nordic countries with the North-German church province increased greatly. This expressed itself, above all, in steps aimed at greater organization. The English missionary bishops led a wandering existence as part of the King's entourage. Bremen now made the diocesan boundaries more fixed. Denmark, where Bremen's influence was great, was at the forefront of this ecclesiastical development. But the missionary foundations for this too had been laid by the Anglo-Saxon Church. Northern Europe in the eleventh century remained a distinct region, held together by maritime communications. Furthermore, the royal families of the various realms within this region tended to be allies and to intermarry : the English Royal House with members of the Danish Royal House, or with the Dukes of Normandy or with Norwegian Kings; and the Swedish Royal House with the Slav princes who reigned by the Baltic Sea.

In this context, the familiar events and personalities from the written sources fall into place. And this shows even more clearly where the decisive influences and the greatest efforts towards the conversion of the Nordic peoples to Christianity came from. How the first Christian Kings in Norway encountered the Christian faith in England is dramatically recalled in great detail in the Icelandic sagas. Olav Tryggvason, the most glamorous Nordic King of Vikings, converted to Christianity in England. Previously he and Sweyn Forkbeard together had attacked London with their long-ships and forced King Ethelred to a costly and humiliating defeat. The Christian mission flourished under King Olav, not only in Norway but also on the North-Atlantic Islands. The sagas ensure that the king's contributions somewhat overshadow any previous achievements by missionaries and through frequent contacts with England. The conversion of the king was the official manifestation of the long prepared change of religion.

Olav Tryggvason was succeeded by Olav Haraldsson, who was to become the patron saint not only of Norway, but of all the Nordic countries. In London, even, there were in the Middle Ages no fewer than four churches dedicated to St Olav. As a Viking general, Olav was a heathen. He conquered Canterbury in 1011, and it was his men who murdered Archbishop Alphege, when the English had shown reluctance to pay a ransom. He was baptized, probably in France, and returned to Norway accompanied by Anglo-Saxon missionaries. In the end, Olav was deprived of his kingdom by his Danish neighbour Canute – and of his life at the Battle of Stiklastad. His relics were placed in Trondheim Cathedral, which thus became one of the most important medieval pilgrimage shrines in Northern Europe.

In Denmark, the official conversion to Christianity had occurred slightly earlier, in the 980s. King Harald Gormsson, often called Blue-tooth, marked the occasion by erecting, at Jelling in southern Jutland, a monument consisting of two massive runestones. One of them bears an inscription, stating that it was King Harald 'who made Christians of the Danes'. The following two kings, Sweyn Forkbeard and Canute, were, as we know, only too interested in England. The Danish-English kingdom formed by Canute by uniting the greater part of England with Denmark included what is now Southern Sweden and Norway. It is hardly surprising that the Anglo-Saxon Church enjoyed a truly great influence in this gigantic Viking Empire. King Canute reigned over his empire from England, where he held court with his English Queen, Emma – and where he found his final resting-place in Winchester Cathedral. During his reign three men were appointed bishops in Denmark: Gerbrand of Roskilde, Bernhard of Skåne and Reginbert of the Island of Funen. All three were consecrated in England. Odinkar, who was to become Bishop of Ribe, was called to England by King Canute, and also sent to France, in order that he might receive a fitting education.

A LASTING INFLUENCE

The Anglo-Saxon mission in the North appears to have culminated soon after the momentous year of 1066. This was the year in which Adalbert, the power-hungry Archbishop of Bremen, was deposed – which explains the diminished activity from that quarter. There was, in contrast, no decline in missionary efforts among the Nordic peoples from the English side, despite the Norman invasion of that very year. On the contrary, this prompted a wave of refugees to seek sanctuary in Scandinavia. Among them, to be sure, would have been bishops and priests removed from office by William the Conqueror.

Certainly, one notes the Archbishop of Bremen's deter-

18

One of the two Jelling runestones. (See text, p.18.) *Below the figure of the crucified Christ, the proud concluding words of Harald Blue-Tooth's inscription read: '...and made Christians of the Danes'. Photograph: The National Museum, Copenhagen.*

19

mined hand in several appointments of Swedish bishops throughout the eleventh century – in Sigtuna, for instance, and especially in Skara, the earliest Swedish diocese. But the missionaries – of whom we know something, and who throw light upon this otherwise rather obscure early phase of mission – came from the English Church. One of these was David who came to the Nordic countries after the Norman invasion. He is inseparably connected with Munktorp in Västmanland, north-west of Lake Mälaren, where he is still revered as the apostle of Västmanland and as the patron saint of the Diocese of Västerås. David is said to have been an abbot, probably belonging to the Cistercian Order, and to have overseen a small community at Munktorp. After his death Munktorp became a place of pilgrimage, and his church has been extended considerably over the years. The earliest part of it, 'St David's Church', shows English features.

Bishop Eskil, a contemporary of David's and a fellow Englishman, was martyred as a missionary in what became the Diocese of Strängnäs, on the southern shore of Lake Mälaren. Strängnäs is the place where he died, Tuna (or *Eskil's Tuna*) the place where he is buried. Eskil had gained the support of a Christian king, Inge, but later fell victim to a heathen reaction under another minor king, Blotsven. Eskil was stoned to death. Only a few decades thereafter, his life and martyrdom were described in a report written by the English monk Aelnoth, who was then working in Odense, Denmark. Eskil was revered as a saint all through the Middle Ages, and sculptures of him can still be found in many of Central Sweden's churches.

The source material that tells of the Nordic missionaries of the eleventh century are exceptionally scarce, and have been exploited to their uttermost. This is not least the case with the sparse references to the English-born Bishop Osmund, mentioned by Master Adam. What little there is tells us that Osmund visited a king of the Swedes named Emund, 'the Old', the son of a king named Olov Skötkonung; that he won further conversions for Christianity;

and that he was 'headless'. This term probably refers to Osmund's independence of the Archbishop of Bremen who (according to Adam) should have been Osmund's true 'head'. There has been much speculation about the 'headless' Osmund. One school of thought argues that Osmund would have received his consecration in one of the eastern countries, perhaps in what is now Poland, and therefore within the Orthodox Church. His work in Sweden, in and around the time of Emund , would have been carried out in the area now covered by the Diocese of Uppsala, namely Uppland, and possibly in Gästrikland. He has been identified as the *Osmundus e Suedia* whose body was buried in Ely Cathedral in the year of 1070, and it is therefore assumed that he returned to England towards the end of his life.

The continuous influence of the Anglo-Saxon Church throughout the tenth and eleventh centuries certainly made a deep and lasting impression on the Nordic churches of the Middle Ages. Due to insufficient source material and also because of its universal character, lacking any particular Anglo-Saxon or other European peculiarities, it is difficult to show the exact extent and details of the imports into Nordic church life at this time. It has, for example, been claimed that the division into parishes – the very core of a national church structure – was introduced into the Nordic countries through influences from the British Isles. This claim is, of course, altogether credible and, if true, also highly significant. But it has to be said that the church provinces of the European mainland were similarly structured.

With regard to worship, the shape of the church year and liturgical traditions – areas where the various churches had their own individual features – it has nevertheless been possible to assess the extent of the Anglo-Saxon inheritance. Research into liturgy has greatly enlarged our knowledge in this respect.

In order to find this out, scholars have had to undertake much painstaking and detailed work, mostly for technical

St John the Baptist and St David, patron saints of Västerås Cathedral. Bas-relief in stone on the west front of the Cathedral. *Photograph: ATA.*

22

reasons. The entire liturgical libraries of the Nordic churches became redundant at the Reformation. What happened to all these precious volumes of vellum manuscripts? They were gathered in and used as 'suitable' material for binding the accounts of the central state administration and similar documents. Although preserved, much intricate and delicate work has been needed in order to trace these strips of vellum and to put together, piece by piece, the pages from which the liturgical life of the Middle Ages again begin to emerge in all its variety and richness.

This piecing together of fragments from the Middle Ages has been done over many years – since the beginning of this century – and the results have been most interesting. In Norway, the medieval scholar Lilli Gjerløw has succeeded in reconstructing liturgical books belonging to the archiepiscopal see of Trondheim (Nidaros). She has been able to demonstrate how greatly these depended on the models provided by the English, although these in turn were part of the liturgical tradition of the Cluny Reform.

In the search for clues to the British influence among the Nordic peoples, some interesting observations have been made by the English historian and theologian, Dr John Toy, Canon of York Minster. He studied the fragments to assess the extent to which British saints are mentioned and depicted within the Nordic liturgical tradition, in so far as this can be established from the martyrologies and litanies, calenders, missals and breviaries. He concludes that 'there was an extensive influence from England on the Northern liturgical tradition, particularly in the early period, up to c.1300'. This influence penetrated so deeply that it remained even during the twelfth and thirteenth centuries, when the Nordic churches had more contact with mainland Europe than with England. The most beloved of the British saints lived on in memory, sometimes more so in that of the Nordic peoples than in that of their country of birth. The cult of St Bothulph is a good example of this. After St Bothulph, the Irish Abbess Brigida appears most frequently in the Nordic material – the Swedish St Birgitta was named after her. Others are St Alban, St Cuthbert, whose cult continued throughout the Middle Ages, St Augustine, the first Archbishop of Canterbury, and the two kings who became national saints, Edmund and Oswald. In later times, certainly, Thomas Becket's memory shone the brightest – but so it did, of course, all over Christian Europe. In the Nordic material, the influence of the English Church is most striking before 1066. We should add that the Anglo-Saxon missionaries who worked in the Nordic countries were also well remembered: St David, St Eskil and not least St Sigfrid. Over long stretches of time St Ansgar, the pioneer in Denmark and Sweden, was relegated to a place in their shadow.

The reconstructed liturgical material provides evidence in other areas, too. Interesting discoveries have been made in the study of diocesan manuals, i.e. handbooks providing the rituals for weddings, funerals, etc. The Swedish scholar Hilding Johansson has written a thesis on the tradition of the *Manuals*, in which he analyses the form for visiting the sick and that for extreme unction, both of which he establishes as derived from the practices of the English missionaries. These manuscripts undeniably bring the reader marvellous close-ups of the life and work of the Nordic church of almost a thousand years ago. The liturgical fragments reveal the means used by the missionaries in their work, through which the Swedish Church was gradually established. Other manuals refer to prayers for farmers working the land, for blessing the bread and for blessing a new hearth and home. Most of this material, and especially that from the lands around Lake Mälaren, describe the Anglo-Saxon church tradition. It includes the 'Ordeals', i.e. the supposedly religious or magical rites performed by the priest in the name of justice, to determine the guilt or innocence of an accused party. This clearly refers back to an old English practice, brought over by the missionaries. The Diocese of Linköping, where the German influence was dominant, was an exception.

In this way it has been possible, albeit in glimpses, to

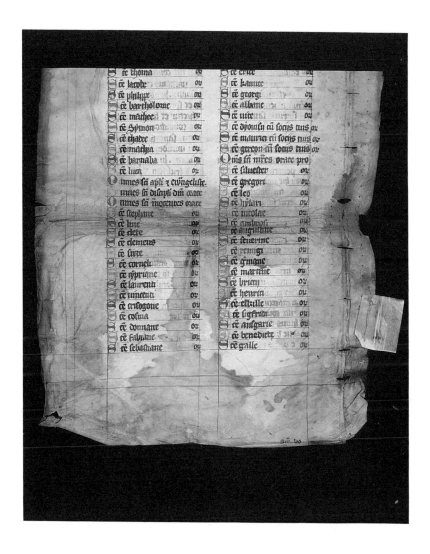

Vellum fragment from a 15th century Swedish missal, showing part of a litany. Among the saints listed (with their Latin names) are – bottom right and above Ansgar – the English missionaries Henrik, Eskil and Sigfrid. *Photograph: The State Archives, Stockholm; from the book 'Helgerånet'.*

25

discover and follow, right from the initial stages, the Nordic peoples' adoption of the Christian faith and liturgical tradition – and to establish, as the dominant influence, that of the Anglo-Saxon Church.

It would be intriguing to know what it was about this Church that appealed so strongly to the Nordic peoples. Part of the answer must be that the Anglo-Saxon culture was in its 'Golden Age'; that its Church was characterized by a great missionary zeal; and that the image of Christ it presented was highly attractive to Northerners: Christ the Hero, and a mighty King. The cross was at the centre – not always the empty cross, but never the cross with the suffering figure of Christ. It was to the Victor on the Cross that they submitted themselves. This was the object of veneration, as in the remarkable poetical work of the seventh and eighth centuries, 'The Dream of the Rood'. Dedicated to the Cross, it originates in the tradition of Helena, mother of the Emperor Constantine, whose dream is said to have revealed the whereabouts of the three crosses of Golgotha. The custom of raising tall stone crosses, in keeping with this particular form of piety, spread via the English missionaries – first to the mainland and then to the Nordic lands, above all to Norway. It was there that the great tenth century Hymn for Good Friday, *Adoratio Crucis*, was created, following the English pattern, in celebration of the Holy Cross.

The mission from England was, as we have seen, extremely active throughout the eleventh century, although the German archbishops were by no means idle. From King Canute's time and onwards, we find clear signs of exertions to refer Nordic church affairs straight to the papacy in Rome, signifying a deliberate attempt to by-pass the Archbishop of Bremen. Following the fall of Archbishop Adalbert in 1066, the Danish kings began in earnest to try to make the Nordic churches independent. In 1104 they succeeded. The Bishop of Lund was made Archbishop and Metropolitan of all the churches in the Nordic countries and on the North Atlantic Isles. This was secured by the

Danish king, Erik Ejegod, in consultation with Pope Paschal, on the occasion of the King's pilgrimage to Rome. The German claim to ecclesiastical power over the Nordic peoples was thus impeded. The recently appointed Archbishop of Lund received official congratulations from England upon his newly independent position, signed by Anselm, the great theologian and Archbishop of Canterbury. Anselm and the Bishop of Lund knew one another, and Anselm had himself acted as intermediary in the diplomatic negotiations between the Nordic churches and Rome.

CHAPTER 2

In Christian Europe

NICHOLAS BREAKSPEAR'S NORDIC LEGATION

The Holy See looked kindly upon the establishment of the new North European church province, since it was wary of allowing the archbishopric of Bremen too much power. Nor was the additional province a small one – in area, it was Europe's largest, albeit sparsely populated and in its northernmost reaches not yet fully organized, either governmentally or ecclesiastically.

Around the middle of the twelfth century, Rome dispatched an envoy to the Northern lands, to oversee their division into additional archbishoprics. The man entrusted with this important mission was an Englishman. His name was Nicholas Breakspear, Cardinal of Albano, and he was born in Abbots Langley in Hertfordshire. No Englishman ever had a greater influence on the development of the Nordic churches. His appointment is unlikely to have been a mere coincidence. As we have noted, these churches had forged far stronger links with the British Isles than with any other part of Europe. Breakspear may well have been deemed, as an Englishman, the best equipped to understand the mentality, and possibly even the languages, of the Nordic peoples.

Papal policy was based on the principle that it is by paying due attention to provincial requirements and interests that unity is maintained and an acceptable balance of political power in Europe as a whole is most smoothly achieved. This principle seems similarly relevant in our time, as efforts are made towards a strong and integrated pan-European unity and fellowship. Breakspear was a representative of the ecclesiastical reform movement of his day, with its demand for *Libertas Ecclesiae*, i.e. the liberty – in actual fact the supremacy, both spiritual and political – of the Church over the secular powers. The aim was to create a kind of federalism – under the unifying authority of the Church – by taking into consideration the concerns and prospects of each individual member country.

Cardinal Breakspear brought with him two new *pallia* (archiepiscopal insignia), one each for Norway and Sweden. His mission took almost two years, 1152–1154. It began with a visit to Norway – to Stavanger and Bergen, and then to Nidaros (Trondheim), which had been designated as the archiepiscopal see. By this time the Norwegian Church was relatively well ordered, and offers of help from Bremen on the vital questions of its organization had been curtly declined. Indeed, the German archbishop's envoy was quite simply shown the door. Nicholas had been handed a task requiring formidable diplomatic skills, but he did come straight from the Pope himself and soon showed that he knew how to play his cards right. The Norwegian church province, established at a synod in the winter of 1152–53, covered a great expanse. This large sea-faring region of Northern Europe was established, in ecclesiastical law, as a province covering the western part of the Nordic area. It also covered the whole of the Atlantic area in which the Norwegian people had encountered and adopted the Christian faith, and where so very many of them had settled. The newly appointed Archbishop of Nidaros was granted no less than ten suffragan bishops to assist him – one each for Bergen, Stavanger, Oslo and Hamar and, for the North Atlantic islands, one each for Skálholt and Hólar on Iceland, one each for Greenland and the Faeroe Islands, one for the Orkneys, the Shetland Islands and the Hebrides jointly, and one for the Isle of Man. (The islands closest to Scotland were later to come under St Andrews.)

This visit by an English cardinal has a prominent place in Norwegian history. The resolutions of the Synod of Nidaros were of fundamental importance to the Norwegian

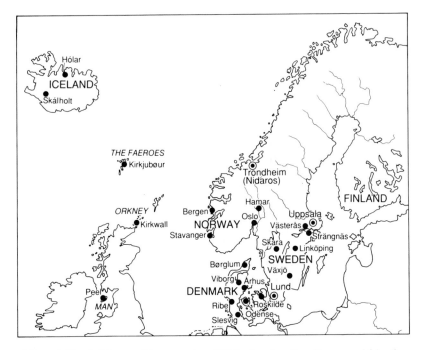

Map of North-Western Europe, circa 1200, showing the dioceses within the Danish, Norwegian and Swedish church provinces of that time. From the catalogue to the exhibition 'From Viking to Crusader', published by the Nordic Council of Ministers in collaboration with the Council of Europe. *Cartographer: Jörgen Myrman-Lund.*

church. Canon law was to be put into practice, and loyalty to the Holy See was to be manifested in payments of the so-called Peter's pence. Breakspear spent nine months in the country, with the longest spell in Nidaros. There he could watch over the formation of the capitular body and church administration for the new metropolitan see, and could watch the cathedral being built, in part with the help of master builders and stonemasons from Lincoln.

The cardinal's next stop was Linköping in Sweden, where he apparently intended to establish a Swedish archbishopric. A kind of provincial council was held during the summer and autumn of 1153. Again, resolutions were made

30

regarding the practice of canon law and of Peter's pence. However, and we do not know quite why, Breakspear found it best to postpone to some future date the establishment of a Swedish church province. On his way back to Rome, he stopped off in the Danish metropolitan see of Lund, where he left the second pallium, intended for a Swedish Archbishop. The Archbishop of Lund was promised a degree of authority over the future Swedish church province, and the title of *Primas Sveciæ*, (a fact that readily lent itself to many a dispute towards the end of the Middle Ages). In 1164, the Swedish Church eventually received its archiepiscopal status with its seat at Uppsala, whereupon the Archbishop of Lund consecrated the first Archbishop of Sweden. He was a Cistercian monk by the name of Stefan. The consecration took place in Sens, France, where the Archbishop of Lund happened to be at the time, and in the presence of Pope Alexander III.

Breakspear had executed his Nordic mission with great skill and he was shortly thereafter elected Pope, under the name of Hadrian IV. So far, he is the only Englishman to have occupied the papal throne and, before John Paul II, the only pope with personal knowledge of the Nordic countries. Hadrian's pontificate saw the beginnings of an ecclesiastical version of Euro-politics, to be developed by his successor, Alexander III, who, to the highest degree, helped to produce that special double feature of our continent: unity in diversity. As Pope, Breakspear went on to repeat his success in achieving both independence for local provinces and subordination to the papacy, by recognizing the independence of the kingdom of Sicily – including all of southern Italy – while at the same time receiving its prince as his vassal. Hadrian's influence in his home country may seem rather more ambiguous: Henry II certainly quoted Hadrian's papal authority in the matter of his conquest of Ireland, but Hadrian then proclaimed the autonomy of the Church of Ireland in its relation to the Archbishop of Canterbury. A recurrent pattern appears: independent churches, respected in their own right, but

31

joined together under the papacy, in an integrated, Christian Europe.

THOMAS OF CANTERBURY, EYSTEIN OF NIDAROS AND ESKIL OF LUND

It is a well known historical fact that the medieval construction of what we might call 'The European House' brought with it well-nigh continuous, frequently dramatic and often violent, splits and clashes. These are, by and large, what medieval European history is all about. Once the Nordic church provinces had been established, they quickly found themselves caught up in the game that this extended family played – the power game that had become a way of life to senior members of that family: popes, emperors and princes; archbishops, chapters and abbots. Events resulting from such confrontations in any of one of these countries or regions caused chain reactions in all the other realms and churches. A prime example – and one of the most spectacular – is the conflict between Henry II of England and his Archbishop, Thomas Becket of Canterbury. Similar situations duly arose in both Norway and Denmark.

The Norwegian Archbishop Eystein Erlandsen strongly championed the cause of 'liberty' for the Church. He was consecrated by none other than Alexander III, and had been in personal communication with Thomas Becket. Incompatibility between Eystein and the Norwegian king, Sven, resulted in Eynstein's temporary exile. He lived for six months in the Abbey of Bury St Edmunds' and visited Canterbury, where work on the famous Corona over Becket's grave was nearing its completion. One might assume this was where he found the inspiration for the Octagon of Nidaros Cathedral. The struggle for the 'liberty' of the Norwegian Church was carried on by Eystein's successor, Erik Ivarsen, who was to leave for the safety of Lund.

In the 1170s Eskil, Archbishop of Lund, was in turn

forced into exile, due to his all too tense relationship with the Danish king, Valdemar the Great. He chose to go to France, and stayed a while in Sens, which Becket, too, had visited. On his return to Denmark, he came to an agreement with the King. Eskil had in fact to give way to Valdemar but, at the same time, it was apparent that the monarchy was very much in need of the Archbishop's support. A reconciliation took place in 1170 at a great church ceremony in Ringsted, Zealand, where Eskil was officiating at the canonization and enshrinement of Knud Lavard, the King's father. That was the year in which Thomas Becket was murdered in Canterbury Cathedral.

Eskil had, in some measure, yielded to the royal will – but he found other ways of furthering the cause of *Libertas Ecclesiae*, by arguing the claim of ecclesiastical supremacy. For one thing, he had at his disposal the powerful liturgical symbolism of the cult of Becket, the martyr of Canterbury, which he initiated in the Nordic countries at this time. Altars were dedicated to Thomas at Lund Cathedral, and a parish church in the city was given Thomas as its patron saint. The cult spread throughout the province. In 1192, when Absalon, the founder of Copenhagen and Eskil's successor, consecrated the first Nordic church to be built with bricks – in Gumlösa, northern Skåne – he placed a relic of Thomas in the altar. Not far from there, at Lyngsjö, there remains to this day a splendid stone font, on which raised figures represent the event of 'the Murder in the Cathedral'. Further Danish altars dedicated to Becket were erected in Roskilde, Ribe and Århus.

In Sweden, there still exist many portrayals of St Thomas, possibly more numerous than in England. He was especially remembered in the Diocese of Linköping, where some districts for many years contributed to a separate Thomas collection for Canterbury. These funds were later ingeniously re-routed to Linköping Cathedral, where Thomas received an altar and, towards the end of the Middle Ages, also a magnificent chapel. This chapel was given a second dedication in 1986, in the presence of rep-

St Thomas Becket. Wooden statue by Bernt Notke, circa 1500, from
Skepptuna. Now in the National History Museum. (Copy in Canterbury
Cathedral.) *Photograph: ATA*

34

resentatives of the then Archbishop of Canterbury. It is now known as 'The Chapel of Thomas Becket and of all Martyrs of our own Time', and is to serve as a special reminder of the links through the ages between the Churches of England and Sweden. A correspondingly symbolic gesture had been made at Canterbury in 1930: the donation, on the initiative of Archbishop Söderblom, of a copy of the noblest of all the Thomas Becket statues in Sweden, and the placing of it in the cathedral crypt. The original figure, carved in wood, was made for Skepptuna, in the Diocese of Uppsala.

BENEDICTINES AND CISTERCIANS

Before the end of the twelfth century, the three Nordic church provinces had been established, the last being the Swedish-Finnish province. The age of the Vikings was over. Their expansionist enterprises were now transferred to the so-called crusades, aimed at the countries along the southern and eastern shores of the Baltic Sea. There, Denmark pursued its active policy of acquisition, sanctioned by the Church – while Sweden extended its domain in eastern Finland.

Meanwhile, ecclesiastical and cultural connections with the European mainland were on the increase. The relationship with the Diocese of Hamburg-Bremen continued to be handled with some circumspection, bearing in mind its proximity to Denmark and its old claims to supremacy which could at any time resurface. Safer relations were to be had further south. Though Eskil had received his education in Germany, his connections with France were closer still, for example in the person of Bernard of Clairvaux. Following his resignation from his large archdiocese, this is where Eskil chose to live, and here we find his grave, next to St Bernard's.

By now Cistercians, favoured by Eskil and his friends at Clairvaux, had begun to arrive in the North. Houses were established in Denmark, Norway and Sweden, and

Font from Lyngsjö in the county of Skåne, Sweden, depicting the murder of Thomas Becket in Canterbury Cathedral and carved only a few decades after the event. *Photograph: ATA.*

later also in Estonia. The earliest was founded in Sweden in 1143 – at Alvastra in the Diocese of Linköping, which then still belonged to the Province of Lund. The Swedish King, Sverker, and his Queen, Ulfhild, actively encouraged the monks of Clairvaux – first by their royal invitation and then by the Queen's donation of an estate given to her as a 'morning present' (on the morning of her wedding day and therefore her personal property and in her gift). The Cistercian chronicles tell of a young monk named Gerhard who begged, quite desperately, to be excused from leaving beautiful Clairvaux for the unknown, cold and barbaric country in the North. Bernard replied that the Swedish enterprise was the Will of God. But he promised the young monk that he would one day be allowed to return, so that he might die at Clairvaux. The promise was kept, once his long and faithful service as abbot at Alvastra had helped to make it one of the richest and most influential monasteries on Nordic soil.

All in all, Sweden was to count eight Cistercian houses; in Denmark there would be eleven. Some of them had belonged to Benedictines who had joined the new order. A number of Cistercian churches still stand, such as the lovely brick-built church at Løgumkloster in southern Jutland, and the Romanesque church at Sorö, Zealand – both in Denmark – and there is Varnhem, in transitional style, in Västergötland, Sweden. Varnhem found patrons among the aristocracy and in the royal household, as did the convent at Vreta, Östergötland. Norway, at this time sparsely populated, had only three Cistercian monasteries. One might add that the earliest of these – Lyse, near Bergen – was founded by monks from Fountains, England. The English influence in Norway was still strong, but the initiative for the Danish and Swedish monasteries came from the mainland. These monasteries transmitted the ideals of piety and of culture expressed at St Bernard's Clairvaux and spreading fast all over Europe. They reached the Nordic countries during the earliest stage of the foundation of their churches – in the case of Sweden, earlier even than its establishment as a church province. This may explain the special attraction the Cistercians had in the eyes of the Northern peoples. Their noble architecture and liturgy and the fruits of their literary labours reached us almost at once, together with their gardening skills and agricultural expertise. Their influence was enormously strong. Other orders would come to match them in importance, but not before a century had passed.

Developments in England were somewhat different. There, Benedictine liturgy had had time to establish itself in the cathedrals, leaving a genuine and lasting impression on church life – never to be erased by the appeal of Cistercian liturgical tradition. The latter was also rather less accessible: the Cistercians lived in their Houses much like the gentry did on their estates, and admission to their services was, mostly, barred to outsiders. In the Nordic countries, a cathedral with Benedictine liturgy was uncommon.

Such an exception was Odense in Denmark, and it is likely that some influence from there found its way into the establishment of the chapter at Uppsala. Other chapters in the North – including the chapter at Lund Cathedral – were so called secular associations of canons. The tradition peculiar to Odense can be traced to the political situation at the end of the eleventh century and the then hopes of the Danish King, Knud IV, to reunite Denmark and England. This Knud later appears as St Knud, Denmark's national saint. The English expedition failed. However, as a part of his preparations for it, Odense had received from him the relics of two English Saints: St Alban, England's first martyr, and St Oswald, King of Northumbria. Thus fortified, Odense and the Island of Funen were to serve as the base for Knud's war of reacquisition. As it happened, he was soon to have more pressing matters to attend to. His kingdom was threatened from the south, and a rebellion arose against his own royal person. He was murdered in the church that contained his precious gift, the relics of St Alban.

Not many years passed before monks of the Benedictine Order arrived in Odense from Evesham in England. They built a church and one of them completed the first biography of King Knud. On this they based their petition for his canonization. Then they buried him in their church – first in the crypt and later in a shrine on the high altar. The murder of King Knud came to exert a strong symbolic power. This had been a king who had greatly cared for his church, and who was murdered in a holy place – a church which was dedicated to England's first martyr.

The part played by the English monks in the canonization and enshrinement of St Knud provides one answer as to why they were given the honour of forming the cathedral chapter. They lived at the cathedral – not as canons, but as brothers of the Order of St Benedict. They followed Benedictine liturgy strictly and remained in constant touch with Evesham. The Danish King had special privileges in relation to their chapter, and they continued their faithful watch over the traditions surrounding the Saint-King of Denmark.

The Chapter of Odense preserved its links with Evesham for at least a century and a half. In the 1150s the Swedish King, Erik Jedvardsson, had monks brought from Odense to Uppsala, where a chapter was to be founded. This chapter, too, might therefore have received, in its initial stages, an English, Benedictine imprint. But this tradition is somewhat uncertain, and this uncertainty extends to King Erik, who allegedly summoned the monks. One legend tells of his 'crusade' to Finland. Another informs us of his murder, by a pretender to the throne, immediately after attending mass. Erik became the Saint-King of the Swedish nation. His relics, placed in a golden shrine in Uppsala Cathedral, are kept and honoured to this day. The Evesham monks from Odense stayed on in Uppsala for several decades, and there – if tradition may be believed – they faithfully kept the memory of St Erik, as they had done at Odense, for Denmark's St Knud. Both kingdoms would in this way appear to have had English support for their national, symbolic saints. There is evidence to the effect that the tradition of St Olav of Norway was equally the object of that special Benedictine attention.

NEW DIRECTIONS

The relations we have so far been able to observe between the British Isles and the Nordic countries belonged to the earlier part of the Middle Ages, and were made possible by concrete circumstances that were, as such, to vanish into history. By the middle of the twelfth century, the Nordic churches' largest number of connections – and the most important – were not with England, but with the European mainland. A new pattern was to be seen in politics, commerce and cultural exchanges within Northern Europe. This was the scenario of the Hanseatic League, which was to affect the ecclesiastical situation in the North continuously up to the end of the Middle Ages and the Reformation.

With the foundation of Lübeck in the 1140s, German merchants gained their first Baltic port, which heralded the start of the West-German infiltration of all North European trade. This was not something altogether new. The trade-routes were the old, established ones: the sea-ways between the countries of the North, and from England and the North Atlantic Islands in the west to the coasts of the Baltic Sea and the Russian interior in the east – the same routes that the Christian missionaries had travelled. The map used by the Hanseatic League looked much the same, with links from Iceland and from London in the west, to Riga, Reval (Tallinn) and Novgorod in the east. What was new, however, was that the initiative and driving force now lay with the merchants of Lübeck and of other cities within the Holy Roman Empire. Their power and influence stemmed from each having its own effective self-government, from the strong unity between them, and from their having at their disposal both capital and a new type of ship, safer and able to carry more cargo than the Viking longships.

The consequences of the Hanseatic influence on the Nordic peoples have been variously estimated. Some think that their fellowship with the mainland brought them material growth and a richer cultural exchange, i.e. positive

40

gains. Others have taken the negative view that Northern Germany's blatantly self-interested expansion was the root cause of the decline of Norway over the latter part of the Middle Ages, and that, from a cultural point of view, North German dominance left the Nordic countries isolated from the rest of Europe. However, no one can deny that trade was flourishing: cod was bought in Bergen, salted down with salt from Lüneburg and sold on the mainland – and so with the herring from the Sound. Butter and cheese, iron and copper from Sweden; furs from Finland and Russia – these were exchanged for grain, beer, silver and hand-crafted products from towns south of the Baltic Sea. Cities grew and flourished: Bergen, Oslo, Visby, Stockholm, Copenhagen and Malmö. All were in constant communication with one another and with expanding, wealthy cities like Danzig (Gdansk), Stralsund, Rostock and, to the west, Brügge (Bruges). London, too, had its Hanseatic office.

German merchants and craftsmen moved to newly founded, fast-growing towns all over the Baltic region, bringing with them burgomasters, guilds, societies and legally binding trade regulations. The German language came to the fore in all these merchant cities. So did German architecture, represented in market squares, town halls, splendid Gothic brick churches, tall and step-gabled burghers' houses and the town walls. Much of this remains. Visby, for example, on the island of Gotland in the Baltic Sea, still has the look of its Hanseatic past. For the Baltic region, the Hanseatic League meant well planned and well functioning towns and the advent of a common city culture.

A solid and lively church life formed an integral part of this culture. The opulent art treasures in many Nordic churches from the last of the medieval centuries – golden reredoses and the images of saints – came from Northern Germany and Flanders, from the cities of trading partners, and still bear witness to the network of the Hanseatic era. Friaries were founded in the growing cities, while the old Orders found themselves more and more isolated in their rural monasteries. In the Northern European city culture late medieval individualistic piety was also expressed in fellowships such as 'the Brethren of the Common Life'. Eventually, there arrived in these cities the preaching of the Reformation which in its first stage was a predominantly urban phenomenon, suggested not least by their Hanseatic burghers.

However, we must not lose sight of the fact that the Nordic countries consisted almost entirely of agrarian communities. Important as the towns were to international communications, to trade and new influences, their populations added up to no more than a fraction of the national total. The life of the Church was therefore practised predominantly in the very many country parishes. There were also vast unpopulated areas, in the far north and east, still waiting to be colonized.

During the Middle Ages, the Diocese of Turku in Finland grew in size and importance. It became a significant part of Uppsala church province – in spite of having only two major cities – Turku, the episcopal city, and, much further to the east, Viipuri. Both had schools and monasteries. Turku Cathedral was named after St Henrik, the Apostle of Finland. Legend calls him an Englishman, one who accompanied Nicholas Breakspear on his Nordic travels and took part in the Swedish enterprises of acquisition and of mission in Finland – where he died a martyr, probably in the year 1156. The greatest medieval Bishop of Turku was Hemming. He was active in the mid-fourteenth century and contributed more than anyone to the development of church life in Finland. Bishop Hemming was beatified by the pope and his shrine is still to be seen in Turku Cathedral. The Reformation arrived too soon for the completion of his canonization.

The Church in Finland was, as has already been mentioned, an integral part of the Swedish Church. But in this eastern part of the Swedish realm the culture was, in several respects, peculiarly Finnish in character. This was because of its situation between the Nordic/Germanic region of

Section of St Henrik's cenotaph in Nousis, Finland (thought to have been erected in 1429). The monument is overlaid with brass plates showing scenes from St Henrik's life. Here he is seen with St Erik, on a 'Crusade' to Finland. *Photograph: The State Department of Museums, Helsinki.*

Europe and the eastern, Slav countries. The whole history of Finland has been shaped by this intermediary position. Finnish church life may, at least in the beginning, have been influenced by the neighbouring Orthodox Church to the east, but later it developed entirely on western lines. The cultural distinctiveness could be seen especially in the oral tradition of Finnish poetry.

From an ecclesiastical point of view, the Diocese of Turku was medieval pioneer country. Mission and coloniz- ation marched, hand in hand, into the regions to the north and east. This, it has been argued, explains why the late medieval Finnish Church was more vigorous than other parts of the Church of its time – more so, even, than those belonging to the central dioceses of the Swedish church province.

ST BIRGITTA AND QUEEN PHILIPPA

With St Birgitta, her prophetic works and her Order, a new spiritual impetus of unifying force was entering the Nordic churches. Birgitta Birgersdotter truly became a dominant figure not only in Sweden, but also in the church life of the neighbouring countries, from the latter part of the fourteenth century to the end of the Middle Ages. Although her thinking and work were in complete accord with the Roman Catholic piety of her time, the intensity and literary power of her writings and their breadth of vision gave an element of renewal to a period which otherwise might have left us with an impression of mechanical piety.

Birgitta was, almost from the beginning, a European figure. When she received in a vision her call to be the mouthpiece of God's justice on earth, she clearly saw it as self-evident that her task concerned, not only her own circle, or even her own country, but the whole world including the Pope, the Emperor and all its princes. This implies that even small countries on the peripheries of Europe, such as Sweden, at this time saw themselves as part of Christendom as a whole, in a world of both spiritual and political unity. Of course, Birgitta's confidence finds further explanation in her special gifts and extremely privileged social status. She belonged, on both her father's and her mother's side, to Sweden's leading aristocracy. Through her mother she was related to the ruling royal house, and her husband, too, belonged to the top echelons of the nobility. They were blessed with eight children. She had great personal wealth. She had not the slightest difficulty in attracting both conversation partners and spiritual mentors

St Birgitta, Vadstena convent church. Figure carved in wood, referred to as 'the ecstatic Birgitta'. Probably identical with a sculpture consecrated in 1435, this image can be seen on countless pilgrim badges. *Photograph: ATA.*

of her choice from the Swedish elite of mainland-educated theologians.

It was after the death of her husband that Birgitta experienced her calling and visions, the documentation of which provides a remarkable literary landmark in medieval Swedish history. Her plans for a new Order began to take shape, and in 1350 she set off for Rome to seek papal approval for them – and to benefit from the special indulgence of that Jubilee year. She was to remain in Rome for over twenty years. From there she embarked, towards the end of her life, on her most important pilgrimage, to the Holy Land.

Birgitta was never to see her own convent. In 1370 her order – *Ordo Sanctissimi Salvatoris* – was declared a branch of the Augustinian Order by the Pope. Three years later Birgitta died in Rome, in the house near the Campo di Fiori which is a Mother House of the Order to-day. Her body was brought back to Sweden – to Vadstena, where her convent church was being built, in careful accordance with her own comprehensive specifications. She was canonized on 7 October 1391, in St Peter's, Rome. Marking the 600th anniversary of this event, Pope John Paul II conducted an ecumenical service in St Peter's, in the presence of the King and Queen of Sweden. At the High Altar, the Pope was assisted by the Lutheran Archbishops of Uppsala and Turku, and by their Roman Catholic 'colleagues' from Sweden and Finland, i.e. by the bishops of the Roman Catholic Dioceses of Stockholm and Helsinki. Birgitta has become a symbol of the ecumenical movement and appears to have contributed considerably to the papal interest in the Churches of Sweden and Finland. She is also spoken of as special, in the sense that she might be chosen to serve as a unifying saint for all of Christian Europe.

Birgitta's Order had an original concept: a convent for sixty sisters and – in a separate building – thirteen ordained monks (= the apostles, including Paul), four deacons and eight lay brethren. The intention was to make possible an unbroken chain of prayers, with the sisters and brothers praying in shifts, and to guarantee the monastery free access to theological learning. Such an unheard of arrangement encountered much hostile criticism, and it would take the support of very influential persons indeed to achieve its realization. Later times brought a reversal: only conventional nunneries now exist in Birgitta's Order. Even greater difficulties – and costs – arose over her proposed canonization. For this to be achieved a notable exertion of royal power proved essential. Her canonization was strongly urged by the English cardinal Adam of Easton, at that time an influential figure in Rome.

Various dynastic connections and agreements between Denmark, Norway and Sweden resulted, towards the end of the Middle Ages, in a Union – at times split by national rebellions and moves towards independence, but nevertheless functioning, at least as a political programme, from the middle of the fourteenth century to the end of the Middle Ages. (The Union between Norway and Denmark lasted until 1814.) The most successful monarch of this medieval Union was Queen Margrethe, whose reign over the three kingdoms began in 1388. She championed Birgitta's canonization and thereby also gained, among aristocratic families devoted to Birgitta's cause, important ideological support for the Union.

Margrethe was succeeded by Erik of Pomerania, the son of her niece. With him, and especially with his queen, Philippa, the convent at Vadstena was to enjoy excellent relations. Philippa was the daughter of Henry IV of England, and sister of his successor, Henry V, the great hero of the wars against France and soon to be renowned for his victory at Agincourt. Philippa came into her own as Queen of the Union and well deserves her place in history, not least in the history of Anglo-Scandinavian church relations.

Philippa was only twelve years old when she became Queen of Denmark, Norway and Sweden. Her wedding to Erik of Pomerania took place in Lund in the autumn of

1406, and was celebrated with a pomp and splendour the like of which this city can hardly have experienced on any occasion before or since. The marriage ceremony was held at the archbishop's residence, 'Lundagård', whereupon the young queen was crowned in the cathedral. Then followed a full week of accolades and festivities. Philippa's royal trousseau and her gifts to the participants were so exceptionally valuable that they were entered in a separate registry, by a specially appointed Nordic commission. This account was later included in the state documents, where they are still to be found.

Philippa made almost immediate contact with the convent at Vadstena, and soon visited it with her husband. Her first lady of the bed-chamber was one of Birgitta's granddaughters, and the queen had already known of Vadstena through one of the knights of her English entourage, Henry Fitzhugh. He made a pilgrimage there shortly after her wedding, to take advice on the foundation, in England, of a Brigittine convent, towards which he had already contributed funds. The result was to be the English convent of St Bridget at Syon in Middlesex, generously supported by Queen Philippa's father and, on his death, by her brother, Henry V. Syon therefore constitutes, right from its inception, a link between England and Sweden – and the Brigittine convent of Syon exists to this day, although it has moved around Europe many times over the centuries.

Philippa dearly loved the convent at Vadstena. She visited it frequently and was received as sister *ab extra*. She bestowed on it a precious relic and endowed an altar – St Anne's Chapel. She was to be of even greater service to the convent, for fresh hostilities had arisen against Birgitta's Order, on the grounds that the convent was also to house men – in a separate building. By 1420 the situation had become critical. Philippa wrote to her mighty brothers in England – to the King and the influential Dukes of Clarence, Bedford and Gloucester, who duly persuaded the Pope to renew his authorization of the Order. It was then, the English royal family who rescued Birgitta's creation.

The convent at Vadstena was granted daughter houses: in England, as mentioned earlier, in Norway, Denmark and Finland, and also in the Baltic territories, in Poland, Germany, Italy and the Netherlands. At the end of the Middle Ages, there were, altogether twenty-five Brigittine houses in Europe. Nowadays we find them, in their various branches, spread over several continents.

While on a visit to Vadstena in the late winter of 1429/30, Philippa fell ill and died at the convent. She was buried in the chapel she had founded. In her will she bequeathed large gifts to this chapel, and the King donated even greater ones. During his long travels abroad, Philippa had served as regent of their kingdoms, apparently with great skill, and she had made herself much loved. With her death, King Erik lost his guardian angel on earth: the remainder of his life was to be full of sorrow and misfortunes. In the end, he was forced to leave his triple kingdom.

Among the many gifts presented by King Erik in memory of his Queen were two golden royal crowns, one made for a king, the other for a queen, which were to be kept in the chapel at Vadstena as the royal insignia of the united Nordic realms. The archives tell us that they were indeed used a few times by fifteenth century monarchs, but that they then disappeared; they were pawned in Lübeck by Christian I, never to be referred to again. It is, however, remarkable that these symbols of Nordic unity were the result of a desire to honour the memory of the daughter of an English king – a memory to be kept alive and cared for in her beloved convent in Sweden.

BEFORE THE REFORMATION

The late medieval life of the Nordic churches did not, of course, in principle differ much from that of the rest of Catholic Europe. Here as elsewhere, we can trace for example the strong influence of the friars in the cities. As early as in the thirteenth century they played a significant

This 15th century embroidery by the Nuns at Vadstena is traditionally known as 'Queen Philippa's Funeral Pall'. *Photograph: ATA.*

role in the Nordic countries, and they enjoyed the patronage of both kings and bishops. They emphasized the importance of popular preaching, a tradition therefore not introduced by the Reformation, or at least not as anything new.

Further, parts of the Bible were already translated into the Nordic tongues. Humanist Biblical scholarship became a cultural factor to be reckoned with, especially in Denmark, where its centre was the beautiful and still well maintained Carmelite monastery at Elsinore.

The medieval Catholic Church was united, but it was not uniform. Local and national features show up especially clearly in liturgical traditions and the veneration of the various saints. The Union between the three Nordic countries during the later medieval centuries is reflected also in their preferred saints. A certain amount of mutual exchange took place. We have mentioned that the English-Swedish Sigfrid received his own chapel in Roskilde Cathedral, Denmark. Olav, Erik and Knud – the three Saint-Kings of the North – consistently appear together in paintings of the late medieval church. However, local saints were also honoured. And many of these were, as we have seen, of English origin: Henrik of Turku, for example, and in the dioceses, Eskil at Strängnäs, David at Västerås and Sigfrid at Uppsala and Växjö. Their popularity showed no signs of diminishing.

As the Lutheran churches never experienced any iconoclasm to speak of, and as the Nordic countries did not suffer the devastation of either of the two World Wars, so it is possible, here to study the rich world of imagery of the late Middle Ages in largely intact vault paintings, reredoses and images of saints. Such a study reveals that the medieval ideal of piety, and its practice, actually grew stronger during the 15th century, to culminate at the beginning of the 16th. In a not very recent, but classic and still valid, book *Helgendyrkelse i Danmark* (The Veneration of Saints in Denmark) by Ellen Jørgensen, the author concludes that the late Middle Ages were by no means a preparation for the Reformation: 'Man hører ingen kritiske røster – før Luther

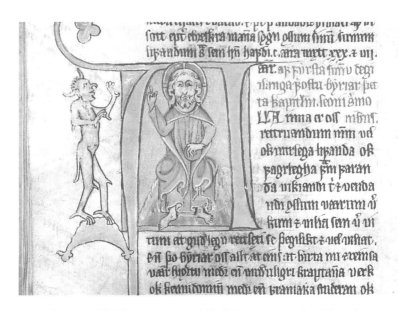

As early as the Middle Ages, parts of the Bible were translated into the various Nordic languages. This detail of the Icelandic 'Arnamagnæan Manuscript Collection', originally from Skálholt Cathedral, dates from the 14th century. *Photograph: The State Archives, Reykjavik.*

løser alle tunger'. (There was not a critical voice to be heard – until Luther gave to everyone a voice.)

Of course there were 'critical voices', but they came from within the Church, and aimed to restore her to what, according to the original medieval view, she was intended to be. No criticism came from the people – there was no forerunner to the Reformation in the North, no equivalent to England's Wycliffe.

There were, however, in both Denmark and Sweden, certain grave anomalies, not least in the disproportionate status of the Church in society. This was perhaps less marked here than on the European mainland but was nevertheless of the same kind, and there are ample examples of strange or downright scandalous appointments to office, where the actions of the Pope himself gave rise to feelings of strong national indignation. It was impossible not to notice the accelerating growth of the Church in material terms, i.e. in terms of church property. By the end of the Middle Ages over 20% of all Nordic land belonged, it is thought, to the Church, rising to over 30% in densely populated areas, such as the plains of Denmark and Sweden. It would, however, be incorrect to describe the churches of these countries as especially corrupt and decayed. That would be historically misleading and do no justice to the deeper meaning of the Reformation.

The late Middle Ages were, in the North as in England, a time of violent contradictions, with feuds between countries and between prominent families. The Church played its part in these battles, as the worldly and the spiritual aristocracies were extensively intertwined, and as land and trade were to a great extent in the Church's gift. It was the nation-state and the power of the secular prince that were in the end to emerge victorious from these confrontations. This was the case in many European countries, and the similarity between the Nordic countries and England is very clear. This is not the place to elaborate, but two features ought to be brought out, to help explain why, after the Reformation, the Churches of England and of the Northern countries were able to survive and flourish as national churches.

The first has to do with the fact that, for these churches, connections between Church an Crown were already close. Further, these were of long standing and here we can see many similarities between English and Nordic church history. Kings and queens had played an important part as early as in missionary times and continued to do so over the ensuing centuries. As we know, William I of England considered himself in some respects as the head of his country's Church, and independent of the Pope. In the Nordic countries, the kings exercised a considerable influence over the Church, for example in the appointment of bishops. Occasionally this resulted in open conflict between king – for example King Erik of Pomerania – and chapter.

In this case the King met with defeat, but in many others, it was the chapter that was forced to give in.

Paradoxically, this was increasingly thanks to the co-operation between the kings and the Pope – paradoxically, as the Pope thereby aided the curtailment of ecclesiastical supremacy by abetting the growing influence of the secular powers. To be sure, the popes did not offer their collaboration gratis, any more than did many others. Kings were able to buy themselves a variety of favours: dispensations from marriage vows, canonizations for their favourite saints, etc. The hunger for monetary recompense on the part of the popes did much to further the Nordic monarchs' maturing view of themselves as national heads of their churches. In this respect, too, the Reformation did not introduce much of a change, except that now the princes could dispense with the costly approval from Rome.

Clear heads were quick to recognize how disastrously this trade was bound to end. To those who revered the classic Augustinian principle of the distribution of responsibility and power between Church and society – between *imperium* and *sacerdotium* – and who held on to the unqualified demand for *Libertas Ecclesiæ*, these papal deals were an abomination. St Birgitta described them as 'stinking of hellish vices'. In the course of the fifteenth century, the authority of Rome was further damaged by the papal schisms and the Conciliar movement. In consequence, the tendency towards national church government grew stronger. This was especially noticeable in the Nordic countries.

The second distinctive feature of the medieval Nordic Church – probably not so marked in Denmark as in the others – was the dominant role of the country parishes. Their importance was due in part to their virtually independent status and in part to the fact that the number of towns was, relatively speaking, so very small. Sweden-Finland for example was very sparsely populated. By the end of the Middle Ages, its inhabitants did not exceed a total of one million, with the towns making up, as late as the mid-sixteenth century, a mere 5%. The population of its largest city, Stockholm, was only 5000. It follows that most church life was lived in the country parishes. This may be a truism, but needs to be stated in order to avoid a false picture. To be sure, urban trends were important; these were the new ones, on which there is much source material. But we also need to gain some impression of the conditions outside the towns, of rural life.

Sunday Mass ruled undisputed over parish life. But in the towns, a wide choice of services was on offer in the various conventual churches and in the many churches tied to guilds and crafts. In England, towns were relatively close to one another; most of the population lived sufficiently close to a town to experience urban life. It should be mentioned that there were by no means as many monasteries in Sweden as in England, where at the beginning of the sixteenth century there were no fewer than 1000 monastic houses. True, the population of England was at this time more than four times that of Sweden, but the predominance of English monastic life was nevertheless proportionately by far the greater. In Sweden there were never more than around twenty monastic houses, and only a few of the chapters grew to a notable size. Moreover, in England there were twenty cathedrals, and other large cities had collegiate churches, with a college of priests and liturgy to match the cathedrals. Nothing of the kind existed in Sweden.

In brief, the rich life of the city churches, cathedrals and monasteries did not imprint itself on the medieval Swedish Church – nor indeed on Nordic churches in general – to anything like the same degree as it did in England. This could explain why, when the Reformation came, the development of liturgy concentrated, in the North, on the creation of a reformed (in fact, a very cautiously reformed) version of the Roman missal. This was the form of service the people knew and loved – the daily offices were of secondary importance.

As previously noted, Swedish parishes enjoyed a remarkable degree of self-government. The very first

This reredos from Nykyrko in Finland, made in Hamburg in 1410, is an example of the many magnificent medieval altar pieces preserved in Nordic churches. The middle section depicts the falling asleep and the Assumption of Mary. *Photograph: The State Department of Museums, Helsinki.*

churches in Sweden had, it is true, been built by kings and by prominent noble or gentle families. They had therefore belonged to them, as had the right of patronage. But the parish churches were built by their parishioners, who therefore had the right to make the relevant appointments and who continued to exercise that right after the Reformation. Another point well worthy of mention is that the workers on the land were free men – never serfs – and were thus represented at the medieval national assemblies, now seen as the forerunners of the Swedish parliament.

The merciless march of the Black Death left a serious demographic decline in its wake. However, as the survivors pulled themselves together, they naturally found themselves with more land per capita. Towards the end of the fifteenth century, the rural population and, in consequence, its clergy, appear in general to have been reasonably well off. Impropriation (whereby a corporation, such as a monastic house or a university college, took over a benefice and its income, appointing a vicar in place of the rector) was relatively seldom practised in Sweden: there were few vicars on meagre salaries. All in all, it would be safe to say that parish priests now made a fairly good living. There are no signs of any anti-clerical feeling, at least not against the parish clergy – the friars were, on the whole, less popular. The churches of the Swedish countryside bore testimony to prosperity. During the fifteenth and early sixteenth centuries many were enlarged. Barrel vaults and west towers were added; and many were embellished with new, and often very costly, altarpieces.

These were the expressions of a rural population that now felt entitled to a goodly measure of self-esteem. During the Reformation it was therefore wise to take into account the feelings and reactions of the rural population – rebellion was never far away. People in the countryside were conservative, jealously guarding their parish churches and the traditional Mass. And this in part explains why the character of the reformed Swedish Church came to be more conservative, or more temperate, than that of other Lutheran churches.

St George and the Dragon in the Cathedral of Stockholm, Sweden, by the hand of Bernt Notke, Lübeck and dated about 1480, is one of the most exquisite medieval representations of a saint in Europe. It is considered a national monument in Sweden. St George is of course also the Patron Saint of England. *Photograph: ATA.*

CHAPTER 3

Reformation and Continuity

ROYAL POWER AND THE CHURCH

The fall of the medieval Church was, in the Nordic countries as in England, initiated by the king – by the monarchy's exertions to gather to itself all political and economic power. The Reformation was to influence the internal transformation of the Church – in so far as there was a transformation.

In his book about the last days of Catholic episcopal power in Denmark, *Nederlagets Mænd* (Men of Defeat), the Danish church historian P.G. Lindhardt writes: 'The successful introduction of the Reformation did not concern 'the Gospel' – not to the leading Catholics and princes of the Church, and not to the Protestant king and his government'. These expressive and, quite possibly, challenging lines conclude his investigation into the condition of the Danish Church as it was when it became the target of the critical reformers. He gives us no indication that the Church was in any way falling apart. Certainly, its bishops lacked many of the primary qualifications one tends to expect in leaders of the Church – but this was not, he argues, the cause of the collapse of the medieval Church in large areas of Europe. The Reformation was welcomed, he writes, as a means for the Danish King to increase his power, and this was to '... lead to the overwhelming defeat of Roman Catholic episcopal power. The personal and vocational qualities of the men of the old church may have been poor. But that was not the reason for their defeat.' The same can be said of the corresponding situation in Sweden and in England.

Given this view, and given that one wishes to understand the momentous ecclesiastical change of the 16th century, one might wish to take a good look at the kings of the countries concerned – at the kings and their royal houses.

Let us begin with the Tudors of England and the Vasas of Sweden. These royal families were, in many respects, alike. Each produced some of the most extraordinary personalities in European history – larger than life; both had quite remarkably pronounced views on the Church; and both ruled throughout the age of Reformation. Their reigns therefore included the whole spectrum of church politics and theological principles, and are marked by those clashes between politics and principles that make sixteenth century church history so dramatic. In the wake of each and every new succession to the throne came more, and more or less violent, upheavals – most certainly including upheavals in church life. On the face of it at least, the church history of this time is, to a marked degree, a reflection of the history of the contemporary royal houses.

The Tudor family had come to the throne one generation earlier than the House of Vasa. Henry VIII had grown up as a son of a king, displaying all the talents and accomplishments expected in a Renaissance prince. Gustav Vasa was the first of his royal line, albeit with a strong claim to represent the leading Swedish nobility during the struggle for liberation from the Danish Union. From the very beginning, then, his mission was to restore royal power in an independent Swedish nation – a mission he accomplished. There is a golden radiance to this feat of his youth – a radiance which he was most particular that the chroniclers should preserve and make the most of. Gustav Vasa was to battle continuously to guard and to extend royal power for himself and for his successors on the Swedish throne. He recognized, at once, that the major obstacle to the realization of his grand design was the Church: its economic and political power would have to be crushed.

Henry VIII's motive for prompting the collapse of the medieval church system was very similar to Gustav Vasa's.

60

The fact that Henry, to begin with, had a private interest – his wish to end his marriage to Catherine of Aragon – is almost beside the point. True, it triggered his breach with Rome. But he was very swift to follow it up by demolishing entire monastic communities and confiscating their property. And by pronouncing himself the Supreme Head of his country's church, he assumed – in his own person and on behalf of his nation – the political authority and powers that had been the domain of the Pope. Gustav Vasa's agenda was much the same. The fact that both empowered themselves to appoint bishops was, of course, nothing new. This was the custom of medieval rulers. However, all at once, papal confirmation and, in practice, free elections by the chapters, were wiped out. The respective national churches were to become established by sheer royal might. In both countries the new system was approved by the legislative powers – by Parliament and the *Riksdag* respectively. Few had the will to argue in defence of papal authority or of monastic property and traditions.

What role, then, did 'the Gospel' – the very heart and spiritual ground of the Reformation – play? Both similarities and differences between Gustav Vasa's Sweden and the England of Henry VIII can be shown. To begin with, there were quite far-reaching similarities. In the 1520s the impetus came from Martin Luther and Wittenberg, even though Henry cherished no sympathies for Luther. Rather the opposite! It was against Luther's view of the Church's sacraments that the King published a polemic, for which he was rewarded by the Pope with the title Defender of the Faith. Henry may later have changed his mind about the sacraments, but that did not improve his opinion of Luther. It was nevertheless Luther's writings that introduced the Reformation to England. It was Luther's thinking that inspired young scholars at Cambridge as early as the 1520s, and Luther's theology that so deeply and abidingly impressed Thomas Cranmer. It was through Cranmer that the Church of England from the beginning received its strand of Protestant 'evangelical' doctrine from Luther's Wittenberg rather than from Calvin's Geneva. Cranmer was married – though secretly – to a German woman of Protestant faith, and he had many German contacts. To find Lutheran features in the Forty-Two Articles (in a later version known as the Thirty-Nine Articles) is therefore no surprise. But this is, by and large, where the similarities between England and the Nordic countries in this the first stage of the Reformation end.

There was no internal change in the Church, neither in its teaching nor its worship under Henry VIII. He did not allow any reformed preaching but held it back. He certainly supported the translation of the Bible into English, but this can be seen as a continuation of widespread humanist interest in the Bible during the late Middle Ages. Towards the end of Henry's life, the reformers felt distinctly threatened by his unreliable and rancorous behaviour. The situation changed drastically after Henry's death in 1547, when the Reformation broke out again. By then, the expansive period of Lutheranism was already in the past. The initiative now came from Calvin's Geneva, which was of decisive importance for the Church of England.

The reformers fared better in Sweden. Earlier than in England, and with the support of Gustav Vasa, they were free to come out with their proclamation and their writings. Gustav Vasa was elected King in 1523, and shortly thereafter appointed the men who were to be his first assistants in his own great reformation of the Church: the two 'companions in harness', Laurentius Andreæ, Archdeacon of Strängnäs, and the young priest Olaus Petri, whose theological education had included a period of study at Wittenberg. Laurentius Andreæ was a humanist – essentially a reformist Catholic – who was to become increasingly informed by the Lutheran view. He was the mastermind behind the King's attack on the economic and political power of the Church, and he was the one who supplied the King with the ingenious – and popular – argument that the property of the Church is really the property of the people. Gustav Vasa was quick to give it his personal endorsement, by reclaiming for himself land granted by his ancestors to Gripsholm Monastery. The nobility saw their chance and soon followed suit. And so the nobility came to depend for their own increasing wealth on the success of the Reformation just as in England. The real blow to Church finances came in 1527, at a diet in Västerås. The King pronounced the country's economy to be in dire straits: the war of independence against Danish rule had inflicted a huge foreign debt. But there was money in the country – money in the hands of the Church. It was therefore decided that the 'superfluous' property of bishops and cathedrals and, as in England, the monasteries, should be confiscated. There was no mention of a confessional change. The line taken was that the Word of God should be 'faithfully' proclaimed, on which there was complete agreement but which, of course, did leave the reformers free to proclaim the teachings of Wittenberg.

The king installed Olaus in Stockholm's main church, Storkyrkan (The Cathedral of Stockholm), where his sermons immediately gained a following. At the same time, the German congregation in Stockholm was granted a Lutheran pastor. Olaus Petri was also appointed as the King's 'secretary'. There is no comparison in England to his public appearances, in speeches and writings, as a representative of the Reformation already in the 1520s. He published a book of prayers, a popular account of the faith, a small book of hymns, a translation of the New Testament – the complete Bible did not appear in Swedish until 1541 – and a reformed order of the Mass in Swedish. He was invited to represent the Protestant view at a public disputation at Uppsala, and he preached at the King's Coronation in 1528.

The 1530s saw further advances for Lutheranism in Swedish church life. First came the appointment and consecration of an Archbishop of the Lutheran persuasion: Olaus Petri's younger brother Laurentius Petri, who was to become the leading figure of the Swedish Church after the

Reformation. The middle of this decade saw England's decisive break with Rome. It is, of course, possible that the actions of the one country influenced those of the other, but there is no real evidence of this. Sweden took its next step in 1536, at a kind of National Council at Uppsala, where a reformed Swedish order of divine service was introduced. This was, as the cautious wording went, to be put in use 'as soon as possible'. A further hymnbook and a catechism followed, as well as a published collection of sermons, or *postilla* (book of homilies). At this point, then, Sweden was ahead of England in the matter of church reforms.

Parts of the old tradition had, in accordance with Reformation teaching, been abolished: the mass for the dead, the veneration of relics and pilgrimage. But no coercion or pressure had been exerted on the congregations. The King, always the pragmatist and with his eye on matters financial, was not slow in confiscating what he described as unnecessary 'popish' items, such as monstrances and chalices, wherever there were more than one, and church bells, too – but this caused serious rebellions. The good town-people had followed suit by grabbing the property of the mendicant friars. It is quite likely however, that most rural parishes hardly noticed that a new church order was about to break through. There were indeed to be some thorough-going changes to church practice. But it was in the towns that these more comprehensive measures of the Reformation were introduced. The rural regions were a different matter. They kept the old customs faithfully, and Gustav Vasa knew he had to tread more softly there.

A serious quarrel – probably of a political, rather than a theological, nature – broke out between the king and the leading reformers. The king accused them of disloyalty to the crown and had them all, except for the Archbishop, sentenced to death. They were later reprieved. Suspicious and hot tempered though Gustav Vasa certainly was, where executions are concerned, he cuts a fairly modest figure compared to his English counterpart. This goes for his marriages, too. Gustav Vasa was to have three successive queens. The first two died – from natural causes; the third survived him.

Gustav Vasa can hardly be said to have been interested in religious questions in themselves. His support of the Reformation had, first and last, practical and political reasons – which meant that his plans for the reorganization of the Church went beyond those of the reformers. In order to reduce episcopal and diocesan independence from the crown, he wished to introduce a centralized administration for the Church, under his royal control. He very nearly succeeded. However, as Archbishop Laurentius Petri survived him, so did the characteristic structure of the Swedish Church – which to this day provides a link with the Church of England.

Gustav Vasa's life lasted until 1560. This in itself caused the ecclesiastical timetable in Sweden to differ somewhat from that in England. Henry died in 1547, and by 1560 England had already experienced two tumultuous turnabouts: under Edward VI, in favour of the Protestants; under Mary I, and no less violently, the restoration of Roman Catholicism. In Sweden, this period had seen the reform work continue, albeit cautiously and, sometimes, not so very smoothly. In England, it had been held back until the death of Henry, when it burst forth to explosive effect. During the backlash in Mary's reign, many Protestants went into exile and others died martyrs. Under these conditions, an ultra-Protestant faction formed – the Puritans – to which there was no parallel in Sweden.

Henry's children had different mothers, different dispositions and different religious views. This brings us back to similarities with Sweden. Gustav Vasa's eldest son, and the first to succeed him, was Erik, born of his first marriage. His mother was a German princess, Katarina of Sachsen-Lauenburg. The other sons were born to him by his second queen, a member of the old Swedish noble family Leijonhufvud. Erik made it abundantly clear to his half-brothers that there was, to his mind, a very wide gap indeed between him and them in terms of rank; only he could claim kinship with an old princely family. The three of them were, for that matter, different in almost all respects. Suspicion and hate marred their relationship – and Swedish history – for the rest of the sixteenth century. The Swedish rulers of the house of Vasa between them came to represent every conceivable religious orientation of the time.

Despite his decidedly anti-Catholic stance, Erik XIV, who reigned 1560–68, cannot rightly be described as a convinced Lutheran. He was intellectually gifted, widely read and artistically talented. There was in him a certain inclination towards Calvinism, as received from Beurræus, a French Protestant and, by royal appointment, Erik's tutor. But Erik's burning scholarly interest lay in the contemporary fields of political science and astrology. The King left the running of the Church to the Archbishop, Laurentius Petri, whose efforts to complete its reformation he nevertheless held back, for fear that a legally sanctioned Church Ordinance, as proposed by the Archbishop, would make the Swedish Church far too independent. Calvinist immigrants had arrived in Sweden and were making their views known. At this time, the leading centres of the Reformation were no longer located in the German cities, but in Geneva and in France and Holland. However, Calvinist influence in Sweden was terminated, mainly due to Laurentius Petri, the defender of Lutheranism, to whom I shall return.

Erik XIV's time was short. Much of it was spent watching with suspicion the external politics of his half-brother, Johan. Johan had married Katarina Jagellonica, the sister of the Polish King, and was playing his own political games in the Baltic region. Erik accused him of high treason and placed him and his spouse under guard in Gripsholm castle. But other worries emerged. A war against Denmark and Lübeck turned out to be less than successful. More ominous still were the first signs of declining mental health. The Vasa family was genetically disposed not only to minor imbalances, but also to insanity. Erik's half-brothers soon turned the situation to their advantage, and soon it was his turn to find himself imprisoned. He died from poisoning, probably on secret orders from his brothers.

With the new King, Johan III, came a new direction for the Swedish Church. Johan was the most aesthetically inclined of Gustav Vasa's sons, and theologically the most knowledgeable. He was no admirer of the Lutheran Reformation, and had even less regard for Calvinism. He allowed Laurentius Petri finally to publish his Church Ordinance. He also re-established the medieval diocesan structure, which his father had undermined, and restored to the consecration of bishops its medieval Catholic ritual. In keeping with his purpose, he revived royal support for the remaining monasteries, for example Vadstena. To his mind, the Swedish order of divine service – conservative though it in fact was in relation to other Protestant liturgies – ought to be brought closer still to the Catholic tradition. Furthermore, he advocated an intensified study of the Church Fathers. So far he had the support of the majority of the clergy. Many of the old ways had, in any case, stayed on within the Swedish Church. But Johan did not stop there; he began negotiations with Rome. His queen, who had made herself well loved in Sweden, was an enthusiastically practising Catholic and kept her own priests at court. Their son, Sigismund, was brought up a Catholic. Soon Jesuits were to be seen about the capital. Nevertheless, Johan's support for the Counter-Reformation was not without qualification. His dream was of a new unity, but with a Catholic Church that ought, he felt, to be reformed in certain respects – not least in keeping with the teachings of the Church Fathers. For example, he called upon the Pope to sanction communion in both kinds (wine as well as bread) for the laity. The Pope remained silent. In the meantime, his younger brother (later to rule as Carl IX) was canvassing support – but for an alternative church policy, in a counter-movement to the King's cause. Most probably, a Catholic-orientated church would, in some form, have been allowed to develop in Sweden, had it not been for that brotherly resistance.

Johan III died in 1592 and was succeeded by his son, Sigismund (by then King of Poland, following the death of his uncle). For some years to come, Catholic Poland and Lutheran Sweden were to be ruled by one and the same King. From the Swedish point of view, the situation was complicated – but it was inconceivable that Sigismund Vasa, despite his Catholic confession, should not succeed his father on the throne. Before his arrival in Sweden, however, an enlarged General Synod met at Uppsala in order to define the religion of the country.

The year was 1593, and the event was the Synod of Uppsala (*Uppsala Möte*). It has been deemed unique, in that it was a true manifestation of autonomy: the free and independent expression of the will of a nation to determine its confession, now that it no longer coincided with that of its monarch. At this Synod the Swedish religion was ratified: it was here declared to be associated with the Confessions of the Universal Church, and further, with the particular type of Church developed in Sweden, in accordance with the Archbishop Laurentius Petri's *Kyrkoordning* (Church Ordinance) and with *Confessio Augustana 1530*, the Augsburg Confession, common to all Lutherans. Remarkably, it was not until 1593 that the Swedish Church officially proclaimed itself as belonging to any particular confessional community – and then only in response to the obvious threat of the Counter-Reformation. Until then, it had seemed altogether adequate to characterize one's church as an extension of the Catholic – or, as one cautiously put it, 'Universal' or 'Christian' – Church, reformed in accordance with the Holy Scriptures.

When Sigismund arrived, he arrived in the company of the papal nuncio, and with his closest advisers, who were Jesuits to a man. Prior to his coronation, he was forced to give assurances that he would respect the Declaration of the Synod of Uppsala. This he did, but with a *reservatio mentalis*. Carl – his uncle, the Duke – decided to take over

68

the royal responsibility of defending the true faith. He took a broad view of this responsibility, and was soon summoning the *Riksdag* and virtually running the affairs of state. After a few years, he threw off his oath of allegiance to his nephew. The King's supporters countered by continuously accusing the Duke of being sympathetic to Calvinist theology. Plans for joint rule by nephew and uncle proved unrealistic. Sigismund tried to assert his position with the aid of Polish troops, but was defeated by his uncle. The Swedish throne was no longer his.

The after-effects of these events were to be felt for generations to come. The Polish branch of the Vasa dynasty had a legitimate claim to the Swedish throne, and this claim caused religious divergence to be seen as a real and present danger to the country's political autonomy. Consequently, persons of the Roman Catholic persuasion were perceived as a threat to national security and were, without exception, expelled from the country.

The respect in which Carl IX is held by the Swedish people in general is most probably due to his role as leader of the resistance against the Counter-Reformation and, in some measure, to reflected glory: his son was the greatly admired Gustav II Adolf (Gustavus Adolphus). In fact, Carl was a man of considerable brutality and very little culture. He had deliberately inched his way to the throne by ruthlessly using all and any means to reach this, his personal goal. He had plotted the dethronement of his eldest brother, and probably been party to his murder. He had been disloyal to his brother Johan in every conceivable way. By using the threat to religion as a means to his own end, he had ousted Sigismund and his descendants. Finally, he forced the Duke of Östergötland, Johan's second son, to resign his right of succession. As the defender of the Protestant faith in Sweden, he eventually gained its throne. Once comfortably seated, he made it abundantly clear that he and he alone – not the people, nor the clergy – would decide the country's confession and church order, in strict accordance with *cuius regio eius religio*. This was, of course, the very principle he had consistently and vehemently attacked in his fight against Sigismund. There now followed a dogged confrontation between the King and the country's leading Lutherans. Carl wanted to reform the liturgy in the direction of a Calvinist divine service. He wrote a new catechism – published anonymously – containing quotations from the Reformed catechisms of Heidelberg and Emden. But the priests kept on their toes. Olaus Martini, the Archbishop, wrote a stream of polemics. It was particularly the Lutheran teaching of Christ's presence in the Eucharist that the archbishops and the clergy were defending, as well as the principle that it was for the clergy, not the Monarch, to interpret the Bible and the Church's doctrine.

Carl IX was, upon his death, succeeded by his young son, Gustav Adolf. The year was 1611, and marks the end of the Reformation era in Sweden. The transfer from one Confession to another with its starting point at the time of the break with Rome, was not completed until the turn of the century. During all this time Sweden had been ruled by kings none of whom can be seen as themselves committed to the Lutheran faith. And yet, this faith was finally secured in the kingdom of Sweden. Soon, under Gustav II Adolf, this country was to be hailed as the leading European power in the fight for the continued existence of the Lutheran Church.

THE REFORMATION IN DENMARK-NORWAY

The breakthrough of the Reformation in Denmark-Norway coincides, in important ways, with that in Sweden: the break with Rome, for example, and the connection with the German reformers. But much of importance was not so similar. The chain of events differed, and these differences were to leave their mark.

Denmark is undeniably closer to mainland Europe than is Sweden – not simply geographically, but culturally, too.

Altar frontal, dated 1561, from Torslunde, Zealand (now in the National Museum, Copenhagen), showing how the three main liturgical acts were performed in Denmark after the Reformation. Note the crucifix and candles on the altar, and the priest's traditional vestments. (There are many paintings of this type in Germany, e.g. by Lucas Cranach the younger.) *Photograph: The National Museum, Copenhagen.*

This is clearly reflected in the history of the Danish Church during the time of its reformation. The Danes were much more acutely aware of the actual presence, so to speak, of Luther and the other German reformers, than were the Swedes. Significantly, the prologue to the reformation of Denmark was set in the adjoining Duchies of Schleswig and Holstein, both belonging to the Holy Roman Empire – and situated just south of Jutland.

The relationship between these two duchies and the Danish Royal family was of long standing and great complexity. Since the middle of the fifteenth century, the Kings of Denmark-Norway had, at the same time, been Dukes of Schleswig-Holstein. Soon after his succession in 1523 King Frederik I handed the two duchies to his son, Christian. The young Duke was an ardent supporter of the Reformation. He had been present at the Diet of Worms in 1521, where Luther's conduct before the Emperor

71

Charles V had deeply impressed him. Responsible, now, for the two duchies, he placed himself in charge of the affairs of their Church. With great determination, he removed all adversaries of the Reformation from their posts, while all who spread the Lutheran teachings received his full support. Soon the Reformation controlled all the important cities in the area: Haderslev, Flensburg, Kiel and Schleswig. As early as 1528, the new, Lutheran form of church government was established, and executive powers over the Church vested in the Duke. These events took place within the Holy Roman Empire, but in a part of it concurrently belonging to the Danish realm. Its rapid change to Lutheranism, so victorious and so close by, cannot but have been a source of great encouragement to Lutheran disciples inside the borders of Denmark proper.

Having succeeded his father to the throne of Denmark as Christian III, he held the reins of government as firmly there as in Schleswig-Holstein. (I cannot here comment on the developments in connection with the succession in 1534–36.) The change of Confession was effected immediately after his coronation in 1537: the adoption of the Augsburg Confession, a new episcopate and the church government firmly held in the king's hands.

The Reformer-King of Denmark-Norway remained a devoted and keen disciple of the leaders of the German Reformation. To him, being the Governor of the Church was a religious calling. He left the practicalities of implementing the Reformation to Dr Johannes Bugenhagen, a Pomeranian pastor recommended by Luther. To him was given the honour of conducting both the coronation and the episcopal consecration that followed it. A new Church Ordinance was speedily in print. There were none of the restraints and none of the sharp turn-abouts that are so characteristic of Swedish Reformation history. Nor did the new Danish church structure show the same degree of independence in relation to mainland Lutheranism.

A further important difference lies in the fact that the breakthrough of the Reformation in Denmark had been preceded by a revivalist reform movement, both extensive and intense, among its people. There was little of this in Sweden, where the significant events were, instead initiated by the King. It is hard to imagine that Christian III could have been so successful in this matter, as soon as he came to power, had not the reform movement already grown so hugely popular – partly because Germany was so close and its influence so strong. The groundwork, then, had been done prior to 1536. In contrast to what was happening in England, individual towns in Denmark and in the Baltic area (such as Viborg in Jutland, Odense on Funen, Copenhagen on one side of The Sound, and Malmö, on the other) had in fact gone over to the new confession of their own volition, before the royal decree. This was the result of the Protestant teachings of some formidable personalities. Hans Tausen, in Viborg and later in Copenhagen, may have been the most influential. The burgher-class was also active through its own representatives. Jørgen Koch, the powerful burgomaster of Malmö, provides a case in point: undaunted, he governed his city in matters both spiritual and secular. Malmö had its own liturgy and hymn-book and, thanks to Koch, the priests could preach what they had learnt from Luther in their church of St Peter in relative peace. They even managed to found their own Protestant theological college, flagrantly disregarding the fact that they lived very nearly next door to the archepiscopal city of Lund. All this took place in the 1520s. There was no equivalent rural development. The peasantry acquired no independent powers for itself in Denmark. Everything that was new emerged in the towns, with their self-assured population and their contacts abroad.

In Norway, the 'Royal' Reformation was not preceded by any corresponding popular movement: there was hardly any independent urban population. The peasantry firmly supported the Catholic Archbishop, and opposition to Christian's reform programme was kept up till the last.

73

But the support for the Archbishop proved insufficient. Christian quashed all resistance, and from then on Norway was governed from Copenhagen, by the King and the Danish Council. The opposition had proved seriously counter-productive, having led to the end of what was left of Norway's independence, political as well as ecclesiastical.

The same fate befell Iceland. The new Bishop of Skálholt had converted to Lutheranism. This left only the Bishop of Hólar, Jon Arason, to organize a defence of the old faith and of the autonomy of the country, which to him counted equally, or more. He was imprisoned and executed, whereupon the *Alltinget* (the Islandic parliament) accepted the Danish *Kirkeordinans* (Church Ordinance). They were also forced to accept Danish troops and a Danish *lensmand* (crown constable), sent by the King.

By the royal activities of 1537 – preceded by the evangelical movement – the Church of Denmark, together with those of Norway and Iceland, had effectively been brought in line with the changes that had occurred in principalities and cities on the European mainland. In Sweden, Gustav Vasa was in charge of the Church, and the property of bishops and monasteries had been transferred to the crown, to the nobility and, in the towns, to the burghers. The Lutheran message was being heard, and protestant worship was on its way. In England, Henry VIII had cut the ties with Rome and, with the backing of Parliament, introduced certain church reforms. His death had opened the floodgates to a far more radical reformation of liturgy and teaching.

These events amounted to no less than a revolution in the church life of the countries concerned – and not only in economic and constitutional terms. The late Middle Ages had emphasized what the individual person, assisted by the Church, could do for the eternal good of himself and his family – by such means as prayers for the dead, pilgrimages and the penitential system. Now all this was to count for nothing – worse, it was denounced as pernicious delusion. The idea that one could make life after death more tolerable for oneself and one's dear departed had in time come to be taken for granted, and permeated almost all the services and prayers offered by the churches. Hence their constantly increasing wealth, in return for which a constant flow of masses for the dead and readings from the Psalter had been provided. And now the reformers declared that it was in no way possible to influence one's own fate after death, nor that of anyone else. One was to concentrate instead on one thing only: the Gospel, and what it offers, free and 'by grace alone' – namely, what was already achieved, once and for all, through the death and resurrection of Christ. This was what they strove to bring home to their congregations – not as something new, but as part of the fundamental continuity with the true catholicity of the Church.

Nor was external continuity lacking, certainly not in the churches here discussed: the Nordic churches and the Church of England. They lived on, quite naturally, as national churches. Royal influence had certainly increased – but this was hardly a novelty. Church and society were in general inseparable, now as before. The congregation and the parish were one and the same thing, both socially and ecclesiologically. The Reformation added nothing new here, nor did it take anything away. Indeed, great exception was taken to radical movements that opposed Church and society. They were seen as dangerous 'dreamers' and sowers of sedition.

And so the national churches in the North, as in England, remained fundamentally the same: *Ecclesi Svecana*, *Danica* and *Anglicana* – while at the same time undergoing an important change. This change is clearly exemplified by the episcopate: quite obviously, no bishop in England or the Nordic countries received, after the breach with Rome, the papal confirmation – essential in the medieval Church. This meant a radical break with canonical unity and continuity. Further, the huge economic and political power wielded by the bishops was severely criticized by the reformers – who demolished it, more resolutely in the North than in England. Nevertheless these churches kept their episcopal structure and their view of episcopacy as being a precious and indispensible inheritance from Catholic Universal Christendom. In this respect there is, in actual fact, unbroken continuity in all these churches. This fact has frequently been overlooked and sometimes doubted, but can today be granted due importance, also from the ecumenical perspective. It therefore needs a special place in our exposition.

EPISCOPACY RECONSTRUCTED

The Swedish Church

When Gustav Vasa was elected King of Sweden in 1523, the country's Catholic episcopate was in crisis, mainly for political reasons. The last effective pre-Reformation Archbishop of Uppsala, Gustav Trolle, had been fighting hard against the nationalist movement and had duly been unseated in 1517. We find him later in the entourage of Christian II, at the time when the latter had placed himself on the Swedish throne by military means. In conjunction with his coronation in Stockholm, these two men caused 'the Blood-bath of Stockholm' – the merciless massacre of more than eighty of the leading nationalists. Among them was the greater part of Sweden's aristocracy, including Gustav Vasa's father and two of the country's bishops. It is unlikely that historians will ever agree on where the initiative lay – with the king or with the Archbishop. However, one thing is clear: this was a major political blunder. The atrocity completely put paid to the great Nordic Union, which in Swedish eyes was now discredited beyond redemption. Further, knowledge of the archbishop's involvement seriously injured the reputation of Catholic episcopacy per se. Trolle was forced to leave the country. Once King Christian had been expelled – following his defeat in Gustav Vasa's war of independence – the Archbishop's chances of ever returning were naturally very slim. But the Pope, stubbornly and against all sense, backed Trolle. He blankly refused to consider any solution that might have been acceptable to the Swedes – which obviously did not bode well for the continued existence in Sweden of the Roman Catholic Church.

At the start of Gustav Vasa's reign five of the seven episcopal sees were, for a variety of reasons, vacant. This of course had to be remedied, as the King fully agreed. The first to be appointed was Petrus Magni, in 1524. He was elected by the chapter of Västerås, and quite in accordance with Canon Law. Being a monk of the Brigittine Order, and finding himself in Rome – supervising the Swedish Church property at Campo dei Fiori, where Birgitta had resided and died – Petrus Magni did, as a matter of course, receive papal confirmation, and was duly consecrated in Rome before leaving for home.

It was this bishop of Västerås who, on his return to Sweden, was instrumental in passing on the historic episcopal succession, the so called *Successio Apostolica*, even to Swedish bishops who, from now on, were to be appointed without papal confirmation. In 1528 he consecrated no fewer than three new bishops, appointed by the King. Several years of Swedish hesitation had passed by then, and Rome had shown no sign of any concession. It now seemed necessary to take this action: the King had not yet been crowned and the coronation could not be further delayed. In the eyes of the people there was something seriously incomplete about an uncrowned King and, indeed, about a coronation without 'proper' bishops – bishops consecrated in accordance with medieval tradition. On the other hand, the theological inclination of the bishops – reformist Catholic or Protestant – was, in popular opinion, a relatively unimportant matter.

It is hardly surprising that Gustav Vasa found the need for bishops whom his people could recognize a pressing one – and that he was careful to continue, in so far as it was open to him, the succession of consecrations. No one was to have reason to criticize him for a breach with the old church order – and certainly not on a matter so central to it as providing the country with proper bishops and priests. Nor must anyone doubt his own 'proper' status as King, crowned by a 'proper' bishop in a manner which would be recognized by all. His sense of urgency is understandable: he had won the throne by armed rebellion, and was himself the first of his dynasty.

Some years later, in 1531, a new Archbishop was to be consecrated. Having long waited for the Pope to stop insisting on the return of Trolle to this office – given that it was impossible for Sweden to accept him back – enough was, finally, enough. A most important event was to take place: the King was about to marry. He had chosen a German princess, Katarina of Sachsen-Lauenburg. Her lineage was flawless, and her parents had not concealed their view of the proposed alliance as rather a risky business. It was imperative, then, to organize the marriage ceremony with the utmost propriety, and it had to be conducted by someone entirely worthy of that task, and of thereafter crowning the new Queen. To this purpose, the 31-year old Laurentius Petri was appointed Sweden's first Lutheran Archbishop. He received his consecration from a bishop who had himself been consecrated according to the Catholic rite – almost certainly the above-mentioned Petrus Magni.

Few topics of Swedish church history have been as thoroughly examined and written about as the episcopal succession and the episcopal consecrations of the sixteenth century – the obvious reason for this attention being that the Swedish Church, including at that time the Finnish church, in these respects differs from other Lutheran churches. Here, not only episcopacy but also the continuity of consecration has been preserved. Interest in this unique situation began in the nineteenth century, hardly earlier. In connection with today's ecumenical movement, this interest has grown. As the Church of England views the so-called 'historic episcopate' as crucial to the unity of the Church, it is, of course, of special interest to be able to show that this essential element has been preserved in the Swedish Church.

Anglo-Catholic quarters have been known to doubt that this could really be so – it seemed rather too good to be true! And in Sweden there was much, sometimes naive, enthusiasm about this apostolic succession and the opportunities it seemed to present the Swedish Church for ecumenical contributions. There is an abundance of church history writing on this subject, including Roman Catholic contributions. The most thorough investigation – of each link in the succession of episcopal appointments and consecrations in the Swedish Church, starting with Petrus Magni's consecration in Rome and ending in the latter half of this century – was made by Sven Kjöllerström, a church historian at Lund University (three volumes: 1952, 1965 and 1974). One of Professor Kjöllerström's reasons for undertaking this comprehensive work was a certain irritation at what he saw as the Swedish Church's childish delight at its 'apostolic succession'. He was keen to find flaws in the argument. But after his many years of investigation he concluded that continuity of consecration had, after all, been preserved in the Swedish Church. The long chain did, after all, hang together – albeit, as he adds, 'by a thread'.

The weakness he locates concerns the practice of episcopacy and consecration not during the 1520s and 1530s, but during the period that followed. Gustav Vasa may have been anxious, indeed, to show himself to have 'proper' bishops in his realm, not least for his own red-letter days – but it did not take him long to feel some apprehension too: even though he had divested them of all fortified castles and lands, these consecrated bishops in their eminent, medieval dioceses might well become too powerful for his comfort. As mentioned earlier, the 1540s saw him make a fresh attempt to further weakening their position in the country. Now he felt safer in his saddle; a German ecclesiastical adviser was summoned, to help with a radical decentralization of the national church government. The dioceses were to be divided into smaller units, each one headed by an *ordinarius*, (usually without a consecration), all in accordance with the manner of the German protestant churches. In addition to these the King also appointed 'superintendents', partly replacing the earlier rural deans. With this comprehensive reform he intended to crush the autonomy of the Church by breaking up the old episcopal structure. It looked as if the plan might well work, but circumstances brought it to a halt: Gustav Vasa's sons did not share their father's aversion to episcopacy. As we have seen, one of them was very particular, indeed, about Catholic continuity. Johan III promptly got rid of his father's German-inspired church government, carefully restored the medieval dioceses and renewed the tradition of episcopal consecration.

Johan III succeeded to the throne in 1569. The old Archbishop Laurentius Petri, who had been consecrated in accordance with the old order, was still alive. At last, in 1571, he was allowed to publish his important work, the Swedish Church Ordinance, in which the character of the Swedish Church is defined. It was not a work that had pleased either Gustav Vasa or Erik XIV – in their eyes, it guarded far too powerfully the autonomy of the Church, not least with regard to the episcopate.

The Church Ordinance of 1571 still ranks among the principal official documents of the Swedish Church. It describes the Church of the Swedish Reformation, in that it points both to a family resemblance with other reformed churches and to its own particular features. Regarding the latter, a notably conservative, or traditionalist, trait needs to be mentioned. Where radical Protestants would say that anything not prescribed in the Bible must be banished from the reformed Church, the Swedish Church Ordinance states, instead, that everything that is a 'good, old custom' should be kept unto, abolishing only what was found clearly to contradict the Scriptures. It would be best, it was thought, to keep one's inheritance and to offer instruction in what was good and valuable in the old church traditions. One consequence of this interpretation is the fact that medieval liturgy was largely preserved within the new Mass. Another, of equal importance, is the continuance of episcopacy, as seen in the Church Ordinance. A separate chapter, 'On Bishops', is rich in detail. Here we are told that the early Church did not distinguish between priest and bishop. However, as the Church grew larger, the need arose for a special office for the oversight of congregations and the ordination of priests. This system is referred to as 'useful and indubitably instituted by God and the Holy Spirit, and thus it was universally approved and accepted, all over Christendom and has therefore remained and will remain, 'world without end'. The Church Ordinance also contains the rite for consecration of bishops, setting out, among other things, how the bishop who presides over the consecration, in his cope and assisted by other bishops and priests, should conduct the consecration by the laying on of hands and prayer.

Laurentius Petri died in 1573, at the age of 74. The consecration of the new Archbishop, together with two other recently appointed bishops, followed a rite worked out by Johan himself. It was magnificent, and contained several medieval elements not included in the Church Ordinance. The crozier and mitre were restored – and so was the act of anointing, despite resistance from the clergy. (The latter element was again removed in the 1590s.)

But how, exactly, was the continuity of the apostolic succession preserved? And where is the weakest link in the chain? Gustav Vasa's successive steps towards a great reduction in the power of the bishops had included the abandonment of episcopal consecration of bishops. Except in Finland. The King had found it wise to consider the Finnish peasantry's aversion to change. He made sure of placing especially reliable clergy in this distant part of his realm, and then gave in on the matter of consecration. In

1554, the Diocese of Turku and the newly founded Diocese of Viipuri, on the eastern border with Russia, each received an *ordinarius* – the King's new name for a bishop. Mikael Agricola, later to be named 'the Reformer of Finland', was sent to Turku, Paul Juusten to Viipuri. (The former had translated the New Testament into Finnish in 1548, and can thus also be called the founder of the written Finnish language.) They were both consecrated bishops in Strängnäs Cathedral, by Bishop Botvid, who had himself been consecrated 'in accordance with the rules'. Juusten was still alive – and Bishop of Turku – in 1575, when Johan III arranged the great episcopal consecration at Uppsala Cathedral. Juusten had been consecrated to the episcopate, albeit as a kind of suffragan, with the title *ordinarius*. Juusten was the last remaining bishop in the realm to have been consecrated. All the others had only their royal appointment – Johan III called them 'paper bishops'. At the consecration of 1575, Juusten was one of the four partic- ipating bishops – though he did not preside – he merely assisted (a fact Sven Kjöllerström has emphasized). But he did – and the sources make this quite clear – take part in the laying on of hands, and did himself perform one of the elements: the anointing. On these grounds he emerges as the link – it may be weak, but is importantly not missing – that leaves unbroken the chain of episcopal consecrations in the Swedish Church.

On the initiative of Johan III both the medieval diocesan organization and the tradition of episcopal consecration were restored. The additional office of 'superintendent' created by Gustav Vasa alongside the 'proper' episcopate was, however, to continue – for two centuries – but not in the old dioceses. Instead they were turned into a kind of flying squad, dispatched to the northern parts of the country and to new provinces that were considered not yet ready to be incorporated into the full diocesan structure. The term 'Superintendent' was also retained in the areas of northern Germany conquered by the Swedes in the seventeenth century presumably in order to conform to mainland Lutheran practice. Superintendents were not consecrated, but were occasionally appointed to diocesan bishoprics, receiving their consecration at that point. As a general rule, superintendents had the right to ordain. In times past, when the Swedish state included the many provinces around the Baltic Sea, many a priest was ordained by a superintendent. It took a royal decree to abolish, in 1772, the last superintendencies. This was done on the explicit grounds that it was for traditionally consecrated bishops, and for them only, to ordain the priests of the Swedish Church – including the priests of the new dioceses.

The decision to appoint superintendents may be regarded as leading into a siding. The main line followed by the Swedish Church across the century of Reformation was the preservation, and later the strengthening, of the episcopal tradition. As a result, the identity of Church's ministry was recognized, and this in turn contributed greatly to the Church's ability to maintain a certain independence vis-à-vis the royal power. With a well defined episcopacy and a house of clergy in the *Riksdag* (parliament), of which the bishops were ex-officio members, the Church could not be ignored or controlled by the monarch. The Swedish Church therefore never quite took on the character of a state institution.

The Danish-Norwegian Church

As we look back again at the development within the Danish Church, and at its immediate effect on the Churches of Norway and Iceland, it is clear that the episcopacy was preserved there, too. The differences between Danish and Swedish church reformation history result from Denmark's closeness to, and assistance from, continental Lutheranism and her lack of those opportunities by which Sweden had been able to build a bridge between the old episcopacy and the new.

A certain Danish disappointment in its Roman Catholic

bishops was not, perhaps, without foundation. As we know, these were by no means incompetent men. But they were lacking theological learning and pastoral experience and therefore they had no chance of understanding, and no chance of withstanding, their country's move towards Reformation. Their frame of reference was determined by their status: all were prominent members of the nobility, they were politicians and they also had the husbandry of their huge estates to see to. Nor did it help that they had been the adversaries of Christian III. Further, the archiepiscopal see of Lund was in a state of confusion – bordering on dissolution – throughout the 1520s. Following the death in 1519 of the last powerful pre-Reformation Archbishop, this vital office was passed on and on, so that there were, in turn, no less than five Archbishops in that one decade. It was a sorry spectacle: a cluster of more or less unscrupulous men, frantically grabbing for a lucrative post. The papal funds were greatly enhanced by the trade in offices but – due to its offensive haggling over the price of the Danish archiepiscopal see – the reputation of the Roman Catholic episcopacy plummeted.

This background helps us understand that what the *Københavnske Recess'* of 1536 (the first foundation document of the Danish Reformation) had to say about the former episcopate was considered fitting: these men had not met the prevailing need for *christelige Bisper og Superattendenter, som det menige Folk kunde lære, undervise og prædike det hellige Evangelium og Guds ord'* (Christian bishops and superintendents, capable of communicating to the people the holy Gospel and the word of God, by teaching, instructing and preaching). Instead they had distinguished themselves by their *'verdslig ståt og prall'* (worldly pomp and circumstance) and by their resistance to the Reformation. They had also aided and abetted rebellion, by siding against the king. They had to be deposed, and their castles and estates handed over to the Crown – these political and economic considerations were no less decisive than the others. It was inconceivable that any one of these men could be entrusted with – or even wish to take on – the task of passing on the succession by the consecration of new, Lutheran bishops. There was only one thing for it: a fresh start – in order, thereby, to keep and to pass on 'the holy Gospel and the word of God'.

The position offered to the new bishops was definitely not a lucrative one. The *Ordinance* of 1537/39 is very specific, and there was certainly no question of their being granted any castles or estates. Their income was carefully prescribed, as was their allowance in the matter of rye, oats, malt and hay and straw for horses, cows and lambs. The number of servants allowed, 'after wife and children', was carefully restricted. At the venerable archepiscopal see of Lund the King moved his *lensmand* (crown constable) into the archepiscopal residence, leaving the superintendent to occupy a cottage nextdoor, an abode consisting of one large room and one small. The occupant of an office that by the end of the Middle Ages had come to mean ruling over five fortified castles and 2,500 estates was now to live in two rooms – with, unlike his predecessors, wife and children.

The duties that went with the job follow in curt terms. This part of the Ordinance begins: 'But in so far as the Superintendents ought to be the true Bishops and Archbishops of the churches, they are now called not to the paltry efforts they have been used to, but to great work.' The sharp tone continues to admonish the bygone bishops. The new bishops would have to show themselves constantly diligent in preaching and teaching in the oversight of everything to do with their dioceses, and in caring for the poor. The most frequently used term for them is 'superintendent', i.e. the Latin for the New Testament's *episcopos* – but it is used, we find, synonymously with that of 'bishop'. The rite for 'ordaining'these superintendents is also laid down in the Ordinance.

This rite sheds light on how the office of superintendent was perceived. The ordination takes place during divine service in the presence of the congregation. Hymns are sung in Latin, but readings from the Bible in Danish predomi-

The consecration of Protestant bishops in the Cathedral Church of our Lady in Copenhagen, on 2 September 1537. Bronze relief (1942), by Max Andersen. On the Reformation Monument, Bispetorvet, Copenhagen. *Photograph: The National Museum, Copenhagen.*

nate, together with the sermon. The duty of preaching the Gospel is strongly stressed, while the liturgy indicates the apostolic character of the office of superintendent. The first reading begins 'Thus spoke St Paul unto his Bishop Titus...'; the second is from the Acts, chapter 20: 'As St Paul bade good night to the priests of Ephesus, he said unto them...'; the third is 2 Timothy, chapter 3: 'Thus speaks St Paul to his Bishop Timothy...' After the readings there follows a summary of the meaning of this office: it is Christ himself who, through his 'preachers' – i.e. through this office – preaches, baptizes, distributes the sacraments, punishes, admonishes and comforts. The liturgy concludes with the president and assisting priests praying, while placing their hands on the new superintendent's head – as the apostles did – whereupon is sung an invocation of the Holy

Spirit. The service continues with Holy Communion.

It was according to this rite that the first seven super-intendents of the Danish Church were, together with one from Norway, consecrated in Copenhagen Cathedral on 2 September 1537. Christian III's choice of *ordinator* was Johannes Bugenhagen, previously mentioned as the priest from Pomerania recommended by Luther. This was the man who had helped organize the Danish Church anew, and who some weeks earlier had officiated at the King's coronation. The breach with universal church order, so strongly implied by the choice for this task of a man who had merely been ordained a priest, appears to have been quite deliberate. But by this the chain of consecrations was broken. In the words of a Danish historian: 'And this displayed the excessive pride of a young Church – thinking it could do away with this venerable tradition.' Nevertheless, the structure of the act of consecration shows that there was no intention of giving up the claim to *successio*, where the meaning of the office of superintendent was concerned. On the contrary, the wish was to preserve it, and to mark its 'apostolic character'.

The choice of holders of the office of superintendent was at any rate a happy one. From their accounts of energetic visitations of the parishes, the sources suggest a very positive view of the work of these, the overseers of the Lutheran dioceses. Peder Palladius' famous *Visitatsbog* (Book of Visitations) provides a close-up of his activities in the Diocese of Zealand. This is the diocese whose bishop in Copenhagen became the presiding bishop of the Danish Church, once Lund had lost its place as its archiepscopal see. Very soon the superintendents were being called 'bishops'. After all, that is what they had always been perceived to be.

CHAPTER 4

Similarities and Differences

Having introduced the main features of the changes in the
Nordic national churches during the Reformation era –
changes nevertheless in conscious continuity with the past
– and having here addressed myself first and foremost to
the Anglican sister churches, I realize that two questions
might naturally arise. Just how alike were these churches,
at the same time young and old, – the Nordic and the
Anglican – which under Gustav Vasa, Christian III and
Henry VIII had broken with the Pope in Rome? And how
much contact did they have with one another, as each lived
through the crises of the sixteenth century – as they went
about their business of building on medieval tradition in
the light of the Reformation?

There is no simple answer to the first of these two questions. We are, after all, dealing with dynamic entities. It is
in the very nature of these churches that they will compare
differently at different times. The era of upheavals was by
no means restricted to the first half of the sixteenth century.
The second half was to be quite as dramatic in many places,
and so was the seventeenth century – certainly in England.
Nor were any of these national churches ever entirely homo-
geneous. Developments at some levels in church and society
did not reach all groups or parts of society, at least not
simultaneously. Add the fact that, due to the changes, each
church experienced its own deep internal divisions, and it
becomes clear that any comparison between them is fraught
with complication. Which section, or which school of
thought, is to count as characteristic of these churches, at
any given time? These questions well describe the dilemma
we face today in our ecumenical negotiations. We cannot
expect comparative church history to be any less problem-

atic. There were, in all these churches, internal tensions –
in some more serious, or more violently expressed, than in
others at the same, or at some other, point in this period
of time. In this respect we may single out Denmark –
including Norway and Iceland – as being, from the middle
of 1530s onwards, the least afflicted. Its Reformation was
at this stage in the process of being completed, effectively
and fairly uniformly. By comparison, Sweden was suffering
more from internal conflicts; and England a great deal
more.

ELIZABETH I AND ERIK XIV

We must bear this in mind when we attempt to investigate
the concrete relations between the Nordic national churches
and the English Church of the sixteenth and seventeenth
centuries, and thereby answer the second of the two questions: How much contact was there between them? To this,
there is a simple answer: Not a great deal, and rather more
superficial than might have been expected. The relationships that did spring up are nevertheless worth examining.

We shall keep primarily to official relations. One of the
first indications of how close the Church of England and
the Swedish Church perceived themselves to be – both
having distanced themselves from Rome – occurs in the
years around the accession of Queen Elizabeth in 1559, and
at the highest level. A marriage proposal was presented to
Elizabeth, the suitor being Erik, Prince of Sweden and, as
of 1560, its King. Plans were drawn up for a Union of
the two countries, to take the form of a lasting alliance, a
perpetuum foedus, with the throne to pass, in due course
and by right of birth, to the issue of the royal marriage.
The fact that the crown in both countries held a prominent
position in the governance of their respective national
churches was, of course, an important consideration, and
was to be reflected in the prospective Union.

Hindsight may tempt us to underestimate the importance of these negotiations – after all, King Erik lost his mind and his throne. But at the time of the proposal it was far from difficult to present him as Elizabeth's equal. For several years in the 1560s the Swedish side invested great efforts in these negotiations, and the idea can hardly have been of no interest to Elizabeth at a time when her position was still relatively precarious and so in need of maximum political support. In addition, Erik was a handsome man, with all the qualities and learning expected of a Renaissance prince. True, he was one in a long line of suitors – one player in a game most cleverly controlled by Elizabeth. But he was certainly no light-weight, not least in view of the compatibility of his country's church with that of Elizabeth's. Although the various draft treaties and contracts concentrated on proposed agreements of a political and commercial nature, significant reference was made to agreement, between the two countries and rulers, on the traditions and objectives of their churches.

The value of agreement with regard to religion and the Church was emphasized in two ways. First, there was a reminder of the known fact that it was from England that the Christian faith had been brought to Sweden: this was evidence of a time-honoured unity. Secondly, both countries had broken with Rome. Gustav Vasa's reformation was greatly praised, as was the 'right' religion of his sons. The ecclesiastical stance of the monarchs was, it would seem, of paramount importance – not surprisingly, perhaps, in the circumstances of a proposed dynastic marriage. Starting from the Swedish King's title, 'King of the Svea people and the Goths', a magnificent parallel was drawn between 'the Gothic victories over Rome', way back in history, and Gustav Vasa's victory over the Roman Church.

There is, however, no mention of the episcopal tradition held in common by the two churches, nor of the continuity of central 'Catholic' features in both the Anglican and the Lutheran interpretations of Christianity. These omissions may have been deliberate, given the then influence of the Puritans. Or they may be explained by the fact that the

90

mastermind behind the Swedish drafts was Dionysius Beurræus, a Frenchman who had served Gustav Vasa and who,
more to the point, was a recent convert to the Reformed
Church. This man, entrusted with the negotiations in
London, became an enthusiastic member of the Puritan
circle there. Most of its members were erstwhile exiles who,
under Mary I, had found sanctuary in Geneva – whence
they had now returned, basking in the reflected glory of
their martyrs, to press for a more thoroughly completed
English Reformation. To them, of course, the episcopal
tradition was hardly attractive, and any remaining Catholic
feature anathema.

Sweden employed several emissaries to bring about the
desired end. A glittering London embassy was created by
Erik's half-brother (and successor) Johan. Johan kept court,
at great expense, in a London house made available for
his use by the Bishop of Winchester. The Swedish prince
became noted for his elegant conduct at the hunt and at
ball-games, and for his good Latin. Of the three sons of
Gustav Vasa, Johan was the one with the greatest interest
in theology. He was also deeply attracted to liturgy, and it
has frequently been suggested that his time in England
inspired the new liturgy – containing clearly Catholic
elements – that he was later to devise for the Swedish
Church. But this is unlikely: the Elizabethan Church could
hardly have held much appeal for him in that respect. The
liturgy of London's churches at the beginning of the 1560s
would not have been particularly splendid. The Queen's
private chapel certainly was not – though there was still a
crucifix on its altar, much to Puritan dismay. One may
safely assume that Johan did not fail to attend worship
during his four months at Elizabeth's court, and he may
therefore have participated in Holy Communion. But it is
hard to imagine him being inspired by the Anglican liturgy,
which under Elizabeth was far more Spartan than a Swede
was used to – though there were, there as here, rural congregations who faithfully kept to the old customs. The Swedish
prince, so passionately interested in liturgy, was to find out

instead about the activities of the Royal Commission led by Bishop Jewell, whose task it was to demolish altars, statues, church paintings and other symbols of Catholicism. It should be remembered that the great Richard Hooker's founding work of Anglican theology – in the form of anti-Puritan polemics – did not appear for some decades yet and had to wait until the seventeenth century for its first real breakthrough.

As every reader will know, Erik XIV made his proposals in vain: the grand design for a dynastic, and so for an ecclesiastical, *perpetuum foedus* came to nothing. The Vasa family's foreign policy turned firmly eastwards and, during the following generation, to the south. Relations with England became sporadic. The dream of a lasting union sank into oblivion. But it was to have a theological epilogue in Sweden: a wave of a highly 'Protestant' Calvinism, with absolutely no 'Catholic' Anglican features. Fired by the Puritan fervour he had found in England, Dionysius Beurræus returned to Sweden armed with inflexible Calvinist propaganda. The Swedish Archbishop countered with an even more unwavering defence of Lutheran theology and the Swedish, traditionalist view of the church. The fight against Calvinism was to be the *leitmotif* of his writings.

DEFENSE AGAINST CALVINISM

From an ecumenical point of view, the diplomatic relations with England at the start of the 1560s turned out to have especially negative consequences. The Swedish gained an impression that the Church of England was an entirely Calvinist community to be guarded against. This was apparently the legacy of the diplomacy surrounding King Erik's proposal, and this opinion was to remain unchanged for centuries to come.

The Swedish Archbishop was not alone in his fight against Calvinist influence. The clergy were increasingly conscious of a Lutheran identity, though it had been difficult to provide for their education in the new situation. The University of Uppsala, founded towards the end of the fifteenth century, only just earlier than that of Copenhagen, was experiencing reduced circumstances. But the diocesan schools took on some of the responsibility, and the Protestant Universities of Northern Germany were accessible. The University of Rostock, especially, saw a great influx of Swedish students. There was therefore considerable support among the clergy for the Lutheran identity of the Swedish Church.

Four elements of Calvinist influence were seen as so extremely dangerous that defending one's Lutheran church against them was perceived as an absolute duty. Two of these figure in the main part of the Archbishop's very first polemic – against Beurræus, on the latter's return from England – which took the form of a defence of the Lutheran view of Christ's real presence in the Eucharistic bread and wine and a justification of the use of images in churches. The Puritans understood the Eucharist almost only in terms of a commemorative celebration, and they were set on clearing the churches of images, in keeping with the Old Testament proscription. The other two elements to come under severe attack were, first, the Puritan belief in Predestination, as being incompatible with the Lutheran understanding of salvation, and secondly, the Puritan rules of morality – again, clearly at odds with those of the Lutherans. Taken together, these points covered vital parts of Lutheran piety and theology. The vehemence of the attack against Beurræus may well have had much to do with his influence on King Erik, but should be seen as issuing also from what was by then a notable show of Calvinist strength in large parts of Europe. The Swedish fight against Calvinism was to continue for generations to come. A wall of defence was built and reinforced, to keep out the Puritan Christians on the mainland, and to keep out the Anglicans, too.

*   *   *

An equally strong guard was kept in Denmark-Norway-Iceland over its Lutheran theology and liturgy. Throughout the Reformation era theological arguments there aimed to preserve the belief in Christ's real presence in the elements of the Eucharist. Niels Hemmingsen, Denmark's leading theologian of the sixteenth century, was promptly sacked from his post at Copenhagen University once there was evidence of his defection from the Lutheran belief in the dynamic realism of the Eucharist. The merest suggestion of Calvinism was perceived to be disastrous. Even Philip Melanchton, Luther's associate, was viewed with suspicion. His theology acquired the name of 'Philippism', and parts of it were branded as Calvinist heresy.

This is not to say that the Danish and Swedish reformed churches were in every way alike. The Danish Reformation was in several respects more radical than its Swedish counterpart. But the Danish-Norwegian-Icelandic version did not let go of its conscious continuity in the Church and liturgy. The mystery of the Eucharist was energetically defended, just as it was by Luther himself. And the Danish Church Ordinance (*Kirkeordinansen*) describes in careful detail the ritual of the Mass. It states that the communicants are to approach the sanctuary, where they are to kneel and receive first absolution, and then the eucharistic elements. Further, the priest is to be told in advance, the exact number of communicants, to enable him to consecrate the exact number of wafers. If more communicants arrive, he must consecrate the equivalent number of additional wafers. The distribution of the Sacrament in the sanctuary was seen as a particularly holy moment in the service. Undoubtedly, it was for this reason that often very magnificent chancel screens were erected in Danish churches after the Reformation. Behind them, at the altar itself, one was to feel that one was entering the Holy of Holies.

The matter of Calvinist versus Lutheran beliefs should not be thought of as solely the concern of professional theologians. There is evidence to show how deeply an awareness of confessional differences had penetrated into the general consciousness. We might take one example from early seventeenth century Denmark, as noted down by a royal court chaplain. Chancellor Christian Friis lies dying. He is a confident man – altogether comfortable in his opinion that his is the true faith. So he gave thanks to God for having been born a man, of Christian parents, brought up in the true faith and, above all, for having been saved from 'the terrible Calvinist delusion of Predestination' (den gruelige Calvinske Vildfarelse de prædestinatione). Obviously for him, certainty of salvation could be built on the teaching of Luther on the unmerited grace of God rather than on the interpretation by Calvin.

We can still see the consequences of the opposing opinions on the presence of images within the churches. The altars were preserved in the Lutheran North, but were exchanged for wooden communion tables in England, like in many Protestant churches, as a result of different interpretations of the Sacrament. In many Danish churches, and still more in Norway, the pictures on the ornate reredos were replaced with Biblical texts referring to confession and communion. The view of Luther and his followers in the North was, however, clear: anything serving as adornment and anything that might serve to instruct was not only to be permitted, but encouraged. Hence in the Nordic countries much is preserved of medieval ecclesiastical art, not least including wall paintings. The tradition of adorning one's church with such images continued in the sixteenth and seventeenth centuries, until the rococo and the neo-classical styles took over.

Finally, as far as morals are concerned, there is ample evidence of how different ethics and social traditions came to be in the Lutheran countries, as compared with cultures influenced by Puritan commands and interdictions. We shall come across a rather drastic example of this, in connection with a large English embassy to the Swedish court of Queen Christina, in the middle of the seventeenth century. The threat of Calvinism, as experienced in the North, did not, however, in the long run come from Great Britain. It was mainland Europe one feared, not least the Netherlands.

In the 1560s, Archbishop Laurentius Petri succeeded in having all Calvinism officially banned in Sweden. In book after book Petri had been condemning Calvin's teachings – not least on Predestination – and his views on liturgy. Eventually he gained the King's support; it was decreed that all persons during Mass must worship Christ as present in the Eucharist. And a law was passed which forbade Calvinists in any way to spread any form of propaganda in Sweden. These non-Lutheran Protestants – in this generation they were French Protestants – soon left the country. Nevertheless, the defence against Calvinism continued. Among the edicts of the Synod of Uppsala in 1593 (referred to above), was one which repudiated not only those of the 'popish' conviction, but also 'Calvinists, Anabaptists and the delusions of all other heretics'. As has been mentioned, there were to be no qualms about openly criticizing King Carl IX for his Calvinist leanings.

During the seventeenth century, Swedish students were only allowed to pursue their studies in Lutheran countries. The clergy wished to place the Calvinist seats of learning on a par with those run by the Jesuits – as equally corrupting of the young. To visit universities in the Netherlands or in England was for a long time to carry the risk of losing one's career in Sweden.

PERSONAL CONNECTIONS

From the end of the sixteenth century, the national interests of England and Sweden were largely divergent. Theological and ecclesiastical contact was infrequent. Among the Nordic countries, Denmark was closest to the English periphery. Elizabeth I's successor, England's first Stuart king, James I, married a Danish princess – Anne, sister of Christian IV. Their wedding took place while James was still King of Scotland alone, and was celebrated three times over – on the last occasion at Kronborg Castle at Elsinore,

Denmark. Here, James had long theological discussions with the above-mentioned Danish theologian, Niels Hemmingsen, and also visited Tycho Brahe on the island of Ven. When James became King of England in the Spring of 1603 there was, again, much festivity – as part of which a performance of *Hamlet* was given in its amended, final version. This play, set in Kronborg, the scene of their wedding, may have been appreciated by James and Anne. They probably did not have to take the words: 'something is rotten in the state of Denmark' too seriously. In England one felt reasonably well informed about Denmark – not least about its drinking habits, to which Shakespeare had not failed to include the odd reference. One was apparently less well acquainted with church life in the Denmark of Christian IV. Hamlet returns from studies at Wittenberg, indicating a Lutheran connection. The priest officiating at Ophelia's burial seems equally Protestant. But allusions to extreme unction and purgatory are also made.

Many commentators have taken Danish church life, as represented in *Hamlet*, to be Roman Catholic. Numerous notes, written by Englishmen visiting Denmark at this time, express surprise over the presence of Roman Catholic traditions in the Danish Church. One such observation was made by King James himself, in connection with a service he had attended in Roskilde Cathedral in 1590. Another, somewhat later, was recorded by the English traveller and travelogue writer, Peter Mundy, on his visit of 1640 to Elsinore. He noted to his amazement that a people 'who call themselves Lutherans' kept in the St Olai Church 'a great Cruciffix on the roode lofft, an Altar adorned with Images, as many parts off the Church elce, as have the Papists'. (Had he returned a few decades later, his amazement would have been greater still – he would have seen a magnificent reredos and one of the most splendid chancel screens in Denmark.)

Relations between England and Denmark were generally more vigorous than between England and the other Nordic countries, and the connection between the royal

The Cathedral Church of St Olai, Elsinore. The pulpit dates from the 1560s; the chancel screen and the reredos, both richly baroque, from the middle of the 17th century. *Photograph: The National Museum, Copenhagen.*

families would naturally have played its part in prompting mutual interest in these two countries. Christian IV's visit to England caused great excitement. A number of Danish nobles briefly took in Oxford and Cambridge on their grand tour of Europe. There were also the trade connections. Elsinore, with Kronborg Castle, was landmark to many a voyager on the Sound. And English literature, including religious writings, arrived in Denmark far earlier and more extensively than in Sweden.

SWEDEN UNDER GUSTAV II ADOLF (GUSTAVUS ADOLPHUS)

But suddenly, in or around the year of 1630, all eyes were on Sweden. The interest generated by this country was greater than ever before, or since. A steady flow of articles and pamphlets containing information about Sweden were printed in England, more precisely, about the victories won by King Gustav II Adolf in the continuous and monumental battle that was raging in Europe between the Catholic Habsburgs and the Protestant powers of the North. In just as much colourful detail, and with just as much bias as if it were propaganda from the Swedish war office or the Protestant parts of Germany, the triumphs of the Swedish hero-king were now revealed to the English readership. Gustav II Adolf was hailed as God's anointed and the true defender of the faith against the legions of the Antichrist. He was God's servant in the liberation of the peoples plunged into slavery by the Catholic Emperor. In England one knew all about the personal piety of the king; his prayers in times of peril were reproduced; he was likened to Joshua, the leader of God's people. Almost overnight, Sweden – Christian Sweden – had acquired a personal face. Sweden and its King emerged as ally and example.

The enormous interest in Gustav II Adolf did not, however, translate into closer relations between the Church of England and the Swedish Church. This was not so much due to the fact that the bright new shooting star in the European firmament was so soon extinguished. As a unifying symbol, he could, after all, have lived on for a very long time. But it was not the official Church in England that had so praised him, and whose faith had been strengthened by his victories, but this interest had been entirely confined to the Puritans. Admittedly, by now they made up a very large part of the population and counted among their number many prominent literary figures, politicians and members of the clergy. But they were in collision with the official leaders of the Church and, importantly, even with the royal family. The praises of the Swedish King always had an undertone of criticism against official England's failure to take up arms in defence of Protestantism. In praising him the people revealed a more or less open criticism of their own King. In comparison with Gustav II Adolf and his noble fight to stop the Catholic conquests, Charles I of England appeared, to Puritan perception, all too closely allied with Catholic France and Spain. Where Puritan influence was strong it could happen that the minister prayed for Gustav II Adolf first – before the prayer for King Charles.

One personal approach was made to Gustav II Adolf from British quarters – an appeal for support in an attempt to bring about a kind of Protestant union. (On this there is a large and detailed literature.) But not even this contact improved relations between the Church of England and the Church of Sweden. The author of the plan was John Dury (1596–1680) a Scottish-born priest who was serving among Englishmen in the North-German town of Elbing, which had been captured by the Swedes. Dury obtained an audience with the King's right hand man, Axel Oxenstierna, and was permitted to put his plan before, among others, the King's personal chaplain, Johannes Botvidi, later to become Bishop of Linköping. Finally, an audience with the King himself was granted. Dury's ecclesiastical stance was, however, fairly indeterminate. Though ordained in the Anglican Church, his soul and heart belonged to the Presbyterians. His ecumenical efforts were somewhat diffuse, and he was never to achieve a position of any real influence. After the death of Gustav II Adolf, Dury continued his ecumenical negotiations with the Swedish government and the Swedish bishops, but without success. He was eventually asked, in no uncertain terms, to leave Swedish territory. Dury then visited a string of European countries in an attempt to promote his views. The *Dictionary of National Biography* describes his life as 'an incessant round of journeyings, colloquies, correspondence and publications'. He regularly reported to Archbishop Laud, but received no real support from him, or from any other English church leader. His indefatigable but inept efforts to put his case had the unhappy outcome of making orthodox Lutheran church leaders all the more anxious to put a stop to any influence from abroad that could conceivably disturb ecclesiastical unity in Sweden.

CROMWELL AND SWEDEN

One of the Puritans who so greatly admired Gustav II Adolf was Oliver Cromwell. To him, the Swedish King was a model military strategist. Using Gustav II Adolf's methods, especially the easily mobile field artillery, Cromwell defeated the royal army. But he looked upon Gustav II Adolf also as a hero of the true faith, the defender of Protestantism all over Europe. The prime objective of Cromwell's foreign policy was to gather together the Protestant countries in a united front against the Roman Catholic powers. This became clear by the Spring of 1653, when he was becoming the effective ruler of Great Britain. Quite naturally, he looked upon Sweden as an obvious ally. In the same year, 1653, he sent a large embassy to Sweden – where Christina had succeeded her father on the throne – headed by one of England's highest officials, Bulstrode Whitelock. Whitelock was commissioned to negotiate trade agreements, but when Cromwell impressed upon him the importance of this task, his first mention was of 'the affairs of Christendom' and of 'the Protestant interest' (*Whitelock's Journal of the Swedish Embassy*, Vol.1, p 33).

In his *Journal*, in two big volumes, Whitelock describes in detail his journey to Sweden and his stay at the court of Queen Christina – and here is a rich source for anyone wishing to observe Swedish society at this time through the eyes of an English statesman. It is also most rewarding from a church-historical point of view, a fact that seems to have gone more or less unnoticed. Whitelock formed his opinions from a strictly Puritan perspective – being the envoy of a regime that had, in effect, dissolved the Church of England. His entries are full of astonished, indeed openly indignant, comments on his experiences in the country he had believed to be the foremost champion of the Protestant cause, but which had clearly not ventured all that far from the ways of the medieval Catholic Church. (We have already noted similar comments on sixteenth- and seventeenth-century Denmark as seen by English visitors.)

The size of the embassy was close to overwhelming, indicating the importance Cromwell attached to the antici- pated ecclesistical-political relations with the Swedish realm. A special government committee had been put to work on the planning and practicalities of the embassy. Sweden's new envoy to London, Israel Lagerfelt, had been involved in the preparations. Staff and attendants had been chosen from the highest circles and consisted of no less than one hundred individuals, including two chaplains and a doctor. It took four sizable ships of war and a number of 'baggage-ships' to transport the party to Gothenburg. Whitelock brought with him one carriage seating eight and one seating ten, each with six horses for his personal use on the journey through Sweden. Queen Christina placed one hundred smaller carriages at his disposal, for the use of the rest of the party and for all the luggage.

One of the participants in the welcoming celebrations at Gothenburg was Ericus Brunnius, Superintendent of the recently established Diocese of Gothenburg (the full status

Uppsala Castle. Mid-17th century copperplate engraving from Erik Dahlberg's *Suecia antiqua et hodierna. Photograph: ATA.*

and title of Bishop was not granted to this diocese until 1664). He was afforded the seat of honour at the dinner Whitelock gave for the town dignitaries, during which he made close inquiries into the ecclesiastical conditions in Sweden. The conversation was conducted in Latin. He was given to understand that special liberties had been granted to 'Calvinist' immigrants. They had their own place of worship and their own services, closed to others. The Swedish people, here as elsewhere, were genuinely of 'the opinions of Luther'. The Superintendent was also able to report that the churches contained both 'pictures and images', and that the liturgical 'ceremonies' were observed with the greatest care. Whitelock was particularly interested to learn that church music was encouraged. This he regarded as something positive.

During the journey through Västergötland, Whitelock could not help noticing, to his great horror, that the Swedish Church had retained a 'papist' colouring. In the sanctuary of Skara Cathedral, he found 'many pictures of saints and other images' and – which appears to have shocked him just as much – the altar itself was dressed in velvet with gold embroidery and adorned with 'a stately crucifix'. There were further crucifixes in other parts of the church, and in the vestry were both chalices and ciboria, containing wafers. (Wafers were forbidden in England at the time, ordinary bread being used.) He concludes that 'none could see a difference betwixt this and the Papists' churches'. From then on, Whitelock never himself attended a Swedish church. He had his own chaplains, and with their guidance carefully observed his chosen form of worship, with them as preachers. Whitelock's notes on divine service at the court of Christina are based on observations passed on to him by his staff.

This was the Winter of 1653–54; the plague was invading Stockholm, and Christina therefore received the English embassy at Uppsala Castle, where her court was in temporary residence. The reception was magnificent. During the welcoming ceremonies, Whitelock made a long speech in English, which was translated into French. The Queen replied in Swedish – protocol required that the Queen speak her own language in all official circumstances, however many other languages she mastered – which was translated into Latin. Whitelock noted down the ecclesiastical purpose of his proposals, namely 'Nearer union and correspondence than heretofore' between 'neighbouring princes and states' to promote the 'common interest and concernment of the true Protestant religion'. Whitelock could have had not the faintest inkling – nor, for that matter, could anyone present – of the Queen's personal reasons for not responding to this point in her own speech. No one, not even her closest circle, knew that she had, already by December 1653, converted to Roman Catholicism.

Whitelock's embassy was to achieve no closer links between the Swedish Church and the Church of England. The attempt had been doomed from the start. For one thing, there was, under Cromwell, no such thing as an Anglican established church. For another, ironically, the Queen of Lutheran Sweden was, for reasons as yet undisolved, not in the least interested in furthering the cause of Protestantism.

What no one knew, Whitelock could not know. He continued with his journal, noting down all that was reported to him by his staff about the liturgy at Uppsala Cathedral. This coincided, they felt, very closely with the English Prayer Book, and was 'too near the fashion of the Popish churches for crucifixes, images, copes, surplices, and the like, and in the manner of their chanting of service, and with ceremonies fetched from the usages of that church and not yet reformed' (Journal I:244 f). The liturgical vestments were somewhat simpler in the Queen's chapel at the castle. But musically – and that was apparently still the only aspect Whitelock and his men actually appreciated – the liturgy there was, according to them, at least as 'excellent good' as in the cathedral.

One episode in particular from the Swedish court figured largely in his Journal. It reflects the contrast between Puritan England under Cromwell and the old

Lutheran habits – habits that in Sweden still seemed self-evidently right, at a time when Pietism and the evangelical movements had not yet opened the doors to puritan ethics.

The setting was the state banquet given in honour of Whitelock soon after his arrival and the offending matter was nothing more and nothing less than the customary toasts or, in Whitelock's indignant words, the habit 'to drink, as they miscall it, healths', to the Commonwealth of England and to General Cromwell. Whitelock refused, point blank, to take part. But the 'master of ceremonies', who was not about to give in, explained that to refuse was simply out of the question. The more the English ambassador was pressed, 'imperiously', the firmer grew his resolve to decline. The toast to The Commonwealth was dropped. But the Swedish host did not give way. Now came the proposal of a toast to Cromwell, and now the disagreement turned into a furious row, 'in words and gestures, full of heat and discontent'. Apparently the toast to Queen Christina was omitted – luckily, she was not present in person – as no one seems to have dared to propose it. After the angry exchanges came nothing but 'a silent discontent during the rest of supper-time'.

It does not take much to conjure up a picture of the great gathering in the Hall of State at Uppsala Castle: the entire Swedish court, deeply offended and with splendid wines untouched before them, very angry at having to miss out on what was to have been such a splendid party. And Whitelock and his men, equally irked, albeit also with a sense of moral satisfaction: they had not budged before the wild customs of Swedish Lutheranism.

Not the best of beginnings for the great Embassy from Cromwell's England. And, although a treaty of friendship and alliance was signed in the Spring of 1654, the end of 'nearer union and correspondence', for the pursuit of common concern regarding 'the true Protestant religion', was not achieved. If anything, the enterprise had served to raise the question of whether religious and ethical values in England and Sweden actually had anything significant in common.

CHAPTER 5

Crossing National Church Borders

ARCH-ENEMIES

Once the national churches of England and the North had cut their ties with Rome, there was no longer any supranational institution capable of unifying them. Regardless of any similar structures and aims, they all became separate units. It is therefore not really surprising that contact between them became more and more sporadic, and hardly ever carried any obligations.

This was to be the case with national churches at some geographical distance from one another, such as the Anglican and Nordic churches, but it also applied between the Nordic churches, i.e. between Denmark-Norway-Iceland as one separate unit and to Sweden-Finland as another. It often comes as a surprise – even to Nordic people – to learn that for centuries after the Reformation there was really little or no inter-Nordic ecclesiastical contact. Few though relations were, then, between England and the Nordic region, they were even fewer between Sweden and Denmark, despite the similarities between the peoples and the churches of these two countries.

There is a simple explanation: during these centuries Denmark and Sweden were more often than not at war with one another. A string of bloody inter-Nordic battles were fought between these 'sister nations', beginning in the middle of the sixteenth century and persisting until the beginning of the nineteenth, with longest and fiercest fighting occurring in the seventeenth century. Until then, Denmark had been the leading power in the North, both economically and culturally. Now Sweden overtook its neighbour – becoming, for one century, a great European power.

It started with Gustav II Adolf (see chapter 4), and during the reign of his daughter Christina Sweden's armies continued to fight wars on the mainland – including one with Denmark. Denmark was defeated and forced to cede territory to Sweden. When Christina surprised the world by her abdication, she was succeeded by her cousin Carl X Gustav. His family ruled the minor German principality of the Palatinate, but his mother had been born a Vasa, and he had been brought up in Sweden. Under him, his son and his grandson – Carl XI and Carl XII – war after war was fought against Denmark. The most calamitous to the Danes – and one of the most dramatic in military history – took place in 1658. Carl Gustav was engaged in military action against Poland when Denmark suddenly declared war on Sweden. He immediately left Poland with his troops, approaching Jutland from the south with lightning speed. Winter was uncommonly cold that year, and the straits between the Danish Islands were frozen over. Against all odds, Carl Gustav managed to lead his soldiers across the ice from island to island, until they were threatening Copenhagen from the west. This was a truly amazing feat which shocked and overwhelmed the Danes. Hoping to save something of his realm, the Danish king could do no more than offer a humiliating surrender. One third of Denmark was the price he had to pay to Sweden. The matter was later somewhat adjusted in Denmark's favour, during peace negotiations following a further war, when the Swedes had met with a more organized Danish resistance – and when western powers had come to the aid of Denmark, in order to prevent Sweden from gaining control of the entire Nordic region. Nevertheless, this was a major catastrophe for the Danes.

Swedish historians have, it has to be said, often been unable to restrain a certain chauvinism when writing about these events – forgetful of what this war, and this peace, meant to Denmark. It was the greatest blow ever to have befallen that country. A Danish historian writes: 'In truth, the old Denmark ceased to exist. What remained was a reduced and enfeebled realm.' From then on, the whole of eastern Denmark (the areas east of The Sound) belonged to Sweden and to the Church of Sweden. Denmark repeatedly tried to recapture her former lands – in more resolute, but unsuccessful, wars. The Swedicization of the conquered regions was swift and effective, achieved not least through the Swedicization of their church life. A new university was founded at Lund, the medieval archiepiscopal see, with the express intent of preventing students from southern Sweden from attending the University of Copenhagen. This put an effective stop to any kind of dialogue between Danish and Swedish theology. Throughout the following century the Church of what remained of Denmark and the Church of Sweden were to continue in total isolation from each other.

RELIGIOUS UNITY

The Nordic national churches were, in any case, not alike in every respect. As we have seen, the Reformation had been achieved in different ways in the different kingdoms, and these differences continued to be reflected in the life and structure of the churches. Like the Swedish Church, the Danish Church had preserved its diocesan organization, with its superintendents/bishops. But in Denmark these answered direct to the king's *Kancelli*, headed by a high-ranking civil servant. In Sweden, the authority of the bishops was protected by a re-established capitular body (*domkapitel*), and in the seventeenth century the bishops were able further to secure their position. Not even Gustav II Adolf could overrule these bishops, once they had mounted guard around their independence.

There was one aim, however, in the pursuit of which both kingdoms followed the same line of development, backed by the leaders of both state and Church. This was the aim of keeping and strengthening church unity in each country. There were occasions when the bishops and the clergy of Sweden had to bow to the will of the government and allow, for economic reasons, a degree of religious freedom – as granted to merchants and experts, for example in mining, who had been encouraged to settle in Sweden and who were of the Reformed confession. These were mainly Dutch and many of them settled in Gothenburg; some were offered high positions within the iron works. But they had to keep their religion to themselves. Calvinist propaganda was still absolutely prohibited. At the same time, the House of Clergy in the *Riksdag* made rules for students who wanted to study abroad, other than at Lutheran universities in Germany. All students who attended universities in the Netherlands or England were required on their return to submit themselves to examination, in order to be tested in their Lutheran confession, before they could be ordained. In the seventeenth century, two leading Swedish bishops were deposed for allegedly espousing 'syncretistic' theological views, i.e. for a certain leaning towards Calvinist theology and a desire to smooth over the distinctions between the Lutheran and the Reformed confessions.

Danish theologians were just as thoroughly on guard against Calvinism. Their main concern at this time was, as ever, Eucharistic doctrine. But this was not the only issue. The writings of the great Danish theologian Hans Poulsen Resen (1561–1638) criticized particularly the rationalist nature of Calvinism. Resen focused on Luther himself – not simply on the Lutheran system – and recognized as central to Luther's theology the awe in which he held the incomprehensible 'mystery', of God's redeeming act. Now, as at the beginning of the Reformation, Luther's presence was felt more keenly in Denmark than in Sweden. However, in both countries alike seventeenth-century theologians moved towards a Lutheran orthodoxy, with its formalist theology. It has to be said, however, that this fact requires a far more careful evaluation than has commonly been afforded. The doctrinal rigour needs to be understood

110

as the armour forged to protect the living heritage of faith; one should not overlook the deep personal devotion and warmth of religious life during this period, as witness its hymn writing and devotional literature.

An essential part of our classical Nordic church heritage stems from this time. One of its most remarkable examples is to be found in Icelandic church life. There, a great hymn writer Hallgrímur Pétursson (d. 1674), a priest who suffered from leprosy, published a collection of fifty *Hymns of the Passion*, a book of exceptional spiritual power, and these hymns have lived on through the centuries. (English edition: Hymns of the Passion; Meditations on the Passion of Christ, translated by Arthur Charles Gook, Reykjavik 1978.) The hymns trace the story of the passion, representing it as a drama of Salvation, but at the same time applicable to the individual believer. Over the centuries, and still today, many Icelanders have known almost by heart these hymns, which expound a classic theme of Lutheran orthodoxy, and still retain their relevance. In the view of Icelandic church historians, it is because of this collection of hymns – with their objective and at the same time personal piety – that Icelandic church life has never been disrupted by revivalist movements: Lutheran orthodoxy was to reach modern times without disruption.

As mentioned above, the overriding principle was to secure religious uniformity. Conditions were far more favourable to this in the Nordic countries than in seventeenth century England, where the religious divisions and tensions between the different groups had become entrenched during the Civil War and its aftermath. In Sweden and in Denmark religious uniformity – as much a political as an ecclesiastical ideal – managed to find almost complete realization. Unity of religion was one of the 'fundamental principles' of Swedish political law.

The introductory paragraph of the Swedish Church Law, passed in 1686 under Carl XI, reads as follows:'In our kingdom, and our other territories, everyone shall confess only and uniquely that Christian doctrine and faith,

Parish church in Reykjavik, Iceland, called 'Hallgrímskirkja' (The Hallgrimur Church) after Iceland's famous hymnwriter, Hallgrímur Pétursson. (See page 111.) *Photograph: Sólarfilma, Reykjavik, Iceland, by courtesy of the Iceland University.*

which is grounded in God's Holy Word, that is the prophetic and apostolic scriptures of the Old and the New
Testaments, set forth in the three main creeds, the Apostolic, the Nicene and the Athanasian, as well as in the
unchanged Augsburg Confession of 1530, accepted by the
Synod of Uppsala in 1593, and also explained in the Book
of Concord...'

In Denmark the Royal Law of 1665 (*Kongeloven*) contains an almost similar paragraph. No one could fail to
understand the meaning of those legally prescriptive paragraphs. There was to be, in the Nordic kingdoms, only the
one religion – the one that rested on the Bible, the Ancient
Church and the Lutheran Confessions. The task of seeing
that this law was implemented without exception belonged
both to the civil servants and to the clergy. Uniformity of
religion was clearly deemed to be of invaluable benefit to
the internal unity of these realms.

The Swedish Empire of the seventeenth century
included a variety of peoples with a variety of languages.
In the light of present ethnic conflicts it is interesting to
note that in the time and place we are reviewing racial
pluralism caused no serious problems. The religion shared
by all these peoples was seen as the decisive unifying factor.
At the same time, of course, 'Unity of Religion' imposed
severe restrictions on contact with countries such as England, where religious divisions seemed to be deep and new
sects numerous.

Certainly, religious unity was the goal also of the English nation – but the divisions within its Church were a fact
that could not be ignored. At the time of the Restoration
of 1660, and for two decades thereafter, laws were passed
which emphasized the fact that the Anglican Church was
the only established Church. But after the Revolution of
1688, and the accession of William and Mary, 'Liberty and
Indulgence to Protestant Dissenters' was granted by the
Toleration Act of 1689. Needless to say, this was contrary
to Nordic national church policy, and was perceived as
threatening.

LUTHERANISM CHANGED FROM WITHIN

The uniformity of each of the Nordic churches was threatened in a different way – from within. The threat came from the revivalist movements which, from the end of the seventeenth century, were spreading throughout the Lutheran lands under the name of 'Pietism'. This movement, which shared certain features with Puritanism, was rooted in the mysticism and individualistic piety of the late Middle Ages which survived within devotional literature even after the Reformation.

It was not the intention of the Pietists to break out of the Lutheran confessional and ecclesiastical community. But they were disenchanted with a church tradition which, as they saw it, was superficial and formal. According to them, every individual had to have an inner experience of faith, and then to be changed, in order to show true seriousness in his Christian life. It was not enough, then, to have been baptized and to observe the external practices of church life. There had to be a spiritual breakthrough. In their view, there was a clear distinction between the truly faithful and the rest, who were merely Christians out of habit. As a result – and this is where the real problem lay – real church fellowship, in the Pietist view, was not that of the national church or of the parish, but that of the group of believers. This concept was potentially explosive. It contained a threat to the whole ecclesiastical system – a system that had so far characterized European Christianity and which not even the national churches of the Reformation had broken. In fact, the main thrust of Pietism was, as has been mentioned, in fact not aimed at such a breach. But the tendency was there, and that was sufficient to alert the leaders of Nation and Church to the presence of danger.

The immediate origin of the Pietist revival was Germany, in the court circles in Berlin and at the newly founded University of Halle. It was therefore, to start with, not at all a popular movement. The originators were Philipp Jacob Spener, court chaplain and dean in Berlin, and

114

August Hermann Francke, professor at Halle. They soon established contacts within the Nordic churches – with priests and students, with the aristocracy and even with the royal families. While Carl XI of Sweden safeguarded, with all his might, the uniformity of the Lutheran national church, his queen was corresponding with Spener and holding prayer-meetings with her ladies-in-waiting at the royal palace in Stockholm. In Denmark Pietism fared even better, and was embraced by the royal family. The pietistic educational institutions of Halle, which also cared for the poor, soon had their royally endorsed equivalents in Copenhagen. Danish-Norwegian Pietism seldom showed any radical tendencies, and was in effect incorporated into the official church. The imprint of the union of Pietism with Lutheran orthodoxy can be found in much Danish theology, and especially in a great treasury of hymns created in the seventeenth and eighteenth centuries by the bishops Kingo and Brorson.

During these centuries, the only notable theological influence to come from England came almost exclusively from non-Anglican quarters. The irony is that it was the Calvinist elements within the Church and the sects in England, which the Nordic church leaders and theologians had always fought with such energy to repel, and it was precisely this influence which now entered their own churches.

The English influence on Nordic piety came, above all, by means of literature. A great flow of Puritan and revivalist devotional literature swept in over the Nordic countries. As David L. Edwards puts it in his book *Christian England:'* The greatest legacy of the Puritan movement was a spiritual achievement which was to be embodied in imperishable literature and to become the heritage of the whole English-speaking world'. Not only of the English-speaking world, one might add. Mainly in German translations this devotional literature soon spread to the North, and first of all to Denmark. Very early on, translations of Lewis Bayly's *Praxis Pietatis* and of works by Bishop Joseph Hall appeared. Bayly's book, which was very widely circulated, contains strict warnings against sinful living. Dancing, comedies, masked balls, card and dice games, jokes and drinking – activities that were perfectly acceptable in Lutheran tradition – were all condemned.

Much literature of this type was translated into Swedish – perhaps even more than was translated into Danish. (This fact has been carefully recorded in a theological-bibliographical investigation by B Hellekant.) In addition to the above-mentioned authors, we find a great many others, for example Richard Baxter. John Bunyan, another dissenter, though not a Puritan, was to reach the greatest fame of all. His books were very soon translated and distributed in the Nordic countries. Here we can see a very different type of piety from that of the classical Lutheranism of the national churches. Nonetheless, this new inspiration was to do much for popular piety in the Lutheran North as elsewhere.

In the latter part of the seventeenth century and the first decades of the eighteenth Copenhagen saw an especially concrete and important English influence on its church life. Some priests had visited England and had been strongly impressed by the preaching and devotional literature there, and this was to colour their own sermons in the churches of the Danish capital. To mention but a few: the cathedral Dean Dorschæus, the Rectors Brochmand and Tisdorph and, eventually, Bishop Worm at St Nicholas Church, Thestrup at Holy Trinity Church, Brinck at Holmens Church and Brunsmand at Vartov. There was much reference to 'the English school', and for some decades it did in fact dominate the preaching in Copenhagen. At the same time, much devotional literature, both German Pietist and English Puritan, was published. There was also a new edition of Bayly's *Praxis Pietatis* and a translation of the Puritan priest Daniel Dyke's *The Self-Deception of the Heart*. One of Dyke's main themes is illuminating: no one must pin their hopes of salvation on merely attending church and receiving Holy Communion. The 'historical faith' is not

116

enough for salvation. 'Internal faith', penitence and the obedience of the heart is what is required.

An important Scandinavian representative of the moderate Pietism within the Church was the Norwegian Peder Hersleb (1689–1757). The son of a priest, he was born in the Diocese of Trondheim and educated in Copenhagen. He was appointed as court chaplain and later Bishop of Akershus (nowadays the dioceses of Oslo and Hamar), and eventually became Bishop of Zealand (*primus inter pares* of the Danish and Norwegian bishops). He was considered the foremost preacher of his time. His collection of sermons – of which, significantly, those on the Passion are best known – show of course the main theme of the Reformation: the emphasis on the grace of God and God's loving forgivness, but also – and equally noticeable – the stress on penitence and the struggle of repentance as well as colourful descriptions of the fallen world and the fallen church. He has remarkably little to say about Baptism and the Eucharist. Hersleb was deeply influenced by German Pietism – but he had also, during his student days at Copenhagen, faithfully attended sermons of 'the English school'. The German influence left him with a great interest in the education system. His collected sermons became popular devotional reading in Denmark and Norway for a whole century, and provided the foundation for a strong Pietist influence in the church life of his home country.

With all due respect to this English school, one must say that something of the original mentality of the Lutheran Reformers had been lost. That feeling of bold, almost defiant joy and trust had been dampened down by so much talk of recognizing one's sinfulness, struggling for repentance and rejection of 'the world' and its pleasures.

COLLABORATION ACROSS THE BORDERS

An important aspect of the Pietist influence in Copenhagen in the early eighteenth century was an interest in overseas mission. On the initiative of the Danish royal family, a Danish-German mission was set up among the Tamils in the then Danish colony of Tranquebar, on the East Coast of India. The enterprise was soon joined by the English Society for Promoting Christian Knowledge (SPCK). The collaboration between the English Society and the Danish-German mission lasted for over a hundred years. It is interesting that acknowledgement of one another's ministry and ordinations presented no difficulties in the mission field. This was not recognized as a problem until Tractarianism began to influence English missionaries in India.

A strong reaction came however from the Archbishop of Canterbury, Thomas Tenison, when he discovered that the Lutheran catechism, translated into Portuguese by the missionaries, and sent to him for approval, was organised in a different way from the usual English translation. Martin Luther had simply left out the prohibition against images (usually the second commandment) – a fact that had rarely aroused much attention – and instead divided the ninth into two commandments. This somewhat autocratic decision was a consequence of the fact that Luther never distanced himself from art in church buildings. Archbishop Tenison did however not let this discrepancy stop him from actively supporting the Anglo-Lutheran collaboration in India. This support was continued by his successors.

There are examples from this period of initiatives towards more comprehensive concord and fellowship between Anglicans and representatives of both Nordic and mainland Lutheranism. In view of our present ecumenical endeavours, it seems important to highlight these attempts – even though they were fairly sporadic and led to no concrete results. They provide evidence of some of the features

118

which the Church of England shared specially with the Nordic national churches. For this reason they deserve a chapter to themselves.

CHAPTER 6

Ecumenical Endeavours

NORDIC STUDENTS IN ENGLAND

Between 1671 and 1674, a young Swedish theologian named Johannes Gezelius was doing his grand tour of Europe. He visited the scholars of the time in various German cities but, most importantly, he studied at Oxford during the Trinity Term 1671, and at Cambridge in 1672. Johannes Gezelius belonged to a Swedish family of scholars who, for many generations, had held leading university and church offices in the easternmost areas of Sweden, which at that time included Finland, the Baltic territories and Ingermanland. The latter is, of course, a province of Russia, but was under Swedish rule for a very long time, before it was lost to Peter the Great. Johannes was born in Dorpat (Tartu), Estonia, in 1647. He became professor at the University of Turku, Finland, and then Superintendent of Ingermanland. Eventually, he succeeded his father, Johannes Gezelius the elder, as Bishop of Turku.

In Finland father and son both made important contributions in the field of Bible study. Their edition of the Bible remains most impressive in its linguistic scholarship. In those days, the greatest experts in exegesis were to be found in England and in Holland, and Gezelius junior could not resist spending a large number of his mainland years in those countries. His father had anxiously warned him of the Calvinism he would be exposed to, but he made agreeable, positive discoveries.

From his time at Oxford, Johannes Gezelius makes special mention of his acquaintance with the Orientalist Edward Pocock (1604–91), one of the many Anglicans who had been relieved of their appointments by Cromwell and

120

returned to them after the Restoration of 1660. It was only such churchmen who enjoyed full recognition in Charles II's England. Pococke was Professor of Hebrew at Oxford; he was at the height of his fame, attracting students and scholars from many countries. His son, also called Edward and also an Orientalist (1648–1727) was a contemporary of Gezelius, who referred to him as 'my friend' (*amicus mei*). Gezelius' esteem for Professor Edward Bernard of St John's was, if possible, even greater. Bernard was a most versatile scholar, renowned in the field of astronomy and a specialist in Semitic languages. He is referred to as '*inter omnes Anglos amicissimus carissimusque*' (among all Englishmen, my very dearest friend).

At Cambridge Gezelius seems to have received his strongest impression of what was for him to characterize the Anglican tradition. Most significantly, he got to know the circle of clergy described as the Caroline Divines. Several of these men, active under Charles I, were still alive and at work at this time. Many, like Pocock Senior, had been driven out by Cromwell, and were able to return only after the Restoration. Among them were prominent philologists and experts in exegesis. Gezelius singles out John Pearson (1613–1686), the author of *Exposition of the Creed*, and Edmund Castell (1606–1685), known for his Polyglot Bible. Many of these men had a strong interest in the Anglican liturgical tradition, the ancient Church and the Church Fathers.

In conversations with them, Gezelius began to understand, more and more, what the Anglican Church stood for. It seemed quite clear to him that it was impossible to equate this tradition with Calvinism and of course not with the Puritans' preferred form of church government – it was, after all, under the Puritans that these men had been persecuted – and that there was, quite plainly, a gulf between the Anglicans and the various sects in England. Given the prevailing Lutheran view, in Gezelius' home country and in general, these conclusions – though self-evident – are fairly remarkable. Gezelius remained true to them, and was never again to call the Anglicans 'Calvinists'.

Gezelius found his first opportunity publicly to stand up for the Anglican Church in 1684. He was then residing at Narva, as Superintendent of Ingermanland, on the border between the Swedish Empire and Russia. A colony of English merchants was living in the diocese with the approval – probably for economic reasons – of the Swedish crown. But Carl XI kept to a strictly Lutheran policy and it was most unlikely that his approval would extend to granting the English settlers their wish to worship according to the Anglican rite. On their behalf, Gezelius now put his knowledge of Anglicanism into action: the leader of this distant Eastern European diocese produced a detailed statement and sent it to his king. This is almost certainly the first official document to contain a theological analysis of the similarities between the Church of England and the Swedish Church.

Gezelius offered a well-considered justification of his view that the Anglicans were closer to the Lutherans than the Reformed churches, also in their interpretation of the Eucharist. He called attention, above all, to the great similarities in respect of *Kyrckio Regemente och Ceremonier*, (Church Government and Ceremonies) – similarities which, he argued, indicated a closer relationship between the Church of Sweden and the Anglicans than could be said to exist between the Swedish Church and many other Lutheran churches.

Gezelius' words had the desired effect. They had reached Carl XI together with a letter from the Swedish Governor-General, and in December 1684 the King granted the Englishmen of Ingermanland their wish. It was now their legal right to hold their services according to the Book of Common Prayer. Gezelius had recommended that freedom of religion be granted to 'those who belong to the English Church' – i.e. not to 'sectarians', but to the Anglicans alone – and this was fully reflected in the royal decree.

The following year, an English priest was appointed to the English congregation in Narva, and a special *congregational order* was ratified by Carl XI. These measures represent a remarkable ecumenical exception, long ago and far away, to the otherwise strict rule of Lutheran orthodoxy. They nevertheless prove that, according to the official Swedish view, Anglicanism was even closer to the Swedish Church than were most of the other Lutheran churches.

At this same time, another young Swedish priest was studying in England. His name was Jesper Svedberg, later to become Bishop of Skara. He stayed in London for a while, then spent a longer spell at Oxford. The year was 1684, shortly before the death of Charles II. Svedberg was of a more practical disposition. He may not have had Gezelius' qualifications for entering into the scholarly explorations of philology and church history that were flourishing all around him, but he was deeply impressed by the eminent theologians who were working along the same classical lines of Anglicanism as twelve years earlier, during Gezelius' visit. Svedberg mentions John Fell (1625–1686) who had been appointed a canon at Christ Church immediately following the Restoration and was currently Bishop of Oxford and Professor Edward Bernard, the man Gezelius had referred to as *amicissimus carissimusque*.

Jesper Svedberg greatly admired what he saw of Anglican church life. He found some of the sermons overly rhetorical and felt than they suffered from a rather too affected literary style, but he certainly had no complaints about their content. He was especially impressed by the 'strict and holy' adherence to the Commandment regarding the Sabbath. Sweden, he felt, had much to learn in this respect – even though England did, on occasion, go a little too far. At the time of Svedberg's stay in London, the Swedish Count Gustav Cronhielm had had his servant row him across the Thames one Sunday – in order to get to church. For this he was convicted of breaching the Sabbath. Both he and his servant were fined and imprisoned.

Jesper Svedberg's positive experiences were to have important consequences when, as bishop, he was appointed by the King to oversee the ecclesiastical conditions of Swedes living in London and in the former Swedish colony by the Delaware River in North America. In both areas he encouraged close contact between the Swedish priests and their Anglican colleagues. In the Delaware colony, relations became so close that an exchange of duties frequently took place – of the kind that we now, in modern ecumenical terminology, refer to as altar and pulpit fellowship or the interchangeability of ministries.

JOHN ROBINSON, BISHOP OF LONDON

The climate in England after the Restoration was favourable to relations between the Church of England and other established Protestant churches. Though such relations were in fact infrequent, they were important in principle, and of interest as the forerunners of ecumenical negotiations in later times. As the Church of England was now represented by men who clearly distanced themselves not only from Rome and the dissenters, but also from the ecclesiastical views of the entire Puritan flank, it became possible for Anglicans and Protestants, in the Nordic region and on the mainland, to discover how much they in fact held in common with respect to church order and church life.

John Robinson (1650–1723) was deeply engaged in the promotion of mutual ecumenical understanding. Before becoming Bishop of London, he had spent nearly thirty years as priest and diplomat in the Swedish capital and at the military headquarters of the Swedish King.

In the 1670s, Robinson was a student at Oriel College, Oxford, where the theological and ecclesiastical milieu was that experienced by Johannes Gezelius. In 1680 Carl XI seized power as absolute monarch of Sweden, upon which Robinson was sent to Stockholm as 'embassy priest' and 'political agent'. As time went by, he was increasingly looked upon as a diplomat, and was eventually appointed England's ambassador to Stockholm. In 1695, he published a book on Sweden, *Account of Sweden, together with an extract of the History of that Kingdom* which reflected his very positive view. He does not elaborate on his experience of the Swedish Church, confining himself to describing Sweden's church life as worthy of respect and the 'long-bearded' priests as 'dignified' and enjoying the complete trust of the people. In 1697 Carl XII succeeded to the Swedish throne. He was then fifteen years old, and Robinson was to develop a closer relationship with the young king than had been possible with Carl XI. Robinson accompanied Carl XII on the military campaigns. His letters tell of the king's regular attendance at divine service, where he always joined in the singing of the hymns. Robinson remained close to the king for precisely as long as the Swedish army remained victorious. He was present at Narva, where Carl XII resoundingly defeated the Russian army, and was in attendance during the subsequent years, when the Swedish victories became a source of awe and amazement to the rest of Europe. Naturally, he became acquainted with many Swedish top officials and officers, and with many Swedish priests. He was on very friendly terms with Jesper Svedberg who, on his return home, had been appointed court chaplain. Later, when the two of them were bishops in their respective countries, they would lend their united support to the Anglo-Swedish ecumenical efforts at Delaware, North America.

In his capacity of English ambassador to the court of Carl XII, Robinson travelled with the Swedish army through Poland and Germany, and stayed close to the king during the long interval in Saxony, 1706–1707. In 1707, at the height of his military fame, Carl XII received John Churchill, Duke of Marlborough. The location was the castle of Altranstädt near Leipzig, to which Marlborough had travelled by coach across Europe. His purpose was to call upon the Swedish King and to gain assurances that

Sweden's plans did not include an intervention in the political developments of Western Europe. The meeting between 'the two greatest men of their time' has been described by Winston Churchill in a colourful chapter of the great biography of the Duke, his ancestor. The contrast between the two great generals – the Swedish King, young and bold, and the victor of Blenheim, cunning and experienced in statesmanship and warfare – is beautifully drawn. Marlborough was assisted by John Robinson, and the conversation lasted about four hours, 'until in fact, his Majesty's kettledrums called him to prayers'. Did Marlborough attend the Lutheran Vespers of the Swedish army? There is nothing in the sources to say that he did.

John Robinson was also present at the Convention of Altranstädt, when Carl XII – by virtue of Sweden's position as guarantor of religious freedom, in accordance with the 1648 Peace of Westphalia – forced through the extension of that freedom to Protestants within the hereditary domains of the Holy Roman Emperor. The Emperor was forced to return around one hundred churches, and to build large new churches (*Gnadenkirchen*) for the Lutherans of Silesia. Robinson had indeed seen, first-hand, how seriously Carl XII took his responsibilities as defender of Protestantism in Europe. He was duly impressed, and this must have influenced the plans he was soon to make for concrete inter-church collaboration. The insight he had gained into the condition of the Protestant churches of Central Europe during his long stay there was therefore the impetus behind those plans.

In 1708, Robinson left his post as ambassador to the royal Swedish military headquarters, returning to England in the following year. He did not take part in the ill-fated march across Russia, and did not witness the defeat of the Swedish army at Poltava. He was therefore able to retain intact his image of Sweden as a great power. Robinson's diplomatic efforts had been much appreciated in England as well as in Sweden. He was appointed Dean of Windsor, then Bishop of Bristol, and finally Bishop of London.

Additional responsibilities were placed in his hands: he became a member of the Privy Council, Lord Keeper of the Privy Seal and leader of the peace negotiations at Utrecht. He was a favourite of Queen Anne's, and was very influential in the Tory party which was now – like the High Church wing of the Church of England, to which Robinson must be reckoned – at the peak of its power. There was less room than ever for Puritans and dissenters.

At the same time, ecumenical negotiations in other directions were begun, and in these Robinson played an important part. The idea came from the continent, but Robinson was to apply it also to the relations between the Church of England and the Lutheran Church of Sweden.

PLANS FOR AN EXTENDED PROTESTANT EPISCOPACY

There is much evidence to show that in the eyes of Europe's Protestants, Anglican church life had fallen into disrepute. The Lutherans of the North disapproved of what they perceived as its Calvinist features, while continental Protestant suspicion was directed at its episcopal element and liturgical tradition. Both camps were to be pleasantly surprised.

A young student by the name of Daniel Ernst Jablonski (1660–1741) provides a case in point. His family came from Bohemia in what is now the Czeck Republic, and they lived in Poland from whence he arrived in Oxford at the end of the 1670s. He belonged to the *Unitas Fratrum*, the Church of the Bohemian Brethren, a Protestant church dating back to the fifteenth century Hussite movement in Bohemia, from which in the eighteenth century the Moravian Church was to develop. Jablonski's maternal grandfather, Jan Amos Comenius, was an innovative educationalist and a bishop of the *Unitas Fratrum*. Jablonski's experiences of Restoration England led him to change – completely – his view of the Church of England, 'that *Ecclesia Anglicana* which he had been taught to dislike and dread'. At Oxford, he became acquainted with bishops and learned clergy of this Church, and studied the Thirty-Nine Articles, Hooker's *Of the Laws of Ecclesiastical Politie* and, above all the Book of Common Prayer. To Jablonski's amazement, he found himself able to conclude that nothing in these documents on Anglican tradition was in any way incompatible with the teachings of Protestantism. Further, he was deeply impressed by the Anglican liturgical tradition – and, above all, by the Church of England's emphasis on the importance of the episcopate. This led him to study Cyprian and his views on this office or, as Jablonski – interestingly – puts it, on: 'the episcopate as the basis of unity in the Church' (N Sykes, *Daniel Ernst Jablonski and the Church of England*, London, 1950, p. 8). Most of his understanding of Anglican theology and piety came from the Caroline Divines. He made many friends at Oxford, and was later to correspond with most of them. (Among these were William Wake, later Archbishop of Canterbury, William Beveridge, later Bishop of St Asaph, and John Sharp, later Archbishop of York.)

In the 1690s Jablonski was appointed court chaplain at Berlin, where his grand plan was born: to introduce the Anglican episcopal tradition into the Prussian Church. Further, he aimed at a 'full union' between Lutherans and the Reformed churches (*'non de tolerantia mutua ecclesiarum, sed de plenaria earum unione cogitandum esse'*). In 1701, the Elector of Hanover's place in the order of succession to the English throne was acknowledged. To Jablonski, this meant that two German electorates were to be included in his plan: Brandenburg and Hanover. By now he had been consecrated a bishop of the Church of the Bohemian Brethren. He explained to his English friends that the difference between the titles 'superintendent', 'senior' and 'bishop' was purely semantic – the result of the desire, on the mainland, to avoid 'the popish associations' suggested by the term of 'bishop'. The function of this office, regardless of its different names, was the same in each case.

Now that the Tories were in power and Archbishop

Sharp, assisted by Bishop John Robinson, had become Queen Anne's adviser, the prospects of realizing Jablonski's plan were promising. Robinson was able to contribute, having a unique knowledge of Lutheran church life, most of it collected from his many years in Sweden and at the Swedish military headquarters, where the episcopal tradition was as firmly anchored as in England. He helped translate the Book of Common Prayer and the Ordinal into German. The King of Prussia and the Queen of England were both informed of the plan, and expressed their interest. Queen Anne was also given a more detailed account of the King of Sweden's contributions to the Lutheran cause in the Habsburg hereditary dominions. It was suggested to her that she might wish to support the cause of the Reformed churches in those same regions. This would lend additional goodwill to the grand plan of wider church unity through a common episcopal church order. Lord Raby, the British Ambassador in Berlin, would be a willing mediator in these negotiations. Leibniz, the philosopher, was deemed the best man to advocate the cause before the Elector of Hanover. Certain marriage plans were also being considered, as a way of uniting the electorates of Brandenburg and Hanover. There were, then, a great many factors which, taken together, seemed sufficient to guarantee the realization of this great ecumenical and ecclesiastical-political project.

But then the situation changed. Blow by blow, all hopes were dashed. John Robinson and Lord Raby were appointed negotiators at Utrecht: two of the leading forces behind Jablonski's grand plan were forced to withdraw their labours, due to their new demanding duties. This was followed by one death after another, among those who had been won over to the cause. 1713 saw the deaths of the King of Prussia and of Archbishop Sharp; in 1714 Queen Anne died. Her demise also meant the end of Tory power. John Robinson became the target of the Whigs, who criticized his leadership at Utrecht and his stewardship as Lord Chancellor. He found it necessary with all speed to get to grips with a completely new political situation. The grand ecclesiastical-political plan had come to an abrupt end.

ADAPTING THE PLAN FOR THE SWEDISH CHURCH

And yet there was a continuation – not on the scale envisaged by Daniel Ernst Jablonski in Berlin, but focused, now, by John Robinson on a target with which he was very familiar. It was quite natural that the Bishop of London should attempt to apply Jablonski's vision of a union between episcopal churches to the Church of England and the church he knew so well the Church of Sweden. He explored the idea with Count Carl Gyllenborg, who in 1710 had been appointed Swedish Ambassador in London.

Gyllenborg had been secretary to the Swedish Embassy for a number of years, and was fairly familiar with the situation in England. The fact that he was made Ambassador in the year the Tories came to power suited him well, as he had excellent connections with that party. He married in the same year. His wife was very wealthy, and had many influential friends among the Tories. The Swedish Ambassador's London home soon became a meeting place for politicians. It hardly needs saying that John Robinson was a frequent visitor. When the time eventually came for Gyllenborg to lay the ecumenical plan before the bishops of the Swedish Church, he referred to the fact that it had been proposed by a number of English bishops. Among those mentioned was, of course, John Robinson. Others had been involved, just as they had been in the earlier discussions with Jablonski, but Robinson's name was the one the Swedes knew well.

Gyllenborg's presentation of Robinson's plan emphasized its dual – political and ecclesiastical – purpose: The Protestant governments should come together for *communitas conciliis et armis*, i.e. to support one another against common enemies through mutual consultation and united efforts; and the English and the Swedish Churches should establish a 'greater intimacy'. The ecclesiastical aspect was not enlarged upon, but appears less vague in the context of Robinson's close understanding of Jablonski's ideas. In 1717, on his return to Sweden, Gyllenborg presented the wishes of the English bishops to Carl XII, who seems to have taken an interest in the project. In a letter to the Swedish bishops the following year, Gyllenborg included a few more details about the thinking behind the Anglican view. According to him, the Swedish Church was thought of as a *systerkyrckia*, or 'Sister Church'. This is the first official document to use that term. Gyllenborg did not bring out more precisely what the proposed 'intimacy' was to entail – but he felt confident enough to state that the English bishops perceived these two 'Sister Churches' to be so like-minded on confessional questions and liturgical tradition that there was 'little or no difference' between them.

THE SWEDISH BISHOPS REPLY

Gyllenborg's proposal is particularly interesting because he could claim that it originated from the English bishops. As we have seen, it was in fact an offshoot of a wider plan for a Lutheran-Reformed-Anglican church union. At the time of its conception and discussion, it seemed to have a reasonable chance of success. As it happened, however, the proposal was delivered to the bishops of Sweden by the wrong person at the wrong time.

The Elector of Hanover, George I, had succeeded Queen Anne. He was far from well disposed towards Sweden – indeed, he wished to acquire Bremen, which bordered on his own electorate, but which belonged to the Swedish territories. In 1710, and for a few years thereafter, it would have been possible for several of England's bishops personally to endorse an invitation to a church union with Sweden – but not now, not in 1718. The Great Power of

131

Sweden was no more. There was nothing further to be gained from that country, except by way of grabbing whatever parts of its dominions that happened to lie close at hand – and George I was in the process of doing just that.

The timing of the proposal was bad, and the choice of Gyllenborg as the messenger did nothing to improve matters. For one thing, there was no theological substance to his letter to the Swedish bishops. For another, he had a reputation for being rashly adventurous. His ambassadorship had come to an inglorious end: he was caught conspiring in favour of Queen Anne's half-brother, the Pretender James Edward Stuart, in whose badly conceived and executed plan to invade Great Britain he had been involved. Gyllenborg was arrested and imprisoned at Plymouth, and then placed on board an English warship and deported to Sweden. This was of course in flagrant breach of the diplomatic immunity enjoyed by foreign emissaries, and as such caused quite a stir all over Europe. Carl XII, who had no knowledge of the plot, was most seriously displeased by the English conduct towards Sweden's Ambassador, and appointed Gyllenborg to a high government office. It was in this capacity that he had written to the bishops. But he had written also with the purpose of providing a kind of sequel to his long diplomatic service in England. Even so, it is reasonable to assume that the Swedish bishops were rather cautious in their reply, knowing as thy did about Gyllenborg's recent escapades.

This was the beginning of 1718, and Sweden was suffering gravely from war-weariness. For eighteen years, war had been waged against her by all her neighbours. Rather than entering into peace negotiations, Carl XII risked a new campaign against the 'arch-enemy' to the west. Under these circumstances, it was not easy to entertain the idea of a church union with England, and almost all the Swedish bishops turned it down. The usual reasons were given: the English Church was Calvinist, and one could not afford to risk the valuable religious unity of one's country. The Bishop of Växjö, David Lund, wrote what was perhaps the

132

most dismissive reply – which more than likely reflected the thoughts of most of the clergy at the time. His words are almost pitiable: 'As it is the case that the Swedish people, in these the most lamentable of times, lack all the comforts of physical well-being, the only and steadfast source of happiness now left to them is their conviction that they partake of the heavenly doctrine in its pure and unassailable form.' Given that the 'brotherhood' offered by the English Church would jeopardize this 'our only and supreme happiness', there was every reason firmly to 'advise against it and decline'.

Only two of the Swedish bishops had any personal experience of the Church of England: Jesper Svedberg and Johannes Gezelius the younger, both of whom we came across in their days as young students in England. The former replied in friendly, but nevertheless very cautious, terms. He had already been criticized by his colleagues for what, in their eyes, seemed a less than strict adherence to Lutheran orthodoxy. They had even turned down his proposal for a new hymn-book, which was to have been his life's great work. The one encouraging reply came from Johannes Gezelius, now Bishop of Turku. Although he could not quite see what the proposed union was to mean, or what purpose it was to serve – something which was in any case not clear from Gyllenborg's letter – he was glad of the opportunity to explain in detail, his view that the English Church was closer to the Swedish Church than any other. He had expressed the same thoughts many years earlier, as Superintendent of Ingermanland, and to good effect. (see p 121 ff). He now repeated them in more detail and with greater clarity.

Gezelius' exposition of 1718 is notable as a forerunner of ecumenical relations to come between the Swedish Church and the Church of England. He starts by describing how he arrived at his view of Anglicanism. It was, he writes, primarily at Cambridge that he had aired his questions regarding the Church of England with the leading theologians of fifty years earlier, whose views had been formed in their youth – which takes us back, in some cases, to the reign of Charles I. Gezelius reports that though these men were themselves unable to provide him with a uniform picture, they had referred him to Richard Hooker. It was on Hooker's work that Gezelius had based his view of the nature of Anglicanism.

This means, of course, that Gezelius had found it necessary to go even further back in time – to the battle, under Elizabeth I, to preserve the identity of the Church of England in the face of Presbyterianism. Gezelius doubted that Hooker's line was always followed by the leaders of the Church of England. Most importantly, however, what followed theologically from Hooker could easily be recognized as closely related to the traditions and teachings of the Swedish Church.

Gezelius had been especially struck by what he saw as Hooker's way of distinguishing his position from 'Calvinism', and it was from this that Gezelius drew his conclusion regarding the close similarity between Anglicanism and Lutheranism. Gezelius was himself first and foremost a biblical theologian with a scholarly philological perspective, and Hooker's sharp criticism of Puritan 'Biblicism' therefore appealed to him. The Puritan interpretation of the Bible was not historical. The Bible was used as if it were a catalogue containing fixed rules of conduct for every situation in life, whereas in Hooker's view the Bible was a part of the living tradition of the Church. The Puritan view entailed the dismissal of everything in the Roman Catholic Church, unless a clear example of it could be found in the Bible, but no such necessity follows from Hooker's view. He – like Luther, and not least like the Swedish reformers – was therefore able to preserve the continuity of everything he felt should be preserved.

The doctrine of the sacraments was another area where Gezelius, from his Lutheran position, found himself in agreement with Hooker. Here, it was abundantly clear that Hooker separated Anglicanism not only from Zwingli's teaching, but also from Calvin's. The sacraments were far more than symbols. And their efficacy was not determined or restricted, at least not in the way that Calvinist believers in the doctrine of predestination would have it be. In Hooker's view the sacraments worked for everyone who wished to receive their gifts: incorporation with Christ through baptism; and 'the benefits of the comfortable Body and Blood of Christ' in the Eucharist.

Gezelius' positive view of a closer relationship between his own church and the Church of England – at least in principle – was not least due to the similarity between the Swedish tradition of ministry and that of the Anglicans. In this context Gezelius does not mention the other Lutheran Churches, but focuses on the Swedish Church as possessing 'ordo episcopalis ... in accordance with the old ways of Christianity', and on the English Church as being in this respect just as 'vigorous'. Undoubtedly this, too, came from his thorough reading of Hooker. According to Hooker, it was quite clear that the Church's ministry was instituted by Christ Himself, and that episcopacy was at the centre of this ministry. Gezelius shared this view and he could refer to what the Swedish reformers had said – that this was in accordance with 'the old ways of Christianity'. His words on this subject clearly show the importance he attached to the continuity of church order in general, and to the continuity of the episcopal tradition in particular. He does not, however, use the word *successio*, nor does he say anything about the act of consecration as such. But this is hardly to be expected in a statement of his time.

Johannes Gezelius sent his detailed reply to Count Gyllenborg in February, 1718. (This letter, Gyllenborg's initiative and the replies from the other bishops have all been analysed by many scholars – but not the connection with the prior Anglo-German negotiations which, to my mind, gives a fuller meaning to Gyllenborg's proposal. Hooker's influence on Gezelius has also been overlooked. This has been due to a misreading of Hooker's name as 'Hooket' – a name of no apparent relevance.) Two months later, Gezelius was dead. He was the only leader of the

The Cathedral of Turku, Finland. Built towards the end of the 13th century, the Cathedral acquired its Gothic features through a reconstruction around 1460. Two famous scholars, father and son – both named Johannes Gezelius, were successively bishops here. After Finland's partition from Sweden, the Bishop of Turku became primate of the Finnish Lutheran Church, from 1817 with the title Archbishop. *Photograph: The State Department of Museums, Helsinki.*

Swedish Church of that time who really knew and grasped the main line of classical Anglicanism, and he had at the last been afforded the opportunity of further expressing his well founded view of the close correspondence between the Swedish Church and the Church of England.

The proposal of early 1718 resulted in nothing, except the documents themselves, which remain. On 30 November 1718 Carl XII was shot dead at the siege of the Norwegian fortress, Fredrikshald. His death meant the end of Sweden as a leading political power in Northern Europe, and came to mean a diminished international interest in the Swedish Church. For a long time to come, Anglo-Swedish ecclesiastical contact was to be limited to matters concerning the church life of Swedes living in London and of Englishmen living in Sweden and to issues of the large scale European emigration to North America. Those contacts were in their turn – though not until the mid-nineteenth century – to lead to a new proposal for firmer links between the Swedish and Anglican Churches, both in the USA and in Europe.

CHAPTER 7

Increasing Connections and Self-Assurance

SCANDINAVIANS IN RESTORATION ENGLAND

1666 was the year of the Great Fire of London. Four-fifths of the city was reduced to ashes. An estimated 13,000 homes and 89 churches, among them the medieval St Paul's Cathedral, were consumed by the flames. But rebuilding soon began, and this required material – not least timber from Scandinavia. The Nordic export trade to England was suddenly flourishing, and with it came a wealth of employment opportunities for Scandinavians in the English capital. Most of those who came – timber merchants, seamen and craftsmen – were Norwegians. Hence the phrase 'by the Great Fire of London, the Norwegians warmed themselves well'.

For a long time, contacts between London and Norway were lively. In Christiania (as Oslo was then known) everything English was fashionable. A merchant-aristocracy emerged, for many generation dominated by the English Collet family. Without too many problems, these families became well integrated into Norwegian society and church life. In the second generation, one of them, John Collett, returned to England, where he became a pillar in the Danish-Norwegian congregation.

Many Danes and Swedes also moved to England in the decades following the Great Fire. Sir Christopher Wren, who besides the new St Paul's Cathedral, was in charge of much of the work of rebuilding, gave several important commissions to the Danish sculptor Caius Gabriel Cibber. The Monument, erected near the spot where the fire

138

started, was decorated by Cibber. The records of the Swedish congregation were later to show many skilled craftsmen at this time: jewellers, tailors, inn-keepers, wig-makers, painters, cobblers, hat-makers, sugar-boilers, carpenters. In addition, as from all the Nordic countries, there were, beside the Embassy personnel, sailors, students and scientists.

In most cases, there is no information at all on the lives and experiences of these Nordic immigrants and their time in England. Only the last category of England-travellers, the students and scientists, have left some source-material behind. Several of them wrote an account of their travels, including their stay in London and their time at the English universities. With increasing frequency students made their 'peregrinations' to Oxford and Cambridge, particularly since the restrictions on visits to non-Lutheran Universities had become less stringent. From the beginning of the eighteenth century, there is also another source: the reports by the chaplains to the Nordic Embassies.

An educated Scandinavian would of course not travel to England un-prepared. A move to England was a great investment, especially for students and scholars, who intended to get well aquainted with academic circles. The minimum was being able to read English and to have a good knowledge of English history and social order. Some of them make a direct mention of the book that provided such introductory knowledge: it was a 'hand-book' of no less than 600 pages, entitled *Angliæ Notitia or The Present State of England,* written by an Oxford academic and writer, Edward Chamberlayne. It was printed in altogether 36 editions over a number of years (1660–1775). This 'hand-book' provided much detailed information on many issues, and in addition no shortage of unrestrained patriotic evaluations; for example, already the Introduction informed the reader that England was 'the better part of the best Island in the whole world'.

Chamberlayne was a royalist and a confirmed supporter

139

of the Established Church. According to what he took for attested knowledge, the Church of England was founded at the earliest possible moment: by Joseph of Arimathea, mentioned at the burial of Jesus, who had come to England to preach the Gospel. Not long after, a church – 'the first in the world' – was built in Somerset. St Paul the Apostle also had preached the Gospel in England, before he went to Rome. Besides these impressive, although rather startling, pieces of information, it is interesting to observe the great importance he attached to the early relations between England and the Christendom of Greece and the Orient. He played down the emphasis on relations with Rome and the papacy, calling the Pope 'The Bishop of Rome', and describing his influence on the medieval English Church as foreign political interference. From the power of this alien 'Sovereign Prince . . . far remote beyond the seas' Henry VIII had liberated the English Church by removing the primacy from the See of Rome to Canterbury.

When the English Church had been thus 'liberated' from the spiritual tyranny of the Bishop of Rome, it had been careful to preserve everything precious in Roman liturgy. With its 39 Articles and its venerable liturgy, the Church of England was 'the most perfect of all Reformed Churches in the world', since it was both a true 'Catholic Foundation, according to the Scripture' and Reformed, truly a 'Via Media', the 'middle way' in Chamberlayne's terminology. The Calvinist influence and the Protestant interlude under Cromwell are quickly passed over. 'The Murder' of Charles I, it is claimed, had been committed by a small group of villains, 'Sons of Belial, that had no fear of God before their eyes'.

The constitutive elements of the Church of England, according to Chamberlayne, include, besides Holy Scripture, the Creeds of the Apostles and the Symbola of the Ecumenical Councils, above all 'a Holy Liturgy, Excellent Prayers, Due Administration of the Sacraments' and the Ten Commandments and the proclamation and teaching of the Gospel. Emphasis is put on the importance of episco-

140

pacy in unbroken apostolic succession: 'We have an uninterrupted succession of Reverend, Learned and Pious Bishops, who ordain Priests and deacons, Consecrate Churches, Confirm the Baptized at a due age, Bless the People, Intercede for them . . .' etc. The section on episcopacy is detailed, not least in its description of the appointment and consecration of a bishop.

For a long time the simplistic view had prevailed in the Nordic Lutheran Churches that the Church of England was a straight-forward Calvinist Church. This view had been formed in meetings with English Church life in the years soon after 1558, when all the exiles returned from Geneva to continue, in their home country, their struggle to 'complete' the Reformation in the spirit of Calvin and other continental Reformers. (See page xxx.) Influences from England on the Nordic countries in the 17th century were predominantly Puritan. Singular examples of Nordic theologians, who may have gained quite different impressions from Hooker and the Caroline Divines and later from church leaders following the Restoration, could hardly have changed that general impression. Eventually the situation changed. More and more visitors from the Nordic countries spent time in England, for shorter or longer periods. They met a Church which, at least officially, turned out to be anything but ultra-Protestant.

The main threat perceived in the Nordic National Churches from ecclesial influences from England was the potential for yet more religious division and new sects. Those who had read and trusted Chamberlayne's account of English church life would have been reassured. The picture given there of the official Church of England was very similar to a Lutheran National Church with episcopal constitution, a traditional and firmly ordered liturgy, and a teaching based on Holy Scripture and on the Catholic Creeds, from the Apostles and the Early Church. Obviously the English too, wanted to preserve religious unity. Chamberlayne's book contained fierce attacks on Presbyterians,

Independents, Anabaptists, Quakers and other sects, which he did not wish to acknowledge as legitimate representatives of English Christianity, and which he hoped would soon disappear. Nevertheless, their names keep appearing in edition after edition of *Anglia Notitiae*.

One Swedish theologian who began his English visit by studying Chamberlayne was Georg Wallin. The son of the Bishop of Härnösand, he was himself to become the Bishop of Gothenburg. He arrived in England in 1710. From the beginning, he was impressed by the Catholic character and the Establishment of English Church life, and he continued on those lines. This is symptomatic of its appeal to those who came to England, especially from the Church of Sweden. It is also an indication of the circles which such a visitor would seek out, and from whom he would learn what the Church of England essentially stood for.

Georg Wallin immediately distanced himself from the Presbyterians and other sects. He particularly disapproved of their criticism of the Anglican liturgical tradition, and their desire to replace the formal prayers in the Service with informal worship. During Wallin's visit to England, a Cambridge theologian had published a book in which this position was severely criticised. It even went as far as condemning such practice as 'ungodly' and a sign of spiritual pride. The name of this high-tempered Anglican writer was Thomas Bennet, of whom it has been said that 'he wrote faster than he thought'. In principle Wallin agreed with Bennet, even though he would not go as far in unilateral condemnation. On return to Sweden he published a whole thesis on the subject, in which he, inspired by the debate in England, wanted to stress the inherent value of a formal liturgical tradition, as it had been preserved in the Church of Sweden as well as in the Church of England. To the criticism by Ultra-Protestants of this worship as 'catholic', Wallin retorted that although this may belong to 'the catholic inheritance', it was not necessarily 'evil'. His reasoning follows the Swedish Reformers, Olaus and Laurentius Petri. It was only the abuses, not what was genuine and authentic, that our Reformers had rejected. And it was not the 'popish' practice but the tradition from the early Church that in this way had been preserved in the Swedish, just as in the Anglican, Church: 'The Halleluja and the Hosanna of the Jews, and the Kyrie eleison of the Greeks, together with the worship of the old Roman Church' (Quoted from Tor Andrae, *Georg Wallin*, 1936).

NORDIC CHURCHES IN LONDON

The activities which led to the establishment of the Nordic Lutheran congregations in London clearly show how the Scandinavians at this time wanted to relate to English church life. Events proceeded along fairly similar lines, both from the Danish-Norwegian and Swedish approach, and in both cases with the full approval and support of both the English government and the Anglican church. Official royal consent was sought via the Embassies, and every care was taken to avoid being classed as a sect. This was of course fully consistent with the fact that the Nordic ex-patriate congregations in London belonged to episcopal churches, which in their respective home countries were intimately linked to the state, and which in every way rejected congregationalism and sectarianism.

In 1672 Charles II, at the request of the Swedish Government, gave the royal consent to the establishment of a Lutheran church in London. A small church was built, but it was mostly used by German-speaking immigrants. The organisation of a Swedish congregation was still in the future. The Danish-Norwegian congregation was first to build a church of their own. It was dedicated in 1696, and the royal consent for this Danish-Norwegian congregation and church building had been given by William and Mary '. . . for the proclamation of the Holy Gospel and the administration of the sacraments according to the faith of the Augsburg Confession'. The official status of the Danish-Norwegian congregation was enhanced by the marriage of

143

the daughter of King James II, later Queen Anne of England, to the Danish Prince Jørgen (George). He was the brother of the Danish King, Christian V, and of the Queen of Sweden, Ulrika Eleonora, the consort of King Carl XI. All his life he was a member of the Danish Church, even though his background was more German- than Danish-speaking, and he occasionally received communion in the Church of England. A Lutheran Chapel was established for him at St James's Palace. This royal connection was of course a support for Danish-Norwegian church life in London, although it may also have been the cause of some division in the long run.

When the Swedish congregation was established in London, and its first Rector was appointed in 1710, everything took place in close collaboration with the Royal Swedish Embassy. The congregation was put under the supervision of the Bishop of Skara, Jesper Svedberg. We have already discussed his visit and his positive attitude to England and the Church of England. At the same time, the Bishop of London was kept well informed about the Swedes and their concerns. This was all the more natural, as the Bishop of London at this time was the eminent authority on Sweden, John Robinson, who has been previously discussed (Chapter 6). When the Swedish Chaplain sought an audience with King Carl XII to request royal support for the building of a Church in London, he brought a letter of recommendation from the Bishop of London. (For further details on this, see Sven Evander, *Londonsvenskarnas kyrka*, The Church of the London-Swedes, 1960)

The urgency for the Swedish congregation to build a church of their own sprung from the fact that they had hitherto met in a small disused chapel, which had previously belonged to a congregation of Dissenters, and any association with them was deeply unwanted. When, after a few years, their own church was at last completed, it had a tower, which although small, was still definitely a tower – a feature which was not permitted on any Dissenter's

144

Chapel. Above the entrance was placed the Swedish national coat of arms, and, in order to emphasize further its status as a National, Established Church, permission was sought and granted to name the building after the Swedish Monarch, who by now was Queen Ulrika Eleonora, the sister and successor of Carl XII. This is still the name of the Swedish congregation and Church in London, even though today a different building in another part of the city is used.

One might reflect that these small Nordic congregations might have been able to join together in a shared church building. An attempt was made at the beginning of the 18th century, but, due to their mutual difficulties in understanding each other's language, in spite of their close kinship, this proved unworkable. The main reason was however the frequent wars between Sweden and Denmark. The definite break was caused when, after the aggressive attack by Denmark on Sweden in 1710, the Danish chaplain insisted on including a prayer for victory for the Danes in the General Intercessions. Understandably, this was too much for the Swedes.

Efforts at gaining the respect of the Anglicans found different forms and practical expressions. In order to show that they were not a sect, a degree of adaption to the traditions of the Church of England was called for in many areas. According to the Anglican calender, both the Anniversary of King Charles I on 30th January, and the celebration of the Restoration on 29th May were kept. The use of liturgical vestments was also adapted to the tradition of the Church of England, with the clear explanation that this was done 'in order that our priest may not be considered a Presbyterian, nor an Independent or any other Dissenter'. Since in practice this meant a break with the Swedish custom, continuous from the medieval Church, of using the traditional chasuble at the celebration of the Eucharist, it is certainly, from the point of view of liturgical history, a somewhat paradoxical development. As the Swedish

145

Church was in some respects more 'catholic' and traditional than the Anglican, this might, for Swedish eyes, seem more than permissibly 'Protestant'. However, in eighteenth century England it was imperative not to appear too close to Roman Catholic customs. It could be dangerous to be seen as too 'popish'.

In any case, the Swedish congregation in London was well aware of its own uniqueness and was keen to mark it out. They certainly did not wish to be counted among the Dissenters. This conscious distinction is clearly expressed on the seal of the Church with the chosen watchword 'ROSA INTER SPINAS'. The Swedish congregation in London was considered to be the 'rose' flowering amidst the thorny wilderness of the sectarian brushwood!

It would seem that the representatives of Sweden and the Swedish Church were very successful in their ambitions to gain the respect of English society. The acceptance by the English King, George I, of the invitation to be godfather at the baptism of one of the sons of the Swedish Ambassador, C.G. Sparre, was not only a political and social courtesy, but an acknowledgement of the Church of Sweden. The Swedish Rector, as well as the Swedish Ambassador in London, enjoyed a socially high ranking. This was true not least of the energetic priest named Jacob Serenius (1700–1776), who was made the Rector in London at the early age of twenty, and who had already achieved a Doctor's degree. He was later to become well-known in Sweden as a prominent politician and a great deliberator in the *Riksdag*, as well as an energetic and innovative Bishop.

Serenius quickly developed a large network of contacts in the higher ranks of English society. He was elected a member of the illustrious Royal Society. The London of Serenius' experience was a glittering metropolis, newly arisen from the ashes of the Great Fire. It was a centre of international trade, a city rich in culture, in literature and music – it was the London of Handel. Among Serenius' most important connections was the new Bishop of

London, Edmund Gibson. He was an expert on Canon Law, and the author of a monumental work, *Codex Juris Ecclesiastici Anglicanae* (2 Vol. 1713). Through Serenius, Bishop Gibson became interested in the Church of Sweden and in Lutheranism. His pre-supposition was that Lutheranism was close to the Dutch Remonstrants, a liberal Reformed Church without any liturgical traditions, and fairly far 'to the left' of continental Protestantism. (It is remarkable to note how very difficult even quite prominent Anglican theologians have found it to grasp the positions of Lutheranism!). Serenius recalls how he and Gibson often, during long walks in the London parks, discussed the relative positions of Lutheranism and Anglicanism, and how he frequently had to emphasize that his Church was in no way comparable to dissenters and sects. To develop this theme further, he, after only a few years in London, published a thesis in which he shows the close comparison of the Lutheran Churches with the Anglican. It is written in Latin and entitled *Examen harmoniae religionis ecclesiae Lutheranae et Anglicanae* (printed in London 1726).

Jacob Serenius was perhaps no eminent theologian, but his thesis is not without interest. The method he used stands well in comparison with present-day ecumenical documents. The Lutheran view is supported by quotations from both the Lutheran confessional documents; and from the Nicene Creed, in order to show that Lutheran traditional teaching is above all an integral part of the universal Christian tradition. Point by point he compares Lutheran Confession with the 39 Articles, and not only with those, but also with the Anglican liturgical tradition in the Book of Common Prayer.

It is fairly obvious that Serenius wrote his thesis with a particular group of readers in mind. He wrote for the High Church wing of bishops and theologians of the Church of England. One of them who, like Gibson, belonged in those circles, is mentioned by name: the Bishop of St Asaph, William Beveridge, who was known for his stress on the ordained ministry of the Church and for his encouragement of the weekly Sunday celebration of the Eucharist. It was particularly among those circles that Serenius wanted to achive an understanding of the Lutheran tradition. This required him to discuss in some depth the doctrine of the Trinity, which provided an opportunity to reject the position of 'Socinianism', a contemporary unitarian movement in England, and also of extreme forms of 'Deism'. He then discussed the Lutheran view of the ministry of the Church, also in order to show the difference compared to Presbyterianism and the Sects. He emphasized that Lutheranism, like Anglicanism, rejected 'Donatism', i.e. the view that the validity of the ministry was dependent on the morality and piety of the individual priest. And he pointed out that it was of crucial importance to the Lutheran Churches, that there was no legitimate priest, except those who had been ordained by a bishop. The expression 'by a bishop' is obviously a reference to the custom in Nordic Churches regardless of other Lutheran traditions. Nothing is said on the rite of consecration of bishops.

The section on the Eucharist is fairly extensive, even though Serenius lightly passed by what may be regarded as a difference between Lutheran and Anglican teaching on the real presence of Christ in the bread and wine of the sacrament. He is more explicit in his defence of the view of the efficacy of the sacrament independent of the mood of the communicant. On this issue, the Lutherans and Anglicans agreed, and they were both criticised – Lutherans by the Pietists, and the Church of England by various Protestant Dissenters. It is obvious that Serenius assumes that there are no problems of 'intercommunion' between Anglicans and Lutherans, at least not if this term is used in the sense of 'mutual eucharistic hospitality', i.e. the current relationship between the Church of England and the Nordic and Continental Protestant Churches; a communicant, who was in good standing in his own Church, was able to receive communion in the other Church, provided the sacrament was administered according to the rite of that Church by one of its legally ordained priests.

148

Particularly with regard to the Eucharist, Serenius' thesis was of decisive importance, even if, in the long run, it met the same fate as so many other ecumenical documents: it was read by a few and then more or less forgotten. But it did happen that, on application, foreigners could be granted English citizenship by reference to Serenius' work. The rule was that every English citizen must be a communicant member of the Church of England and must receive communion at least once a year. It now became possbile to argue, by reference to Serenius' work, that those who were regular communicants in an Established Lutheran Church were of the same status. This was in principle an important acknowledgement. This rule, however, was questioned by the Tory party, who wanted to restrict citizenship only to those who were able to prove that they were already Anglican communicants, i. e. members of another Church within the Anglican Communion. Bishop Gibson, who had received Serenius' book, was however able to defend the current practice of applying the rule to Lutherans as well as to other Anglicans by referring to Serenius' exposition of Lutheran teaching on the Eucharist. Generally speaking, relations seem to have been cordial between the Lutheran congregations, both the Danish-Norwegian and the Swedish, and the Church of England.

Jacob Serenius certainly contributed to the increased understanding between England and Sweden. In order to improve knowledge in his home-country of English culture and social economy, he published a book with the rather quaint title: *Engelske Åkermannen och Fåraherden* (The English Farmer and Shepherd); mostly a compilation of various English writings, with the purpose of raising interest in England among Swedish politicians and industrialists, and as a link in his campaign of raising money for the building of a new Church in London. A greater contribution was his large English-Latin-Swedish Dictionary, which also included a small thesis on early medieval Swedish-English relations: *De veterum Sveo-gothorum cum Anglis usu et commercio dissertatio.* It was a chauvinist

149

review, which also told of the important role of English Missionaries in the conversion of Sweden to the Christian faith.

Altogether Serenius had achieved a great deal during his ten years as the Swedish Rector in London. His greatest cause of fame in Sweden – the claim that he introduced confirmation according to the English custom, a claim which he made himself – is however unfounded. It may be true that he embraced the idea of a solemn ceremony to bring the Christian education of the youth to a close with great enthusiasm, but he was neither the first nor the only one to do so. Besides, this was not a direct comparison with confirmation in the Church of England, where confirmation is a sacramental act, administered by the bishop. In the Church of Sweden, confirmation may be administered by a priest, and the custom has emerged from the educational system of the Swedish Church itself.

During the eighteenth century visits to England by Swedish theologians and scientists became increasingly common. There were apparently no difficulties in establishing good contacts with English bishops and priests and with the learned circles of Oxford and Cambridge. One such visitor, well worth a mention, was the later Bishop of Kalmar, Martin Georg Wallenstråle. He was the son of the previously mentioned Bishop of Gothenburg, Georg Wallin, and he spent several years in England in the 1760s. Wallenstråle's letters and diaries, parts of which have been published, contain various informative details of academic and ecclesial circumstances in England. His father's successor in the see of Gothenburg, Erik Lamberg, hade also studied in England for several years. Not least in Gothenburg there were frequent and lasting contacts with England.

But of course not all Swedes and other Nordic visitors to England found it easy to adapt to the social and ecclesial customs of the country, or were able to make themselves at home in their own congregation in London. For later generations the most famous of all the Swedes who lived in London in the eighteenth century was Emanuel Swedenborg (the son of Bishop Jesper Svedberg). He lived in London for many years, and also died there. He was buried in the Swedish Church, were his remains stayed, until they were moved to the Cathedral of Uppsala in 1908. He was however of no particular importance for relations between the Church of England and the Church of Sweden. His 'New Church' was a separate foundation, quite apart from them both, and his contacts with the Swedish congregation in London were fairly sporadic. He was regarded as a rather odd person, whose appearance in his old age was unkempt and somewhat strange. Swedenborg himself complained that in the Service at the Swedish Church, he felt no peace from 'the spirits', which constantly contradicted the preacher. He is still remembered in London today, especially on the site of the Swedish Church in his day, which is nowadays a London park named after him: Swedenborg Gardens, restored and re-opened in 1993.

An increasing number of the Swedes and other Nordic visitors to England towards the end of the eighteenth century, with a theological or other interest in the Church, were more attracted to John Wesley and the circles around him, than to other English clergy and their sermons. One by one they testify in the account of their travels to the great impression made particularly by John Wesley. They found his personality just as attractive as his sermons. John Wesley's sermons 'are for the heart, they build on the right foundation' the learned collector and librarian Johan Hinric Lidén, for example, tells one of his friends in Sweden in a letter. Also the Chaplain to the Court, Carl Magnus Wrangel, who on the English pattern, founded the Swedish society 'Pro Fide et Christianismo' in 1771, was deeply attracted to Wesley and the Methodists during his visit to England in 1768. And there were others: Bishop Erik Lamberg, the Secretary to the Swedish Embassy and later the Ambassador to Madrid, Malte Ramel. It was John Wesley and his sermons that they appreciated most in English Church life.

There was of course an aspect of Wesley's preaching which resembled the characteristic Lutheran tradition, and which came closer to this than the otherwise 'enlightened' preaching which was common in contemporary England. That this could be the reason why a Nordic Lutheran felt a particular kinship with Wesley's devotion is quite obvious from Lidén's letters; it seems that Lidén's judgement was also somewhat coloured by pietist influences. The great attraction in Wesley's preaching was, in his view, in the concentration on 'the crucified Saviour and the faith in the merit of Jesus'. And he adds: 'The people (in England) had never heard anything like it'. The judgement of 'the learned' in England on such preaching was that it ought to be condemned as 'enthusiastic and heretical' (*Lidén, J.H., Förtroende brev från,* utg. 1961.; Confidential Letters by H.J. Lidén, 1961). A corresponding type of Christ-centered preaching was certainly still the norm in Sweden, and it was this theme that the Swedes recognized in Wesley. Justification 'by the merit of Jesus' was a main theme in Lutheranism, including among those who were influenced by Lutheran 'enlightened' orthodoxy and of course no less among those who were influenced by the Pietist Revival.

That the Swedes were attracted to Wesley was not particularly strange. He was the great man in the Church of England at the time. And it is worth stressing the word 'in'. In the lifetime of John Wesley, the Methodist revival was still a movement within the Established Church. That the members of the Swedish National Church had a preference for him during their time in England did not in any way mean that they had chosen a different way other than that of the official Church.

CHAPTER 8

The National Church in Crisis

THE REVIVALIST MOVEMENTS

The nineteenth century was a time of great tension, not least from the perspective of church history, which makes it difficult to trace the patterns of development.

Looked at in the context of the national Church, the picture becomes clearer. The identity and way of life of the National Church was under serious threat. It survived, but only after having been re-examined and renewed in various ways. A simultaneous study of the Nordic churches and English church life, using the comparative method, brings out the main features of this development.

Let us begin by concentrating our attention on the Revivalist movements. During the first half of the nineteenth century, these movements swept across the Nordic countries, leaving hardly a county or a region unaffected. (The only exception was Iceland, where there was no Revivalist movement.)

The chain of events was fairly similar, although there was only sparse contacts between the Nordic countries. All these movements were rooted in the teaching of the Christian faith, which the Lutheran National Churches had obviously imparted very successfully to the vast majority of the population. Knowledge of the central content of the Christian faith had indeed been imparted through sermons and through the persistent educational efforts of the clergy, through Luther's Small Catechism, the Hymnal and other devotional literature. The tradition was that of Lutheran orthodoxy, coloured by the pietistic view.

But now the awareness grew that something was missing. It was no longer considered enough to trust in one's

153

baptism, to believe the Christian message, to practise personal prayer and attend public worship on a regular basis. The emphasis shifted to the desirability of a personal experience of salvation, and so the necessity of a personal, spiritual breakthrough, leading to a new way of life and the rejection of this world with all its vanity, became mandatory. To form independent groups for fellowship and mutual support of the likeminded, and to keep a distance from all others, became indispensable. This attitude can be seen as a continuation and sharpening of tendencies already present in earlier traditions: Puritanism, Pietism and among the Moravian Brethren.

Revivalist movements were a general Protestant phenomenon. So were the tensions they created in relation to existing church life. There were strong similarities and a variety of links between the movements in the Nordic countries and their counterparts on the Continent and in Great Britain.

The desire was to make the spiritual life more prominent, more evident in the actual personal experience of the individual, and more obvious in the way of life of the believer. Official orthodox Lutheran teaching had of course always stressed the importance of personal acceptance of the Gospel: 'justification by faith' presupposed personal commitment. It is not that the churches had forgotten to stress the fundamental requirement of Christian living in obedience to the commandment of God and in faithfulness to one's calling in the world, but this message had been preached to the Church as a whole. It was trustworthy because it was founded on the Word of God, and its authority was underpinned by the 'proper calling' (*rite vocatus* – i.e. the legal ordination and institution) of the bishops and priests who taught it.

For the Revivalists, the reason for trust was vested in the individual, in the layman as well as the priest. Only he was trustworthy who had experienced a proper 'conversion', i.e. who had experienced personal salvation in a clear breakthrough, and who had conducted his life in a new way, different from the 'worldly' ways of his surroundings. The Revivalists certainly acknowledged and listened to priests; many of their leaders were in fact priests but unless they were 'converted' priests, they were not considered to have any spiritual authority.

The Revivalists' view of the marks of the true Church proved a serious threat to the national Church. The ecclesiastical authorities, which in all these countries were intimately united with the institutions of the State, took drastic action to try to stop these developments. Already during the first half of the eighteenth century, the Pietists were prohibited from holding private meetings by the so called *Konventikelplakat* (the Conventicle Act) both in Denmark-Norway and Sweden-Finland. Parochial unity must not be broken. The teaching authority and the rights and responsibilities of the priests to expound the faith officially must not be undermined, nor usurped by lay ministers. It is important to remember that such legislation only applied to the internal affairs of the Church and to its own members. In each of the Nordic countries there was officially only one Church. At least in theory that established Church included the entire population.

This is a difference compared to the situation in England, where ecclesiastical pluralism was already a fact. In England, the law of the land still assumed that only those who were loyal to the Church of England as the established Church could enjoy full citizenship and the right to stand for Parliament, to hold public office, to teach etc. Towards the end of the 1820s and the beginning of the 1830s Parliament, in spite of fierce opposition from the bishops of the Church of England, repealed a number of these laws. This gave dissenters, such as Baptists and Quakers who had broken away from the Church of England, a stronger position in society. Roman Catholics also gained a better position. Hitherto they had been barred from all these privileges.

By now the Methodists had also formed their own

155

denomination. The movement towards this can be found already in the work of John Wesley. He ignored the parochial structure of the national Church. 'The world is my parish' is a famous saying of his, a courageous, proud proclamation and hardly exaggerated. Wesley's preaching was very influential and spread far afield. By the time of his death in 1791 there were reportedly 70,000 Methodists in Great Britain and 60,000 in America. But the concept of 'the parish' had been shattered. Wesley's 'parishioners' were those who had experienced personal salvation and who had voluntarily joined a congregation for mutual spiritual support. Such an association was not called a 'parish' but a 'society'.

John Wesley became the wellspring of spiritual renewal and confident certainty and boldness to preach the Gospel among his contemporaries in Great Britain and in many other places. The inspiration from Wesley continued in the Evangelical Revival in the nineteenth century, thereby contributing to the renewal within the Anglican Church. The same can be said of the revivalist movements in the Lutheran national churches in Scandinavia. They brought a new enthusiasm for devotion and contributed lasting values to the spirituality of these churches. However, over against the idea of a national church, they proved a source of tension, which sometimes became a destructive element.

Already several studies have been made of the Revivalist movements from a sociological point of view. They spread like popular movements within certain defined layers of the population, and in particular among those classes who at this time gained a stronger, more independent place in society. The sense of greater commitment and increased responsibility also in religious matters became an important notion among these groups. It is difficult to determine what was the cause and what the effect in these issues.

It is clear that many countries in Europe went through a period of social upheaval at this time. In England, this had started already in the eighteenth century. In the Nordic countries the first half of the nineteenth century brought a similar change. New interests and concerns led to new differentiations within the community. The old social order, with its hierarchy and well-defined structures in which the national Church was an important, well-integrated part seemed to be in a state of flux. Religion became either a 'private matter' or the concern of the popular movements, which in fact remained within the framework of the national Church. So the national Church survived. And it has shown itself capable of survival, not only in the turbulence of the nineteenth century, but for almost another century since.

Theologically speaking, the Revivalist movements were usually conservative. When criticised by the ecclesiastical authorities, they were able to respond that they only held on to the old tradition: salvation through the blood of Christ and through him alone. On the other hand, the theology propounded by the church leaders of the day could be seen as a deviation from the 'true faith and teaching'. The Revivalists detected a theology tinged by rationalism and moralism. The main theological orientation among church leaders and theologians at the beginning of the nineteenth century was the so called 'Neology', which showed a strong resemblance to the Deism current in eighteenth century England. 'God, virtue and immortality' were the main themes and there was hardly anything about sin and grace and salvation through Jesus Christ. Such tendencies the Revivalists also discovered, to their sadness, in the new liturgical rites and the official service books, in the teaching manuals on the Cathecism and in the Hymnal. This was the reason why the people of the Revivalist movements in Scandinavia were no longer able to find their spiritual sustenance in the worship and sacraments of the established Church. In many places the criticism of the Service Books and the baptism rite itself became the cause of schisms between the National Church and the Revivalists in Scandinavia.

The leaders of the Revivalists believed themselves to be

building on the inheritance from Luther. And in many ways they were right. It was however a Lutheranism deeply coloured by Pietism. Their teaching on redemption stood out against a dark canvas. The world was evil and man, prior to conversion, was totally corrupt. On these points they had lost several important aspects of Luther's view. Martin Luther himself experienced great joy and delight in God's creation. He took an open and active interest in culture. He recognized God's work in the given structures of society. He commended every honest effort at home, in the family and in the community as a service and 'worship' of God.

Even so, the Revivalists could build on Luther. They read with preference the sermons of Luther, and they often named their chapels and congregations after him. They found support in him for their Christ-centered spirituality. And they found great inspiration in his teaching on the Christian vocation in the world and inspiration for ernest study of the Bible – for a life in obedience to God – in general contentment. They were usually conscientious and successful in their professional life, though they seldom participated in cultural activities: art, music and literature were preferably to be abstained from.

A great many of the nineteenth century Revivalists combined their Lutheran inheritance with a way of life similar to that of the Puritans. This was done without reflection on the fact that this union was one of essentially different entities and that it actually implied a break with traditional Lutheran morality and lifestyle. Thus there emerged within the Lutheran national churches a tension similar to what can be seen within Anglicanism as the tension between Evangelicals and Catholics ('Low Church' and 'High Church') on issues of morality and social order.

The demands of 'pure living' made by the Revivalists' leaders in the Nordic countries often led to a break with both the priests and the people in general. These conflicts often homed in on the use of alcohol, card-games and dancing. The issues of abstinence often became very prominent.

It is a well-known fact, both that alcoholism was very widespread with devastating effects on a vast number of people, and that it was by and large the Revivalist movements that provided the cure. But it is also quite obvious that it was for theological reasons that many people objected to the too close linking of the Abstinence Movement with the faith and teaching of the Church. It might appear, they argued, that the abstainers were better Christians than others. Their concern was to defend both the freedom of the Christian under the Gospel and the openness of the national Church.

NORWAY'S HAUGE AND FINLAND'S RUOTSALAINEN

The exclusive attitudes of the Revivalists often strained relations with the National Church almost to breaking-point. Even so, the majority of Revivalists stayed within its framework. This was due, to a large extent, to the personal opinions and charisma of their great leaders. One example from Norway and one from Finland will serve to illustrate this.

The church historian Einar Molland writes about the great Norwegian Revivalist Hans Nielsen Hauge (1771 – 1824) and his followers; 'Haugianerne er Norges puritanere'('The Haugians are Norway's Puritans'). Hauge is in many ways a typical leader for the early Revivalist movements in Scandinavia.

Hauge's work as a lay preacher extended across vast areas in Norway, though from a sociological perspective it was limited to the peasants. He was, however, himself also a pioneer as an energetic industrialist and business executive. His conflict with both ecclesiastical and civil authority arose not because of matters of doctrine, but because he broke the law defined by the Conventicle Act, which forbade anyone other than priests to engage in public preaching. This led to a custodial sentence and he was detained

159

for several years. Imprisonment took its toll on his health, but he nevertheless remained loyal to his church. He encouraged his followers to faithful attendance of Sunday worship in the parish church and to reception of the sacraments from their priests. The Haugian revivalism consequently remained within the Church, and it continued to be led by priests who were themselves personally involved. Thanks to the leadership of Hauge's successor, Professor Gisle Johnson (1822–1894), this movement was consolidated, and as a result of these fortunate circumstances, it became a source of great enrichment for the Norwegian Church. The fruits of this can still be seen in the high level of lay-led activities, the general sense of lay-responsibility and the lively interest in mission in the Church of Norway. It is of course also discernable in the strongly pietistic leanings in much of Norwegian church life.

In some cases the new spiritual movements feature characteristics central to Lutheran doctrine. This can be clearly shown in the great Revivalist movements in the Evangelical-Lutheran Church of Finland. A remarkable spearhead figure was the self-taught poor peasant Paavo Ruotsalainen (1777–1852). He had developed his own theological approach, based on eager and frequent study of the Bible, a few of the main pietist devotional books that he could get hold of, but above all of Luther's Small Catechism. That he had taken to heart.

And that was in fact how the Lutheran Catechism worked for those who took it seriously, who used it as a devotional guide for Christian living. The great issue for Paavo Ruotsalainen, as for large groups of his contemporaries, revolved around the quest for 'certainty' about personal salvation: 'How can I know for certain that I am a Christian, that I have been saved?' Luther's Small Catechism provided a clear answer. In the edition used in the early days of Ruotsalainen in both Sweden and Finland an introductory question 'Are you a Christian?' first met the reader. The answer was given immediately with a clear and simple 'Yes'. Then the next question followed: 'Why are you called a Christian?' and the answer: 'Because I am baptized in the Name of the Father, the Son and the Holy Ghost. By baptism I am clothed with Christ, and I believe and profess that Christ is my Saviour who will sanctify me'. The purpose of the Catechism was precisely to help people to know this for sure.

Luther pointed to an objective truth, not to subjective emotions, but to Christ as Saviour and to the sacrament of baptism. And it was precisely this objective truth that Ruotsalainen took hold of and imparted to others in his far-reaching work as a spiritual guide. He opposed with great energy those who trusted in subjective feelings and got carried away by their enthusiasm at charismatic meetings. He pointed instead to the 'way of the cross' and the 'school of the cross' which a Christian must submit to. It was the Christian duty 'quietly' to bear whatever this might mean, and to 'wait on God' in humility and faith.

It may seem strange to us today to think that this severe attitude to the faith was able to attract such a warm response from such large groups, and that it survived for several generations. Those who carried the inheritance from Ruotsalainen further put far more emphasis on the 'evangelical' tone, the joyful aspects of the Christian life. Latterly it was to a large extent the priests of the Church who took over the leadership.

However, the ferment from Ruotsalainen lives on deep down. An example of this was given when the Lutheran World Federation held its General Assembly in Helsinki in 1963. Finland's President, Urho Kekkonen, the man who, as President for altogether 25 years, most certainly exerted a far greater influence on his people than any other politician in this century, made a speech at the opening ceremony. Most people in the audience were probably expecting a conventional speech of welcome. The Finnish President, however, took the opportunity of making a personal statement, telling the story of how he had always brought the Christian faith with him from his family home.

This home had been completely steeped in the spirituality of Ruotsalainen. In this way, he said, he himself had also learnt to understand and appreciate Martin Luther.

THE INTERNATIONAL LINKS OF THE
REVIVALIST MOVEMENTS

The influence of the Revivalist movements on the national churches in Scandinavia led to a somewhat changed interpretation of the Christian faith within Lutheranism. This revised understanding has a great deal in common with that of other Protestant denominations, not least with the so called evangelical movement in Anglicanism. Consequently, there is a strain of Pietism, or 'Evanglicalism', in modern Lutheranism as practised today. This may be called 'Evangelical Lutheranism'.

International links were an integral aspect of the Revivalist movement from the very beginning. Neither parish nor national nor denominational boundaries proved any hindrance at all. This could already be seen in the eighteenth century in the work of the Moravians in Scandinavia. German Moravians sent missionaries called 'Diaspora Workers', to the Nordic countries. They gained several followers, who were then also open to Revivalist influences from other sources.

At the beginning of the nineteenth century two missionaries arrived from Great Britain: John Paterson, an English Methodist, and Ebenezer Henderson, a Scottish Presbyterian, both Revivalists without any particular denominational allegiance. Their intention was to become missionaries to the Danish colony of Serampore, near Calcutta, so in 1805 they arrived in Copenhagen, hoping to travel from there to India. However, because of the Napoleonic wars sailings were disrupted, so the two missionaries never reached India. They started instead some ecumenical work in the Nordic countries, first in Copenhagen and later in Gothenburg, Stockholm and Turku. The fruit of their

162

labours was impressive. In 1819 John Paterson visited Finland, where he was warmly welcomed by the Bishop of Turku, Jacob Tengström. As a result, the Finnish Bible Society was established as early as 1812. Soon Bible Societies after the English model were formed, also in Denmark, Sweden and Norway. *Evangeliska Sällskapet* (The Evangelical Society) for the purpose of distributing religious tracts also sprang up in Sweden at this time. The Norwegian Bible Society founded in 1816, very soon became a widespread organization with a number of diocesan committees and strong support from the Norwegian bishops.

The inspiration behind all these organizations sprang from the enthusiasm for Evangelical revivalism of these two Britons. It is interesting to note the immediacy of the response. They were very successful in gaining the support of leading men in Church and nation from circles not previously involved in revivalism, and in securing their commitment as board members. The virtue of spreading Christian education among the people was clearly appreciated. Support was also found among the friends of the Moravians throughout Scandinavia. Besides the national Bible Societies, the British and Foreign Bible Society started up branches in several countries, among them Sweden. (The Swedish branch was started because the British Evangelicals disliked the Swedish Lutheran tradition of allowing the Apocrypha to be included in the Bible.) The British agency was opened in Stockholm in 1832 and was active right up until 1885, during which time it distributed some three million Bibles in Sweden. The Bible Society in Norway was largely financed from England, and 'travelling preachers' who traversed Norway, distributing Bibles and devotional tracts, were also sent from England. This English 'mission' continued until the end of the nineteenth century.

The Bible Societies in the Nordic countries were highly esteemed. In Sweden, Bible societies were formed in individual dioceses. Similar societies, *Traktatsällskap* (tract societies), were also formed for the purpose of distributing tracts and pamphlets written in the spirit of revivalism. These Societies also provided fellowship and a formal structure for binding together the people of the Revivalist movements. The British initiative had great effect. It gave inspiration for evangelism. To the circles surrounding the Evangelical Society and the Bible Societies can be attributed also the first attempts to found independent societies for Overseas Mission.

A 28-year-old Methodist from Scotland, George Scott, was appointed to run the British Bible agency in Stockholm from its inception. He was also the preacher at the English Chapel, a small Methodist chapel in Stockholm. In spite of all the stringent prohibitions limiting religious freedom in Sweden, permission to build this chapel had been obtained in order to provide a place of worship for a few English Methodists, among them the prominent industrialist Samuel Owen. Scott's work in Stockholm marks the beginning of the spread of Methodism in Sweden. He was also behind a number of new initiatives in co-operation with leaders of the Church of Sweden. The most important of these was the foundation of *Svenska Missionssällskapet* (The Swedish Missionary Society) in 1835 as an inter-denominational society, with many influential personalities from the highest establishment among its trustees: the Minister of Justice, Mattias Rosenblad, Bishop (later Archbishop) J.O. Wallin and others, including the Methodist Samuel Owen. Scott also brought new enthusiasm to the distribution of tracts by the Evangelical Society and encouraged the work of the Bible Society.

The most important aspect of George Scott's work in Sweden was, however, his influence on the great leader of Swedish nineteenth century revivalism, Carl Olov Rosenius (1816–1868). This lay preacher from the growing revivalism in *Norrland* (the north of Sweden) had begun theological studies with a view to ordination to the priesthood in the Church of Sweden but found himself in a crisis of faith, which Scott helped him through. The Methodist certainty

164

of personal salvation became a tower of strength for him, and he soon became Scott's assistant at the English Chapel and later took over that work. He became particularly influential as editor of the Revivalist periodical *Pietisten* (The Pietist), which was distributed in large editions across the country. Rosenius' published sermons and homilies soon became very popular and are still used today as devotional literature among low church groups of a later generation. The influence of Rosenius also reached wide circles in Finland and Norway, and, to a lesser extent, the Danish island of Bornholm. (In historical writing about the Swedish Church, Rosenius is described as a 'Neo-Evangelical' Revivalist, but the simple term 'Evangelical' seems sufficient for international usage.)

During the time of Rosenius the greater part of Swedish revivalism was brought together in an organization called *Evangeliska Fosterlands-Stiftelsen* (The Swedish Evangelical Mission) along the lines of the Scottish Presbyterians, whom they felt to be kindred spirits. There was however a difference: It was possible to preserve structural links with the Church of Sweden, and *Evangeliska Fosterlands-Stiftelsen*, although an independent organization with its own chapels, preachers, periodicals, publishing company and even a society for overseas 'mission to the Gentiles', managed to remain fully within the institutional framework of the Church of Sweden. A certain ambivalence of this kind has always attended this 'Evangelical' stream of Swedish Lutheranism – fully independent while preserving loyal membership of the national Church. Nowadays almost all its preachers are priests, ordained by bishops of the Church of Sweden. In the 1870s, however, a large part of this Society broke away and formed a new, partly Lutheran-Pietist, partly Congregationalist denomination under the name of *Svenska Missionsförbundet* (The Swedish Covenant Church). So the Revivalist movement led to a degree of schism in Sweden, which was largely avoided in the other Nordic countries.

*   *   *

For the Swedish Evanglical Revivalist movements, direct, personal contacts with Great Britain were formative, not least the influence of George Scott on Rosenius. In the other Nordic countries, British influence was less obvious. Inspiration from abroad took different routes. New ways of thinking were brought to both Denmark and Norway through publications spread by the Bible Societies. In Denmark Pastor Bonne Falck Rønne in Lyngby, near Copenhagen, was a pioneer in Christian social work and also in arousing interest in overseas mission. It was he who initiated the formation of *Dansk Missionsselskab* (The Danish Missionary Society) in 1821. It had a humble beginning as an association from among the lower middle-classes. To begin with neither encouragement nor support was received from any church leaders, but this association not only became the cradle of the first missionary organization of the Danish Church: it also anticipated the consolidation of the entire Danish Evangelical movement in the so-called *Indre Mission* (Home Mission).

Det Norske Misjonsselskap (The Norwegian Missionary Society), the first of a number of similar organizations, was also founded in a democratic manner as a result of a broad interest among the people. This was a little later, in 1842, and it immediately received considerable support. This new society very soon became a nationwide organization, an association of independent, local societies. Across the country people had informed themselves about revivalism and mission, not least from British sources. In this way interest and the will to act had been aroused, and at the same time an independent Christian national organization had been created, whose remit reached beyond the boundaries of the national Church.

In Finland contacts between revivalism and the national Church were distinctive, because of the great change inaugurated in 1809, when Sweden was forced to hand over Finland to Russia. Finland enjoyed a remarkable independence within the Russian Empire. It became an independent state, a duchy under the Tsar with its own legal system, and the Evangelical-Lutheran Church remained the established state Church. Strangely enough this Lutheran national church came under the authority of the Tsar, who was also the head of the Russian Orthodox Church. Tsar Alexander I showed every respect for these arrangements. He was in fact very keen to support the national Church of Finland, in which he saw a guarantee of unity and civil order in the country.

The Tsar regarded the Revivalist movements as a possible ferment of disunity, which ought to be kept under control. Conflicts between church leaders and Revivalists could lead to drawn-out legal wranglings, which in the last instance were brought before the Tsar himself. Alexander I showed considerable restraint in sentencing Revivalists. Tougher measures are noticeable under his successors. The challenge to the church leaders was to prove to the Tsar that religion was not a threat of national life nor a cause of civil disobedience. The desire of the Revivalists to form independent associations for overseas 'mission to the Gentiles' in Finland, as they had done in Sweden and in other countries, met considerable opposition from the regime of the Tsar. Permission to found *Finska Missionssällskapet* (The Finish Missionary Society) was not given until 1858.

As we have seen above, contacts among Revivalists always crossed national boundaries. There was mutual understanding and reciprocal response, there was an exchange of periodicals and other devotional literature, translations were made of psalters and hymnals, there was practical co-operation in mission, or at the very least, mutual encouragement. About the middle of the nineteenth century an international organization, the Evangelical Alliance, was formed for the purpose of strengthening this fellowship and looking after common interests. The participants in the international conferences of the Alliance included Scandinavian delegates. The Evangelical Alliance can be considered a forerunner to the Ecumenical movement, although entirely from the revivalist perspective..

Among the movements which can be called 'Evangelical Revivalism' in Scandinavia, the main, strongly dominant, inspiration came from Great Britain. In the context of Anglo-Scandinavian ecclesiastical relations, it is in fact these contacts between Revivalist Christians which were the most extensive and the most influential. They took place, however, along routes other than the official channels of the church leaders.

NEW INTERPRETATIONS OF THE NATIONAL CHURCH

It would of course be quite wrong to describe the developments in the Church in the nineteenth century only from the perspective of the popular Revivalist movements. Sadly, this has too often been the case in the literature on the subject. Too often the desperate attempts by the national churches to prevent and circumscribe all independent movements by prohibitions and penalties are set against the enthusiasm of the Revivalists. This appears as merely a negative, rigid defence of traditional structures and ideals from the past. In reality, things were very different. Many of those who defended the tradition of the national Church and wanted to hand on that inheritance, were also fired with a zeal for renewal. They defended something in which they really believed. They argued the case for continuity precisely because they had discovered indispensable values in the received tradition of a given, common inheritance, which they wanted to hand on intact to the future.

The first decades of the nineteenth century saw a dramatic shift in European culture, away from rationalism and materialism towards spiritual, eternal values. Emotions and feelings now gained prominence, in place of reason and prosaic pragmatism. Nature itself was conceived of as ani-

168

mated. This change in outlook led to a new appreciation of history. The past deserved great interest. The culture and mentality of specific peoples became fascinating subjects of study. The hitherto prevailing French Classicist style in literature was in decline. This new culture and mental attitude is commonly known as the Romantic period.

This cultural re-orientation became highly significant in theology and in church life. Emotional life and religious experience took prominence over virtue and reason. The priest was above all a 'steward of the mysteries of faith', and as such should not be overloaded with 'worldly' duties on behalf of secular society. The identity of the Church should be seen in the light of its own history. Tradition was again highly esteemed.

As we shall see, this re-orientation led to important results both in Scandinavia and in England. Scandinavian culture, at this time, found most of its inspiration in Germany from the German Romantics and the 'Evangelical Revival' on the Continent. These new tunes reached the young generation at the beginning of the century. Henrik Steffens (1773–1845), a Norwegian who had studied in Germany, at the feet of Schelling, the famous philosopher, brought the thinking of the Romantics to Copenhagen. There he influenced a large number of young men, who were soon to reach worldwide acclaim during the Danish 'Golden Age': Thorvaldsen, H.C. Andersen, Kirkegaard and Grundtvig.

In Sweden the change in spiritual climate becomes most obvious in the preparatory work towards the publication of the new Hymnal in 1819. The best examples come from the great hymnwriter J.O.Wallin (Archbishop of Uppsala, d.1839), whose hymns gradually changed towards 1819 from stressing moral virtue to centring more and more on the doctrine of redemption through Jesus Christ.

The change in attitude towards spiritual matters, for which the Romantics had paved the way, contributed greatly to the views held in leading church circles in the nineteenth century on the questions surrounding the issue of the continuity of the national churches. These matters were debated more or less simultaneously in the Scandinavian countries, in England and in many other places. In many ways the same questions are being posed with equal relevance today, towards the end of the twentieth century.

Although the questions were often the same, the answers often differed radically. Four different attitudes can represent the situation in the Nordic national churches of the nineteenth century. The first two examples come from Swedish church history; one shows a radical liberal stance, the other a consequent, considered conservatism. Thereafter we will look at two famous examples from Denmark.

The first example is found in the ecclesiastical reform programme developed by Professor Johan Henrik Thomander (1798–1865), later Bishop of Lund. For him, the thought of the Romantics was obviously the starting point. Thomander began his career as a poet and translator. He was the first important translator in Sweden of the dramatic works of William Shakespeare. His theological view represented a corresponding shift from orthodoxy and rationalism to 'Evangelical Revivalism' and interest in medieval mysticism. Politically he embraced a liberal view, according to which free interest groupings should replace the given structures of society, which had hitherto been regarded as instituted by God.

From such stand points, Thomander presented a programme of reform for the Swedish Church in the form of a proposal for a new Church Law (1837). He pleaded for his views for decades in his writings and in the *Riksdag* (Parliament). His idea was to separate out the ecclesiastical and religious sphere as an independent area of interest, which demanded its own organization and its own, specifically qualified, spokesmen. The differentiations in society at large made such a distinction necessary. It could not be argued that society as such was Christian, nor that State and

Church were identical. On the national level, the 'internal' affairs of the Church should be handled, not by the *Riksdag*, but by a Church Assembly (a kind of Synod), with members elected by the Church itself. At the top there should be a Central Board. At the local level, one and the same council, the *Sockenstämma* (Parish Meeting) had hitherto taken all decisions concerning both secular and ecclesiastical affairs. A similar separation was necessary in local government.

It was not only Thomander who voiced thoughts like these, nor were tried and tested models lacking. About this time synods were introduced in some German states. But in Sweden it was Thomander who presented an overall, considered reform programme to this effect. His ideas were adopted in part. In the 1860s the Church Assembly of the Church of Sweden was established, and at the same time secular and ecclesiastical affairs were separated at the local level by the institution of two separate councils. (The ecclesiastical Central Board only came into existence in the 1980s.)

Similar reform programmes (partly inspired by Thomander's ideas) were proposed in Finland at the same time. These were more thoroughly adopted (by means of a new Church Law of 1869). In Denmark, Norway and Iceland the system created at the Reformation, i.e. church government in the hands of the state Government through the Ministry of Ecclesiastical Affairs, in principle remained unchanged. In return, especially in Denmark, as we shall see, great freedom was enjoyed by the national *Folkekirke* (The Danish National Church). In England criticism of the power of the state authorities to make decisions on issues concerning the Church gradually increased, but the system of synodical government of the Church was not fully established until almost a century later.

Against this whole way of thinking – the idea of separating the secular and the spiritual and of transforming the national Church into a religious body independent in prin-

171

ciple – stood another equally well-considered, conservative view of state and church: conservatism, a totally genuine, well-integrated and well-founded philosophical view of society, which had also sprung from the Romantics. Those whose views were founded on this conservative idealism saw the whole of society as one organism, built on the family, blood-relations and the traditional class system (nobility, clergy, bourgeoisie and peasants) as a hierarchy culminating in the monarchy. This entire social system was sanctioned and sanctified by religion and embraced by the national Church.

It is not hard to find advocates of such conservative ideas among the leaders of the various churches. On Swedish soil it was above all professor Henrik Reuterdahl (1795–1870), later Bishop of Lund, and finally Archbishop of Uppsala, who most consistently defended the old order in opposition to the radical reforms encouraged by Thomander and others. Reuterdahl took a long view of state and church in their historical perspective. He was himself an eminent scholar, specializing in medieval church history. In his view, State and Church in Sweden formed an indissoluble unit, and in this inherited system he found indispensable values. He felt almost physically sick at the thought of some people considering themselves to be better Christians than others, more virtuous than others, and in consequence deliberately cutting themselves off from the community of the ordinary parish.

Reuterdahl lived to see almost all the reforms he had opposed being adopted. His failure to prevent them was almost certainly fortunate. The process of religious fragmentation would most probably have gone even further, had not the church leaders shown any signs at all of comprehension and willingness to tolerate a degree of relgious diversity. But Reuterdahl's fight had not been entirely in vain. The importance of the national Church and the inspiration from its own history was to prove its strength in the following generations.

Reuterdahl approached the issues of the day in church

and in society as an historian. Among his contemporaries there were others, whose conservative church politics had a more theological, philosophical foundation. (In Sweden above all E.G. Bring, A.N. Sundberg and N. Flensburg, all three professors of the Univeristy of Lund, and later bishops, Sundberg succeeding Reuterdahl as Archbishop of Uppsala, and all three finding support in the historical philosophy of the German philosopher Hegel.) They saw the identity of their church first and foremost in its formularies of confession, e.g. in the Lutheran confessional documents of the sixteenth century. Supported by the Augsburg Confession they strongly defended, for example, the position of the ordained ministry of the Church.

At this time reference to formularies of confession had become a frequently used method in the German protestant churches, and it was to become the commonly used method of argument in all the Lutheran churches. The written confession became normative.

Church leaders and theologians, in Scandinavia as in Germany, mostly supported what has been called Lutheran Neo-Orthodoxy. They were anxious to defend the Lutheran national church against liberalism and revivalism. The conservatives wanted to stress the value of having a Church which embraced the whole of the nation and the importance of preserving its character as a Lutheran church. In this way the identity of the national Church was defined as its belonging within an international and confessional tradition.

Danish church history shows two completely original attitudes towards the constellation of the national Church and revivalism. They both stem from the two giants in Danish nineteenth century culture: N.F.S. Grundtvig (1783–1872) and the internationally renowned and not least in modern times influential philosopher, Søren Kirkegaard (1813–1855).

Grundtvig's understanding of the identity of the Church was also built on the foundation laid by the Romantics. For

173

Grundtvig, the revolt of the Romantics against Rationalism led to a re-discovery of the Bible and a kind of what he called 'old-fashioned' Lutheran piety. But he was to go further. His next great discovery was Nordic mythology and Old Icelandic literature. There he found the Nordic personality in all its original strength. Thus his own creativity as a writer and poet was awakened. Grundtvig was a priest, but he often found himself in fierce opposition to church authorities. These confrontations led to disciplinary actions and from time to time he was barred from exercising his ministry. During these periods he had all the more time for his writing.

Suddenly, out of all these conflicts, mingled with his biblical and historical research, sprang a quite unique interpretation of the nature of the Church and the place of the Bible within it. The pivotal point in this 'discovery' was that the Church preceeds the Bible. For protestant theology this, however self-evident it may be, was in fact quite a revolutionary insight. This approach broke completely with the intellectualistic tradition of Lutheran orthodoxy. The Protestants had, Grundtvig thought, exchanged the Roman Catholic Pope for a 'Bible-Pope' and a system of dead doctrine. The Word of the Bible does not come alive except in the midst of the gathered congregation, in worship, and in the celebration of Baptism and Holy Communion. The Word of God must reach us as the 'Living Word' in an existential context. Neither orthodox teaching, nor right feelings nor correct morality that can make a congregation 'come alive'. On this point Grundtvig parted company with both Rationalism and Pietism. Christianity was for him above all a cultic drama, and it was this kind of Christianity that should be found in the national Church, and that should be its distinguishing mark.

To this 'historical ecclesiology', as he called it, Grundtvig added his view of human life. The only equivalent is found as far back as in the work of the early Fathers, especially Irenaeus. But it was of course also the Lutheran tradition that raised its head. According to Grundtvig,

174

The Memorial Church to Grundtvig in Copenhagen, built 1921–1940 (after drawings by P V Jensen-Klint). The western front recalls the face of an organ, as a sign of Grundtvig's importance as Denmark's greatest hymn-writer. The architecture itself is also, in spite of the enormous proportions, a reminder of Danish rural churches with their characteristic stepped gables. It has been called 'The Apotheosis of the Danish Rural Church'. In its own way, it wants to be a tribute to 'The Danish Folk-Church'. *Photograph: The National Museum, Copenhagen.*

175

Christian life, and life in the Church, should be ordinary, truly human life, and nothing else. It is in the midst of ordinary, daily life among the people to whom I belong, speaking my own mother toungue, as part of its history and culture, that my faith in Christ should live and be put into practice. It is hard to think of any ecclesiology which could be more markedly that of the national Church.

Consequently, Grundtvig's work also included the creation of a new format for 'living' education, a school marked by national sentiments and a degree of personal freedom – the *Højskole* (a type of College of Higher Education), which, as an educational format, spread across Denmark to other countries. The Christian aspect of this form of school is found in its deliberate intention of fostering the personal development of the individual and of teaching the culture and customs of its people, including civil rights and social traditions. *Menneske først og Kristen saa* (human first and then Christian) was Grundtvig's motto.

One aspect of Grundtvig's influence on the Danish Church was, paradoxically enough, that he who was so strongly devoted to the national Church, also, in part, forced a kind of break from that Church. Grundtvig's followers, who soon formed themselves into a sort of popular Revivalist movement, secured the right to be exempt from membership of the local parish. They gained the right to form their own electoral units, tantamount to independent congregations within the framework of the national Church. This was an example of the liberalism of the day, and by this arrangement a formal split in the Church was avoided. Both the Evangelical Revivalist movement (Home Mission) and this 'Grundtvigianism' belong within the established Church which (since 1849) is known as *Den Danske Folkekirke* (The Danish National Church). The word '*Folkekirke*' (folk church) is in itself a witness to the great value accorded to the people, the democratic will, and the specific national characteristics of the people. The official name of the Danish Church is an indication of how strongly it is influenced by the nationalistic ecclesiology of Grundt-

176

vig. And it is also most certainly due to Grundtvig's re-interpretation of the inherited ecclesiology that Denmark still, without too many problems, keeps to its tradition of the national Church organized as an established state Church.

But such an extremely nationalistic ecclesiology could not remain unopposed. The integration of the Church, as such a well-established and highly honoured and respected insti-tution, in such harmonious reciprocity with society can in itself give rise to strong criticism. That is what happened when Søren Kirkegaard made his fierce and dramatic con-tribution directed against the highest authorities in the Danish National Church.

Kirkegaard's attack was prompted by a comment made in an obituary commemorating the recently departed Bishop of Zealand, the highly respected and much loved J.P. Mynster, who had died in 1854. It was the description of Mynster as a *Sandhedsvidne* (Witness to the Truth), made by his successor-to-be, H. L. Martensen, which made Kirkegaard explode. Verbatim, the comment on Mynster read *et af de rette Sandhedsvidner* (a genuine witness to the truth), not only in word and insight, but in understand-ing and action as well, he was a *led i den helige kaede af sandhedsvidner, som straekker sig gennem tiderne fra apostlenes dage* (a link in the holy chain of witnesses to the truth, which extends throughout time from the days of the Apostles onwards). This, in Kirkegaard's view, was sheer blasphemy. The Bishop of Zealand, a well-heeled and socially well-connected member of the privileged elite, what did he have in common with his Master, Jesus Christ, the crucified, and with his apostles and martyrs? Only one who, following Christ, suffered persecution and humiliation could be a genuine witness to the truth. A church leader in the society of the established upper classes was a rep-resentative of a triumphalist Church. The least one could demand from such a man was his admittance that he was in no way a witness to the truth.

Kirkegaard's attack met strong reaction. It was not only directed against a recently departed prominent church leader, it was an attack on the national Church itself. How could Kirkegaard possibly argue that it was only the ascetic Christianity of monks that was genuine, they fumed. It was not only the upper classes that were upset. The entire Movement inspired by Grundtvig also opposed Kirkegaard. For the followers of Grundtvig, it was a genuine Christian attitude to accept the society in which one lived, to thank God for all the good things it provided for one's benefit and well-being. Following Christ did not mean denying and abstaining from all this.

Kirkegaard's contribution had sprung from a different background, and a lifestyle other than that of upper- and middle-class society. He also had a longstanding hostility towards Bishop Mynster. But his attack cannot be regarded as an ecclesiastical reform programme. It must be seen as an existentialist, philosophical comment, an issue of Kirkegaard's radicalism as a philosopher and writer, and at the same time as a religious expression. The point was that a Christian, as he saw it, should live his ordinary, daily life in humility and trust in the grace of God.

Grundtvig and his followers never quite understood and never felt themselves in the firing-line of Kirkegaard's criticism of the established Church. It was an aspect of Grundtvig's view of the national Church that he never identified the institution of the national Church with the 'true Church of Christ'. At the end of the day, the national Church was nothing but a social institution, a framework for the true life of the Spirit. Given that distinction, he could accept both the institution of the State and the historical-ecclesiological reality in its true spiritual and dramatic dimension.

This was also the major difference between Grundtvig's ecclesiology and the ecclesiastical programme presented in England at this time by the Oxford Movement, although the background and purpose were in many ways similar:

Romanticism provided the starting-point; the historical rootedness in the traditions of the Church and the strong emphasis on the objective, sacramental tradition of worship were the same. In Anglicanism, the Oxford Movement brought the most important contribution towards the upholding of the historical tradition of the Church against both rationalism and subjective revivalism. The Oxford Movement requires a chapter of its own, not least because of its formative influence on Anglicanism, but also because of the reactions to which it gave rise in the Nordic churches, and because of the important part played by its ecclesiology in later ecumenical dialogues, Anglo-Scandinavian and others.

CHAPTER 9

The Oxford Movement and The Nordic Churches

ANGLICAN RENEWAL

1833 is commonly considered the year of the birth of the Oxford Movement. One of the starting points was a book written by John Keble, poet and Oxford Professor, entitled 'The Christian Year'. This book of daily devotions, which has since been reprinted in numerous editions, draws a parallel between the liturgical year of the Church and the shifting seasons in nature, focusing not on rationalistic argument and moral virtue but on a different dimension of the life of the Church, in which the continuity of tradition stands out as a major theme. Thus this book was able to pave the way for a new movement in the Church.

The year 1833 also saw protests against the undue involvement of the state authorities in the internal affairs of the Church. Already towards the end of the 1820s some circles in the Church had reacted against what they considered the high-handed decisions of Parliament on issues concerning the Church's own business, where the integrity of the Church ought to be respected. These were issues of religious freedom and new civic rights for those who were not members of the Church of England. In 1833 Parliament decided to abolish a number of medieval episcopal sees in Ireland, a reasonable move, given the drastic decline in population throughout the last centuries, which had left the Anglican Church in those regions with a much smaller potential membership. But the decision was an intrusion into the integrity of the Church; it concerned the internal organization of the Church, and at a very vital point: episcopacy. This decision by Parliament met with very strong opposition. It was referred to by Keble as 'the National Apostasy'. He saw the parliamentary Act as a treachery, a betrayal by the authorities of State, who ought to act as the defenders of the Anglican Church. This became the signal for a whole group of men in Oxford who wanted to work for the integrity and renewal of the Church.

Many Oxford academics joined ranks with Keble. The most prominent among them was John Henry Newman, who, alongside his academic career, was the Vicar of the Church of St Mary the Virgin, Oxford, where he exercised great influence, not only as a writer, but also, and perhaps even more, as a preacher. Newman and his friends, especially Hurrell Froude and Edward Pusey, published a series of pamphlets entitled 'Tracts for the Times', in which they developed a distinctive interpretation of the nature of Anglicanism and a programme of renewal for the Church of England. This series gave name to the whole movement, which became known as 'Tractarianism'. The Tractarians saw the tradition of the Church of England as a *via media*, a middle way between Protestantism and Roman Catholicism, or even more clearly, as an organic, unbroken continuation of the medieval *Ecclesia Anglicana*, as the national branch of the universal, Catholic Church. Newman went furthest in his denial of all identification with the rest of the Protestant world, and in 1845 he converted to Roman Catholicism. The leadership of the Tractarians transferred to Edward Pusey, and from then on the movement was usually called 'Puseyism' (which was also the term normally used in contemporary reactions in the Scandinavian countries).

All these are commonly known facts. If, however, we want to understand what happened in Anglicanism simultaneously and in comparison with developments in the Nordic national churches, we need to elucidate in somewhat greater depth the content and convictions of the Oxford Movement.

The first thing to note is that Tractarianism had deep roots in Evangelicalism in the Calvinist stream of English spirituality. It was the inheritance from the revivalists that came to the fore when the Tractarians opposed the system of the state Church and also took a stand against earlier English high church circles with their rationalizing theologians and politically-minded bishops. From the Evangelical Revival came the strong emphasis among the Oxford men on personal sanctification, a feature which had also been the distinguishing mark of John Wesley and Methodism. It was above all the Swedish Scholar, Yngve Brilioth, who drew attention to this in his nowadays classic and still much used and often quoted work *The Anglican Revival. Studies in the Oxford Movement* (1925). The continuity between personal Evangelical inheritance and the new ecclesiology is particularly evident in Newman. The Oxford Movement was in itself a Revivalist movement, which at the same time pointed to objective tradition as fundamental to the Church.

Objectivity was found above all in the sacraments of Baptism and Eucharist and in episcopal ministry. Episcopacy in unbroken succession from the apostles of Jesus was in itself the sign and guarantee of the true identity of the Church. Or, as it could also be negatively expressed, without episcopacy in unbroken, continuous succession, no real, genuine Church. The men of the Oxford Movement could find support for this point in earlier exponents of Anglicanism: Hooker, for example, who defended episcopacy against the Puritans under Elizabeth I, or the church leaders around Charles I, the so-called 'Caroline Divines' who stood against the Puritans in the seventeenth century. The negative formula, directed against other denominations in other countries, is however not to be found in these earlier writings. The interest in 'un-churching' other denominations was a new idea proffered by the Oxford Movement.

The Oxford Movement wanted to find 'the true Church' in their own Church, the Church of England, in its charac-

Dr Yngve Brilioth, later Archbishop of Uppsala, receives the Lambeth Cross from Archbishop William Temple. The Lambeth Cross was created in 1939 for presentation to foreign churchmen in recognition of long association with the Church of England. Dr Brilioth was honoured above all for his important contribution to the study of the Oxford Movement. *Photograph: Associated Press, by courtesy of Lambeth Palace.*

teristic, visible form. They attempted to prove this not, as was common in Protestant denominations, by reference to their Confession as a 'true' exposition of Holy Scripture, nor by reference to its members as being truly 'converted', saved and sanctified. But by reference to the sacraments and their administration by the 'historic' ministry, the Church of England could be said to be a 'true Church' in unbroken continuity with the Church instituted by Christ. Here was a challenge to all non-episcopal churches, and at the same time to many aspects of their own tradition of a national church. Ecclesiology had been extended beyond national boundaries. In the long run, this was an important gain towards new ecumenical thinking.

By stressing so strongly the continuity with the early Church, the interest in the early Church and the Fathers was naturally awakened, and with it went an equally keen interest in diminishing the importance of the Reformers and their followers. Following the focus on the sacraments, on liturgy and on the apostolic succession of the ordained ministry came a deep sense of the place of worship as sacred space. The importance and value of decorating the church building and of ancient liturgical practices were re-discovered. Added to this came a new sense of the value of personal, spiritual discipline through regular liturgical devotions. This liturgical interest became more and more significant in later Tractarianism. It also led to many bitter conflicts between high church priests and ordinary parishioners. But gradually, much of this liturgical awareness became an integral part of Anglican worship in general, and also an inspiration for other churches.

The most urgent task was to find a new ecclesiological clarity and credibility. The Oxford men found what they sought in this historic 'continuity', and they did not hesitate to describe their church as 'catholic'. This was brave. The Roman Catholic Church was for most people still the feared enemy. And the Roman Catholic Church at this time showed no signs of ecumenical attitudes. There was also, in England, a considerable minority of Roman Catholics, who for centuries had been severely oppressed. Given these circumstances, the Roman Catholics were not particularly impressed when the Anglicans suddenly wanted to claim that the Church of England was the true, Catholic Church.

THE NORDIC CHURCHES IN THE EYES OF THE OXFORD MOVEMENT

The search for the identity of the Church was, as we have seen, a relevant pursuit in the national churches in Scandinavia as well. What was known in England about such converging interests and possible opportunities for co-operation? How did the leaders of the Oxford Movement consider the Nordic Churches?

Already in 1833, the same year as the Oxford Movement, according to most scholars, began, a comment was made on where a church might be found, outside Anglicanism, which might be considered to measure up. That year, a handbook, *The Churchman's Manual*, was prepared for a conference on the Church. It was printed in Oxford the following year. This manual lists the churches which can prove unbroken continuity with the early Church, the Church of the Apostles, and which, in that sense, may be considered truly 'catholic'. The list included, besides the Church of England and other Anglican churches throughout the world, one other Church, which could also claim to be 'Protestant Episcopal' with full apostolicity and catholicity: the Church of Sweden.

The author of *The Churchman's Manual* was Arthur Philip Perceval, a priest from an aristocratic family, who joined the Oxford Movement with great enthusiasm and contributed greatly with extensive writings. Among his works, the collections of documents on the high church revival are the most valuable, while his own theological productions show a somewhat imaginary inclination – he attempted to prove, for instance, that the Patmos of the Book of Revelation is in fact a reference to Ireland, and

185

that the Virgin Mary is buried there, on the Hill of Tara! In the preparation of the *Manual* he was, however, assisted by a rather more prominent theologian, William Palmer (usually referred to as 'Palmer of Worcester College' to avoid confusion with a contemporary of his with the same name who was also active in the Oxford Movement). It was William Palmer who was responsible for the acknowledgement of the 'catholicity' of the Church of Sweden. Palmer's own writings focused throughout on episcopal ministry and on *'successio apostolica'*. The note on *Apostolic Succession in Sweden* is found in a collection of documents illustrating the Oxford Movement and its theology which Palmer published in the early 1840s. He had taken the precaution of first checking this with the Swedish chaplain in London – since 1840 Gustaf Wilhelm Carlsson. The Swedish pastor was able to confirm these facts; Swedish episcopal succession, from the Middle Ages onwards, is unbroken.

It should, however, be said that these two theologians from Oxford, who were the first in England to point to the Church of Sweden in this context, can hardly be regarded as typical representatives of the Oxford Movement. They had both belonged to earlier high church circles before joining the Tractarians. The main leaders of the Tractarians were not satisfied by reference to the plain fact of unbroken succession, but, as was soon to become evident, they greeted the claim that a church like the Church of Sweden could possibly possess any degree of 'catholicity' at all with considerable scepticism. This has been accentuated by the Swedish Scholar Carl Henrik Lyttkens in his thesis *The Growth of Swedish-Anglican Intercommunion between 1833 and 1922 (Bibliotheca Theologiae Practicae*, 24, 1970. I am indebted to this thesis for much of what follows. It is a very extensive and well-researched analysis, providing detailed knowledge of the dialogue between the Church of Sweden and some Anglican churches which started in 1833 and which has since been of great ecumenical importance.)

*　　*　　*

With or without sceptical comments, the Church of Sweden had been brought into a new perspective. It appeared to possess a unique quality as a Protestant, Lutheran Church and at the same time in full possession of its episcopal structure and with its succession unbroken from the Middle Ages onwards. This historical fact was in itself not a new discovery. The Church of Sweden was certainly aware of it. It had also been noted by earlier high church groups in England, and it had been counted among those characteristics which identified the Swedish Church as, in English eyes, a fully acceptable 'sister church'. But now there was something else which made the apostolic succession in Sweden particularly interesting to Anglican theologians. Now their real concern was the ecclesiology of the Anglican Church itself. If it could be proved that the Anglican tradition with its claim to 'catholicity' outside the Roman Catholic Church was in some way part of a larger, historical context, Tractarian ecclesiology could, to some extent, be confirmed. Since they were unwilling to accept the Roman Catholic Church as 'true' – it had, they thought, in various ways forfeited its claim to truth – they looked to the Greek Orthodox and other Eastern churches as potential partners. It was also desirable to find a partner from within the Protestant family of churches, a church which could at least be deemed to be 'almost' authentic, with preserved continuity. The only possibility was the Church of Sweden.

Long before the Oxford Movement entered the scene, the leaders of the Church of England had shown their respect for the Church of Sweden many times. They were aware of its position as an established national church, not to be confused with the sects. In the same way the other Nordic churches had been equally respected, as had other Protestant denominations on the Continent. Ministry, Baptism and Eucharist had been mutually acknowledged, performed according to the customs of each church within its own area. With the advent of the Oxford Movement, this was no longer to be taken for granted. Suddenly the Church of Sweden was considered in a different light compared to the other Nordic churches and other Lutheran churches. Now the determining factor was 'catholicity', and in 'catholicity' participation in 'the historic episcopate' was an indispensable ingredient. Only the Church of Sweden could show evidence of that.

However, it was soon to become very obvious that the leading men in Oxford were in fact rather dubious about the claims made even for the Church of Sweden. Already in his first approach to the Swedish chaplain in London in order to ask for confirmation of the assumed facts, A. P. Perceval had expressed his scepticism. He did not think the difference between the Church of Sweden and other Lutheran churches was very great. If it was possible to confirm what he assumed about succession in the Church of Sweden, it might of course be interesting, but it would not, he thought, make any real difference, unless the Swedes themselves were able to appreciate properly the value of this succession and to order their lives accordingly.

It is particularly interesting to discover how the central figure of the Oxford Movement after Newman, Edward Pusey, viewed the Lutheran churches. He did not, it seems, place the Church of Sweden in a class of its own, in spite of its peculiar history of episcopal succession. He did not think much of the Lutheran Churches in general, although for Martin Luther himself he had the highest regard and only the strongest possible praise. Pusey's admiration for Luther has rarely been noted, though it has been brought to attention by recent research. (See Leighton Frappel in Perry Butler (ed.), *Pusey Rediscovered* (1983).) In Luther, he found a dynamic, genuine spirituality. As a young student of theology in Germany, Pusey had read Luther thoroughly, and for his appreciation of Luther he would use strong words. He counted Luther as the greatest Christian since Paul. Lutheranism, however, had perverted the inheritance from the great Master, and the Lutheran churches had ended up in a sterile intellectualism. That was not Luther's fault. It was the theologians of Lutheran orthodoxy and the Enlightenment who were responsible. Even so, he had some symphathy for a few German Lutheran theologians – Spener, 'the Father of Pietism', for example, and among his contemporaries, Schleiermacher. But as things were generally in the Lutheran churches (Pusey commented on the situation in Germany) he had no desire to explore closer links in that direction.

The possibility of closer relations with the Evangelical-Lutheran and indeed episcopal Church of Sweden was obviously not very high among the priorities of the Oxford men. The first impulse was nevertheless awakened. What was the reaction in Sweden? And how did other Nordic theologians and church leaders respond to the Oxford Movement?

REACTIONS IN THE CHURCH OF SWEDEN

The Chaplain to the Swedish Embassy in London, G.W. Carlsson, was the first to be given an opportunity to react. When he was asked, already in the early 1830s, about episcopacy in the Church of Sweden, he certainly confirmed that the succession in Sweden had remained unbroken from the medieval Church onwards. But in addition to his official reply he made it clear, in no uncertain terms, in a private letter to the enquirer (Perceval), that he himself did not share these 'superstitious and anti-biblical' views on apostolic succession (quote by Lyttkens, p.24).

It was G.W. Carlsson who wrote the most extensive contemporary account of the Oxford Movement for Swedish readers. He was certainly well informed about the ecclesiastical situation in England. He was Chaplain to the Embassy and Rector of the Swedish Church in London for twelve years, and he was known and respected in the highest circles. In his autobiography he recalls how he was presented to the young Queen Victoria and 'kissed hands', and how he often received royal hospitality. He dined with the Bishops of London and Winchester. His contacts appear to have been mostly with the older, high church groups of the established Church, but he was also in touch with the Evangelical, socially concerned low church wing. The London City Mission merited his particular study. Among the circles in which he moved, opinions of the Oxford Movement were clearly not very high. During the years following Newman's Tract 90 (1841), in which he had interpreted the Thirty-nine Articles in conformity with Roman Catholic teaching, a stormy debate against the Oxford men had raged, which of course influenced Carlsson's article.

The account given by the Rector of the Swedish Church in London was published in a major series of articles in the conservative periodical *Svenska Biet* (The Swedish Bee) in 1844. It must, by and large, have had a deterrent effect. He described the Oxford Movement above all as a hierarchical ecclesiastical structure, putting great stress on their teaching about Apostolic succession. Episcopal ordination in unbroken succession right back to the apostles was the determining criterion, and it was only through that episcopal ordination that 'the Holy Spirit dwells in the priesthood'. The Holy Spirit enters the priest at ordination. And further: only in this way, through episcopal succession, is it possible to seek communion with Christ. It would in fact be dangerous for people – 'precarious for their souls' to attempt any other way. The Oxford Movement had started off in a way of which G. W. Carlsson approved. In a situation of divisions and ecclesiastical wranglings, it had upheld the integrity of the Anglican Church and drawn attention to its primacy as an episcopal church. But it had, in Carlsson's view, gone astray, so that it now seemed to stand 'on the same platform as Papism'. That was apparent on such controversial issues as the sacrifice of the Mass, the doctrine of purgatory, the reverence of relics and icons and the worship of the saints. And it had provoked opposition by reinstating old liturgical practices which had been laid aside in England during the time of the Puritans, e.g. the position of the priest at the altar and the use of candles and vestments.

It was quite natural that the chaplain in London had first-hand knowledge of the Oxford Movement and that he was able to give detailed reports on it, including the crisis it had run into in the 1840s. But he was not alone in the Church of Sweden in keeping himself well informed about the Oxford Movement and forming an opinion on its theology and ecclesiology in various writings. I want to recall three such opinions, formed at a high level in the Church of Sweden. They are interesting because they reflect typical positions on church matters in Sweden at this time. They also explain why there was lasting reluctance in the Church of Sweden to take up invitations from the Anglicans to form closer links on the basis of similarities with regard to apostolic succession. The three theological writers in question are Carl Fredrik af af Wingård, Lars Anton Anjou and Henrik Reuterdahl.

At this point I would also like to make a general observation. There were in fact here, way up in the North, those who were remarkably well informed about events in the rest of the world, and not least in the churches. It has often been assumed in recent times, since the modern Ecumenical Movement began in earnest, that earlier church leaders were fairly ignorant of the wider world. That is a misconception. Looking at the situation in Sweden, it could certainly not be deemed to be lacking in information about church life in other countries.

Carl Fredric af Wingård was a man who certainly made it his business to provide an international perspective. This he began to do during his time in Gothenburg, where he had succeeded his own father as bishop. His knowledge of English was excellent. He had learnt English particularly through frequent contacts with George Scott, the Scottish Presbyterian minister, whose activity in Sweden we have previously discussed. In a biography on af Wingård we are told that he took several theological periodicals, especially English ones. In 1823, 1830 and 1836 he gathered the clergy of the Diocese of Gothenburg – three times – to regular clergy conferences (*Prästmöte*), and on all three occasions he himself contributed an international 'Overview of the

191

State of the Christian Church'. As Archbishop of Uppsala he went a stage further and extended his 'overview' to a book in excess of two hundred pages, *Öfversigt af Christna Kyrkans senare händelser och nuvarande tillstånd* (An Overview of the Latest Events and the Present State of the Christian Church), published in 1843. In that book he gave a particularly extensive review of the Orthodox and Oriental churches and of church life in Great Britain and in the USA. The Lutheran churches in Germany and the other Nordic countries were given comparatively scant treatment.

af Wingård was well informed about 'Puseyism', which he feared might provoke a serious crisis in the Church of England, more 'dangerous' than the previous controversies with various dissenters. The purpose of Puseyism he acknowledged with great respect; it built on the words of the Creed: 'One, Holy, *Catholic* Church'. It attempted to defend 'the firmness but not the faults of the Catholic Church', and 'the freedom but not the internal fragmentation and lack of stability of the Reformed Churches'. Pusey himself had however not made any great impression on af Wingård. He seemed to be too close to Roman Catholicism. In spite of his determination and his great learning, he seemed 'too stern, like someone dressed in a hairshirt, observing all the prescription of the morality of monks'. The stress on the Church and on tradition by the Oxford Movement won af Wingård's approval; it was certainly a matter of urgency to find a basis for the unity of the Church, but rather more dubious to put quite as much stress on tradition as the Puseyites did – there were of course many traditions, and in any case, tradition must be subject to Scripture.

The emphasis on the ordained ministry of the Church and on *successio apostolica* by the Oxford Movement was of course given due space in af Wingård's review. It is interesting to observe that the Swedish Archbishop took this as a reference to the ministry as a whole: 'This does not mean the more limited sense of only episcopacy, but the whole priesthood and *Potestas Clavium* (the Power of the Keys)'. With that extension he was able to let his report

192

on the stress on ministry and apostolic succession in Puseyism refer to what he himself wanted to stress in the Swedish
situation. He used every opportunity to speak of the high
and exalted position of the priesthood, in order to stem the
demand from the Revivalists to give the laity a share in
priestly functions. From that point of view he could
approve with great satisfaction of the Anglican exposition
of its doctrine on the ministry in contrast to the 'system of
the Presbyterians'. Archbishop af Wingård was keen to
speak to his priests about the spiritual importance of the
priesthood, and of ministry as a vocation, not delegated by
the congregation, but given from above, from God. He
passed lightly by what the Oxford Movement wanted to
stress: the importance of episcopacy. Nor did he make any
mention of the vague 'proposals' which had arrived from
there concerning the potential importance of the 'historic'
episcopate in the Church of Sweden for future church
unity.

It was to the then Professor of Church History in Uppsala,
L.A. Anjou (later a cabinet minister and finally a bishop)
that the Swedish Chaplain in London had turned when
he sought confirmation of the unbroken succession of the
Swedish episcopate from the Middle Ages onwards. It was
certainly to the best possible specialist knowledge that he
then gained access. Anjou was in fact an expert on Swedish
church history during the Reformation period. He published his detailed research in three volumes (1850–1851),
which were also translated into English (1859). What he
said there about apostolic succession has largely been confirmed by later research. There is no doubt about the actual
facts. The events have been discussed in an earlier chapter
(see Chapter 3 above).

Through the Rector of the Swedish Church in London,
the result of Anjou's research on succession had been
imparted to the early circles of the Oxford Movement. What
did Anjou himself think of the actual, ecclesiastical importance of this succession? He proved, like many of his

colleagues on the bench of bishops, to be politically conservative, and a consistent opponent of all demands for increased rights from the low church Revivalists. He wanted to stress throughout the proper position of the ministry of the Church. On this point he even went a step further than Archbishop af Wingård had done in the books to which we have just referred. Anjou made clear the special place and tradition of episcopacy *within* the ministry of the Church. This is expounded in a church periodical in 1850, in an essay entitled '*Om kyrka och prester*' (On the Church and the Priesthood). There he wrote without qualms: 'The Episcopate traces its origin to the apostolic period', and again about the early Church: 'The preservation of the purity of the confession and of the unity of the Church with that of the apostles depended primarily on the bishops'. In such phrases Anjou came very close to the views of the Oxford Movement on episcopacy. But he was quick to warn against what he called 'false episcopalism', in which the ministry was not subject to Scripture, and where a tendency to 'hierarchism' and 'papalism' was close at hand. However, he made no direct reference to the Oxford Movement in the Anglican Church. His main concern was presumably to guard against the Roman Catholic Church.

It is quite obvious that a new awareness was growing in the Church of Sweden, not only about the place of the priesthood, which it was neccessary to defend against the demands of the Revivalists, but also of episcopacy. This can be clearly seen from the 1850s. Previously, episcopacy had often been understood as primarily a cultural and educational position, and as a political office. Before the Constitutional Reform in 1866, the bishops had been ex officio members of the *Riksdag*, and also governors of all schools at both higher and lower levels. This did not necessarily imply a lack of interest or ignorance of theological issues. Culture and education was far from secularized. Even so, the nature of their priorities was sometimes a moot point. It is significant that when Esaias Tegnér, the brilliant

194

humanist and famous poet, who was Bishop of Växjö from 1824 to 1846, encouraged Christopher Isac Heurlin, his friend and later his successor, to accept the appointment to the see of Visby, he was of the opinion that this appointment might not necessarily require Heurlin to take up residence in the diocese. Occasional visits to the diocese once a year to preach at the end of the year ceremony for the schools, and every sixth year to preside at the obligatory clergy conference, would be quite sufficient. Bishop Tegnér also complained loudly on those few occasions when he was told that he absolutely had to wear episcopal attire. However, soon enough a more liturgically aware approach to episcopacy again became the norm in the Church of Sweden. This is noticeable with, among others, Lars Anton Anjou and even clearer with Henrik Reuterdahl.

Archbishop Reuterdahl continued the tradition commenced by af Wingård of publishing reviews of church life in the major churches in Europe. In his review of 1849 he discussed ecclesiastical developments in England, and he made it quite clear that in many ways he supported the 'Puseyites'. In Reuterdahl's view, the criticism against them came from those who embraced 'Zwinglian-Calvinist' teaching. His only disagreement with the Oxford Movement concerned their views of State and Church, which he opposed. In that area Reuterdahl's sympathies lay with William Gladstone, the Anglo-Catholic statesman, who, unlike the 'Puseyites', defended the links between State and Church.

When it came to the interpretation of the Eucharist, Reuterdahl defended Pusey. It was Pusey's views on the Eucharist which had led to him being barred from the pulpit, because it was it was held that he taught Roman Catholic doctrine. Reuterdahl reported on this controversy and commented, without hesitation, that no Lutheran could possibly have any objection at all to Pusey's understanding of the Eucharist. The fact that this neo-Anglican movement had led to many conversions to Roman Catholicism was of course a pity for the Anglicans, but it certainly did not change what, in Reuterdahl's view, was a very positive understanding. The need to make a definite decision on the issue of Anglican-Swedish intercommunion was to fall to him, as Archbishop of Uppsala, in the middle of the 1860s. We will come back to this later. What is so far obvious is that neither Reuterdahl nor other leading figures in the Church of Sweden were lacking in knowledge of what went on in the Anglican Communion and of the latest developments there. But before we continue, something ought to be said about how other Nordic churches had followed these developments.

REACTIONS IN THE REST OF SCANDINAVIA

In Denmark, it was Grundtvig in particular who made it his business to study Church and society in England. He made very thorough study visits to England, no less than three times: in 1829, 1830 and 1831, – just before the birth of the Oxford Movement. In many ways he was more impressed by the spiritual culture of the time, by the approach of the Romantics to literature and to historical research, than by theology. He deepened his knowledge of Anglo-Saxon culture in the early Middle Ages and compared it to the Nordic *'Oldtid'* ('the olden days'), and he was impressed by the sense of realism and the spirit of industrial and commercial endeavour in contemporary Britain. What he saw of church life was the older variety of the high-churchmanship. He could speak very positively about episcopacy, but when it came to personal spirituality, he felt more akin to Methodism. The English experience contributed strongly to what later became his ideal of a national church: such a church ought to be deeply rooted in the culture of its own people and nation, and it should support religious freedom. He was not, it seems, in any way drawn to Tractarianism. Nor was the movement in Danish church life which was named after him.

Theologians in the Nordic countries learnt of 'Puseyism'

196

particularly from articles in German theological periodicals. It seems reasonable to assume that in this way a fair, though hardly congenial, view of this Movement was communicated. Pusey himself never hid his negative view of German Protestantism. Nor was there any interest in the German Lutheran churches at this time in episcopacy, which was so highly valued by the Puseyites.

In the Nordic area (apart from Sweden) it is only in Danish theological periodicals that I have found descriptions in the mother tounge of the new movement in English Church life. Denmark had a rich output of theological periodicals in the nineteenth century. Two particularly extensive essays are to be found on the ecclesiastical development in England. One was published in the ambitious *Tidskrift for Udenlandsk Theologisk Litteratur* (Journal of Foreign Theological Literature) in 1844. This was a translation of a German thesis of almost one hundred pages, entitled *Den anglikanske Kirkes tilstand* (The State of the Anglican Church) by H.F. Uhden. The chapter on Tractarianism is quite objective. However, in the paragraph on apostolic succession the author allows himself the liberty of pointing out that it is not possible to prove that the succession of bishops during the first centuries of the early Church was in fact unbroken.

The other extensive work in Danish on Church life in England was published in 1850 in *Theologisk tidskrift* (The Theological Review), a periodical which was also read in Norway. This was a thesis of no less than 132 pages, entitled *Brudstykker om de kirkelige forhold i England* (Fragments on the Ecclesiastical Situation in England) by P. W. Becker. The author was one of Denmark's most prominent historians in the nineteenth century, although he never embarked on an academic career but remained a *sognepraest* (parish priest) in rural Zealand. The thesis on England was later reprinted in the collected works of Becker (1874). This is a most eminent description, certainly the best of what was written on the subject in Scandinavia. Becker had researched the situation in England thoroughly, both with regard to church history and university life. His description of the Oxford Movement was completely neutral. Newman's and Pusey's theology is described as an organic continuation of mainstream Anglicanism from sixteenth century Hooker onwards. He reports on the new Anglican ecclesiology, starting with William Palmer and A. P. Perceval, right through the whole series of the *Tracts for the Times*. Without any subjective comment he describes the new Anglican view that authentic sacramental ministry is only available in Churches with unbroken episcopal succession, that is to say, among churches outside Roman Catholicism and the Eastern Orthodox Churches, only in the Anglican Churches and in the Church of Sweden.

For the Danish Church, as for others, such a view was precarious. Becker pointed out that Anglican theologians usually found some extenuating circumstances which improved the situation for the churches which had lost their succession; the prevailing circumstances in the sixteenth century really did not give them any other possibility. Nowadays there was no other cure for these churches except to accept bishops who had been ordained in England. Becker's account was, as I said, strictly objective, but it is not difficult to imagine how many church leaders in the Danish and the Norwegian churches as well as in the Protestant Churches on the Continent must have found this understanding of ministry in the new high church Anglicanism rather arrogant.

Even so, Becker finished his desciption with quite a respectful summary of the theology of the Oxford Movement. His opinion was that although this movement had stirred up fierce controversy, it had in fact brought out many very valuable aspects, which he hoped would be adopted. For many, it had re-awakened an almost forgotten understanding of the Church and of tradition. Not least Newman's sermons and other writings were a rich source of spiritual insight.

'THE ENGLISH CHURCH AND THE SCANDINAVIAN BODIES'

About the middle of the nineteenth century there was a growing desire among Anglicans to extend geographically the area of ecclesiastical communion. This might be due to England's increasing international inolvement and the efforts to build up the Empire. The new Anglican ecclesiology implied the opposite tendency. The older high church had shown a more ecumenical attitude, which could be seen, for instance, in the establishment of the new episcopal See of Jerusalem. This had been agreed jointly by both British and Prussian authorities. Leading Tractarians were critical of this move. It was not possible, they argued, to integrate in this way two such very different ecclesiologies.

In the same way they began to take a sharper attitude towards the Nordic Lutheran churches. An anglo-catholic theologian, William Palmer (not the William Palmer we have met already, but William Palmer of Magdalen College, Oxford) directed his unmitigated criticism against the Nordic churches. He made his disapproval clear in no uncertain terms. All Lutheran churches as well as the 'Calvinist' ones were, in his opinion, fundamentally heretical. They rested on their own agreements on common confessions, which represented nothing more than human opinions, while the 'true' churches were bound together by episcopacy in unbroken succession. Of the national churches in Scandinavia, he would in fact not regard the Danish and Norwegian churches as real churches. And the Swedish Church fell, on closer inspection, under the same judgement.

These views were further developed in an (anonymous) article in the anglo-catholic periodical *The Christian Remembrancer*, in 1847. Here it was pointed out that the Church of Sweden was totally lacking in the 'Catholic spirit'. Now and then doubts were also raised as to whether the Church of Sweden really had preserved its apostolic succession. This statement, it was argued, needed further underpinning by more modern research. It was such an incredible supposition, even in the outward, literal sense! In any case, the Church of Sweden had not lived up to this tradition.

Since the question of intercommunion with the Church of Sweden nevertheless continued to be raised from time to time, Pusey eventually found reason to pronounce on this issue himself. He did so in an article in *The Guardian* (1867), entitled 'The English Church and the Scandinavian Bodies'. The title itself shows that in Pusey's view the Nordic Lutheran churches were in no way to be regarded as 'churches'. He used instead the word 'bodies'. Not even the Church of Sweden could be called a 'church', since, like the others, it had accepted the Lutheran Confession and must consequently, like all other Lutheran churches, be deemed heretical. This argument was developed in a special commentary on the Lutheran doctrine of justification by faith. According to Pusey, the Lutheran view was completely individualistic, and this discriminated against its entire ecclesiology. Unless the Church of Sweden would distance itself from its Lutheran Confession, there would, according to Pusey and his closest allies, be no foundation for 'catholic intercommunion' even with this church. (For further information on these issues, see Lyttkens, Chapter I:1.)

CONTACTS – NEVERTHELESS

The Nordic churches had not asked to be evaluated by the theologians of the Oxford Movement, nor, one might add, with appraisals just as indiscriminately black-and-white as those by which Lutheran theologians had for a long time written off Anglicanism as simply a Calvinist denomination! The sweeping characterisations, by which Pusey and others spoke of the Lutheran churches obviously lessened the possibilites of building any bridges at all between Lutherans and Anglicans. Even so, determined attempts

200

were made, as early as in the middle of the nineteenth century, and they were not without results.

Initial contacts of a preliminary exploratory nature were made with Lutheranism, if not by the main anglo-catholic theologians in Oxford, at least by those who continued and developed the Oxford Movement. From England, from an organization called The Anglo-Continental Society, contacts were also sought for the purpose of explaining to foreigners what the United Church of England and Ireland stood for, and of furthering the principles of the English Reformation on the Continent. This organization intended to extend the understanding of the importance of 'historic episcopacy' as fundamental to the unity of the Church.

But initiatives came also from another direction, from the Episcopal Church in the USA, where there was an increasing interest in immigrating Scandinavians. Even though they were Lutherans, they did come from a church with an episcopal constitution, which, the Episcopalians thought, might provide a basis for simply integrating them into the American Episcopal Church. It might be possible to gain support for such a strategy in the Nordic churches, at least from the Church of Sweden.

There was in fact a precedent. In the eighteenth century, there had been an exchange of services between Episcopalian priests and those Swedish Lutheran priests who were sent to the parishes on the east coast of the USA, where Sweden had once had its own little colony, Delaware. This exchange did of course presuppose the mutual recognition of ministry and sacraments, and it had been legitimized and encouraged by the respective European mother churches. When priests from Sweden were no longer available, the Swedish Lutheran congregations had eventually transferred to the Episcopal Church. It was now thought to be possible to continue along those lines and to receive in the same way the whole wave of Swedish immigrants who during the nineteenth century poured into the Mid-West. However, this proved a very much more intricate business than it had been a century earlier. By now, there was a self-conscious Lutheran Church in the USA, and the Swedish immigrants were mostly influenced by low church Revivalism. They formed their own 'synod' within Lutheranism and had no desire whatsoever for any episcopal government. The leaders of the American Episcopal Church did not have much of a clue about this. Quite unawares, they contacted the Archbishop of Uppsala.

The Anglo-Continental Society developed lively activity in the 1860s. The Secretary, the Revd F.S. May, who was a keen initiator, was responsible for relations with the Scandinavian churches. He started a correspondence with some Nordic priests, Jens Vahl in Denmark and Sven Libert Bring in Sweden. Neither of them was particularly influential, but May had found their names, and they were eager correspondents. Jens Vahl is famous above all as a scholar of history of mission and as a theologian of a definitely low church brand, active in the *Indre Mission* (Home Mission). Bring was eventually made Professor at the University of Lund, during the time that the Lutheran Neo-Orthodoxy dominated the Theological Faculty. May's correspondence with Bring provided the Englishman with knowledge of how professedly Lutheran theologians put great emphasis on the sacraments and on the ministerial priesthood. He then published detailed accounts of church life in Scandinavia in the Annual Reports of the Anglo-Continental Society. Those reports certainly gave English readers a rather more positive and nuanced view than the summary statements by the men of Oxford.

It is worth noting that the Anglo-Continental Society intended to make links with all the Scandinavian national churches. The Danish and Norwegian churches were not to be excluded, even though the Church of Sweden had prominence, due to its historic episcopacy. It is interesting that F.S. May had the idea that the English priests in Gothenburg and Stockholm ought to work under the authority of the respective diocesan bishops of the Church of Sweden, and that corresponding arrangements ought to be made for Swedish priests in England. This thought is equally relevant today.

It is against this background that a remarkable ecumenical breakthrough – remarkable at least in its day – was made in 1866, at the consecration of a new English Church in Stockholm. The initiator was F.S. May. The new church, which was a predecessor of the present English Church in Stockholm, was dedicated to St Sigfrid and St Peter – 'St Sigfrid' of course with reference to the English Missionary Bishop of Scandinavia. The Bishop of Illinois, H.J. Whitehouse, officiated. His reason for accepting the invitation to do so is obvious: there were numerous Swedish immigrants in his own diocese in the USA. The invitation had been issued by the Bishop of London (later Archbishop of Canterbury) A.C.Tait. (Overseas Anglican congregations were at this time under the jurisdiction of the Bishop of London.)

The consecration of the English Church in Stockholm in 1866 became particularly significant because the Archbishop of Uppsala, Henrik Reuterdahl, was invited to participate, and he was present and took a full and active part in the whole service. Reuterdahl has been mentioned several times. In most discussions of church history, Reuterdahl is only described from the perspective of his oppression of the Revivalist movements. Here another aspect is apparent. He was clearly aware of his episcopal position and the ecumenical responsibility that went with it. It was not for nothing that he had worked for decades as a medievalist scholar. This research had given him a sense of what the episcopal role traditionally ought to involve. It is symptomatic that soon after becoming Archbishop, he made an investigation of what might possibly be lacking in the episcopal vesture in the individual dioceses. He encouraged his fellow bishops to make sure that everything was available and in usable order, including the staff and mitre.

At the dedication ceremony in Stockholm he appeared, as a newspaper article puts it, in full episcopal vestments with complete insignia, and having been invited, he took a full part in the service, both in the consecration itself and the following Eucharist. A further three bishops of the Church of Sweden also took part together with the Archbishop. These were the three prominent bishops, Sundberg, Bring and Flensburg, who represented Lutheran Neo-Orthodoxy in the Church of Sweden, or as it is also commonly called, 'the High Church Movement of Lund'. They had at least one thing in common with the Anglican Church: a strong interest in the ministry of the Church. All three had been Reuterdahl's colleagues as professors of the Theological Faculty of the University of Lund, and like him, they were all well informed about developments in the Anglican Church, including its internal diversity. They had all been asked prior to the service if they wished to participate in the Eucharist as well, and they had all, without hesitation, said yes. The article reports that the Archbishop took part by reading part of the rite of the Church of Sweden during the Act of Consecration, that he 'made a speech', (i.e. preached the sermon), and that, after Communion had been given, he gave the blessing from the altar.

Whether or not the liturgical participation of the Archbishop and the Swedish bishops present at this Anglican service of consecration and celebration of the Eucharist ought to be seen as an act of 'catholic intercommunion', to use the anglo-catholic terminology of the day, is perhaps debatable. The liturgy of the Eucharist followed the Anglican rite, and there were, of course, no interpolations from the Swedish rite. In any case, it was a remarkable ecumenical manifestation that took place at the Consecration of the English Church in Stockholm on 13 June 1866. It is also quite obvious that these events took place with a clear, considered intention from both sides.

There was yet another positive statement on Anglicanism by Henrik Reuterdahl during his time as Archbishop of Uppsala, which was perhaps even more challenging. He made an official recommendation, in the form of a letter from the House of Clergy in the *Riksdag* (*Cleri Comitialis*

Cirkulär), that those Swedish immigrants in the USA, who went to live in places where there was no Lutheran church, ought to join the local Episcopalian church. This caused great upset among the pastors of the Lutheran Church in America, and it was a recommendation which the Swedish Church did not have the courage to uphold in the long run. It was a sensitive issue in the American situation, and it proved itself to be so again, as soon as the Swedish mother church took an initiative towards closer links with the Anglican Communion.

CHAPTER 10

From Lambeth to Uppsala

AROUND LAMBETH 1867

In September 1867 the then Archbishop of Canterbury, Charles Thomas Longley, gathered the bishops of the Churches of the Anglican Communion for a three day long conference on various issues of common concern. The meeting was held at Lambeth Palace, the official London residence of the Archbishop of Canterbury for the last 700 years. The Palace has lent its name to the international Anglican bishops' conference, which since 1867 has been held, more or less regularly, every tenth year. Ever since its very first meeting, this conference has had a certain importance also for the Nordic churches, and in particular for the Church of Sweden.

The Lambeth Conference, which is the Anglican equivalent of the *Concilium* or synod of bishops, in the Roman Catholic Church, is a visual expression of the episcopal tradition and structure of the Anglican Communion, the feature which had been so strongly accentuated by the Oxford Movement. Representatives of other churches could only be invited to attend the Lambeth Conference if those churches had a corresponding episcopal structure and constitution. This is not to say that the first conference reflected the views of Tractarianism. It was rather the other way round: the need was felt to confer on measures *against* the Oxford Movement. Proposals for subjects to discuss during this first Lambeth Conference included 'Putting down the Ritualists'. Another proposal concerned a renewed emphasis on the Thirty-nine Articles, the doctrinal document from the English Reformation period, which Tractarians had attempted to tone down. Even so, the time was felt to be right for holding a bishops' conference, precisely as a unifying factor for the worldwide Anglican Communion. A 'synodical' counterpart to the Lambeth Conference, including clergy and lay representatives as well as bishops, has only been created in modern times – the Anglican Consultative Council. The Lambeth Conference includes only bishops. Consequently, the relations of the Lambeth Conference to the Nordic churches have rested entirely on the principle of episcopal communion. At the same time, these relations have served to give a clearer focus to the position of episcopacy in many churches. This has been obvious at least in the Church of Sweden.

When the plans for a central organization for the worldwide Anglican Communion were realized in the Lambeth Conference, this was of course an ecclesiastical manifestation of the power of the growing British Empire. Even so, it should be said that the idea was not born in England. It arose among bishops on other continents, where Anglican missions had led to the establishment of independent Anglican churches, which had grown to become units of considerable size. The suggestion to hold the first conference came from Canada, and the debates held during it were particularly relevant to the Churches in South Africa and the USA. The timing, 1867, can be seen against the background of contemporary events in North America. That year, the Dominion of Canada was created, marking a new independence and self-respect for the British colony which covered the vast area north of the USA. (Only then was the definitive border between the USA and Canada drawn.) The USA experienced new developments at an explosive rate in the years immediately following the Civil War after the momentuous day, 9 April 1865, when General Lee capitulated to the Commander-in-chief of the Northern States, General Grant.

For the South, all this meant much upheaval, but the greatest expansion took place in the Northern states. At once all the necessary resources for an extensive building programme of railways, for new initiatives in industry and agriculture, were made available, and new immigrants arrived in great waves. In some areas in the Mid-West the poulation increased by over 50% in a few years. The Churches grew as well not least the Anglican and the Nordic Lutheran churches. In this context, the thought of closer co-operation was repeatedly expressed: would it not be possible for these two communions to unite and become one episcopal church? This idea, among others, was brought to the Lambeth Conference by the North American bishops. For these Bishops, it was not only a theoretical issue, nor simply an ecumenical idea, but a matter of ecclesiastical strategy in an area were development and success and ever increasing self-respect seemed to be available beyond measure.

It should be said straight away that the first Lambeth Conference was something of an experiment, without much preparation and lasting only a few days. The various proposals made in advance of the Conference ought therefore not to be taken too seriously. Even so, the suggestion that delegates from the Church of Sweden should be invited was brought up from various quarters, among them Charles Kingsley, famous as a leader of the 'social revival' in the Church of England, F.S. May of the Anglo-Continental Society, and the Bishop of Illinois, Henry John Whitehouse – the bishop who, assisted by Archbishop Henrik Reuterdahl, had consecrated the English Church in Stockholm. Having made contact with the Archbishop on that occasion, Bishop Whitehouse had great hopes of direct co-operation with the Swedes in the American Mid-West. It was about this time, since the middle of the 1850s, that Sweden experienced the first great wave of emigration to the USA.
  Another issue also appeared, which gave added interest to the possibility of inviting the Archbishop of Uppsala as a supporter and adviser at the Anglican bishops' conference. The Bishop of Natal in South Africa, J.W. Colenso, faced trial for heresy, and this was of course a most delicate and intricate business, intensively debated. The suggestion to

include a Swedish delegate in the first Lambeth Conference was probably somewhat premature. It was rejected for the simple reason that this Conference was concerned with private discussions among the Anglican Bishops themselves on internal matters. Advice was however sought from Henrik Reuterdahl concerning the matter of the Colenso affair, and this is not without interest, especially from the point of view of Reuterdahl's response.

The trial of Colenso for heresy was part of the wider scene of the extremely tense relationship between biblical faith and modern science current at the time. Darwin's *On the Origin of Species* was published in 1859. The following year another book, entitled *Essays and Reviews* – by some 'liberal theologians' – in Oxford caused much upheaval, suggesting as it did that the Bible should be read 'like any other book'. Colenso, who was basically a scientist before he became a missionary and eventually the Bishop of Natal, followed the same lines. He published various exegetical works, in which he wanted to show, by using mathematic formulas, that the books of the Old Testament were unreliable at various points. They could not be regarded as 'the Word of God', even though it was possible to 'gain a glimpse of God's Word' through them. This was too much for the Bishop of Cape Town, Robert Gray, to whom Colenso was directly responsible. The conflict between them led to Colenso's deposition from the see of Natal and to his excommunication, in 1866. The whole affair attracted international attention, and Reuterdahl had kept himself informed via his new Anglican friends. Bishop Gray, who was completely obsessed by his persecution of Colenso, took every opportunity to bring up the matter, not least during the Lambeth Conference. As soon as he heard that 'intercommunion' had been established between the Church of Sweden and the Anglicans (that was how the events at the consecration of the English Church in Stockholm had been somewhat over-interpreted), he turned to Reuterdahl for support against Colenso's 'heresy'. Bishop Whitehouse was the intermediary. He himself was furious over this whole affair, and with the entire American Episcopal Church behind him, he had supported Colenso's excommunication. His view was that all 'branches' of what he called 'the Reformed Catholic Church' ought to join together in this cause. He obviously counted the Church of Sweden as part of 'the Reformed Catholic Church' on parity with the Anglicans.

Reuterdahl, however, was not willing to lend his support, neither on behalf of the Church of Sweden, nor privately. First of all, he did not consider himself to have the right to pronounce on a charge against a Bishop of Natal. In terms of 'internal', spiritual matters, he could of course acknowledge communion with this church, but not in 'external', legal and organizational matters. Secondly, he wanted most definitely to avoid making a charge of heresy on an issue of biblical theology.

When reporting this undeniably 'sober' stand taken by the Swedish Archbishop in this over-heated affair of Colenso, it is worth remembering that Reuterdahl himself was a prominent scholar, well-known in his own country, not only for his pioneering work in using the method of source-criticism in historical research, but also, in his younger days, as a scholar of Biblical exegesis. He had himself been criticised for his 'heretical' exposition of Scripture. In any case, he did not wish to become involved in the heresy trials of Anglican bishops, nor did he want to make any too hasty decisions on the question of inclusion in their episcopal college. This was certainly a well considered position, even though it would have been interesting to see what might have happened if he had made a contribution. The issues of biblical theology were of course crucial in all those churches which, ever since the Reformation, claimed to build primarily on the Word of God. A discussion at that time between a Lutheran church leader and the Anglican Bishops might have been important.

LAMBETH 1888

The second Lambeth Conference took place in 1878, but, from the ecumenical perspective, it was the third, which took place exactly ten years later, in 1888, that became really important, not least for relations between Anglicans and the Church of Sweden.

It is the so-called Lambeth Quadrilateral, a statement about the unity of the Church in four distinctive points, that has made the 1888 Lambeth Conference a milestone in recent church history. This text deserves to be quoted in full, since it became one of the foundations for all Anglo-Scandinavian dialogues throughout the next century. The Conference documents indicate that the purpose of these four points was to serve as a basis for the re-unification of similar churches. (These four points had in fact been accepted, in almost similar wording, by the Bishop's Conference of the American Episcopal Church – again a contribution from the energetic sister church in the USA.)

The four points were as follows:

a. The Holy Scriptures of the Old and New Testaments, as 'containing all things necessary to salvation' and as being the rule and ultimate standard of faith.

b. The Apostles' Creed as the Baptismal Symbol; and the Nicene Creed, as the sufficient statement of the Christian Faith.

c. The two Sacraments ordained by Christ Himself – Baptism and the Supper of the Lord – administered with unfailing use of Christ's Words of Institution, and of the elements ordained by Him.

d. The Historic Episcopate, locally adapted in the methods of its administration to the varying needs of the nations and peoples called of God into the Unity of His Church.

It was the fourth point, about the 'historic episcopate', which was to attract most attention. Here was a clearly expressed basis for exploring closer relations with the Church of Sweden. For other Churches, this point proved a

211

great stumbling-block. This was to become a much debated issue in ecumenical discussions for years ahead.

But the first three, cleverly worded points should not be by-passed. They have proved to stand up very well, not least in discussions with other Lutheran churches. These phrases express what also from a Lutheran perspective ought to be acceptable as an adequate and sufficient basis for Church unity. The fact that a special point is made about the ordained ministry of the Church might also be considered fully in line with Lutheran tradition, even though the focusing on episcopacy was to make for great difficulties. At the 1888 Lambeth Conference, there was in fact a minority who expressed great concern that this particular point might shut the door to many close, but non-episcopal, churches – a fear that has certainly proved to be well-founded. (See A.M.G. Stephenson, *Anglicanism and the Lambeth Conferences* (1978), p.85ff).

On the whole the Lambeth Quadrilateral is impressive evidence of creative ability. Behind it lay a strong determination to seek a firm and robust definition of the nature of the Church and a foundation for church unity.

Starting from the Quadrilateral, two committees worked during the Conference to find realistic possibilities for developing closer communion with churches of a tradition and structure similar to that of the Anglicans. This is interesting as an example of a growing will to understand the Church as a supra-national organism, in the way that it had once been, before the great ecclesiastical schisms. Re-unification with Rome was not a realistic possibility. The churches which might be considered were those which, in spite of the break with Rome, had kept everything essential in the tradition from the early Church – Holy Scripture, the Catholic Creeds, Baptism and Eucharist, and Episcopacy in historic succession. The churches with which re-unification might become a possibility were the Eastern Orthodox and the Scandinavian – at least the Church of Sweden – as well as the Old Catholics and maybe the Moravians.

This was the conception from which Anglican ecumenism was to take its shape for decades to come. According to the committee report from Lambeth 1888, this included the welcoming of every opportunity for closer links with the Swedish Church, which in its 'standard of doctrine' is so close to our own. A concrete plan for how this should be put into effect was, however, not part of this statement.

RANDALL DAVIDSON'S TRAVELS IN SCANDINAVIA IN 1889

So what happened about contacts with the Church of Sweden after this important declaration by the 1888 Lambeth Conference? The answer is: not very much, at least not for the next twenty years.

Various opinions as to why nothing happened have been offered. The most obvious comment to make is probably that this is anything but unique: a conference makes interesting and more or less challenging statements, but nobody is given any particular mandate to follow them up. Whatever the cause, there is nobody, either from the Anglican or from the Swedish side, who can be directly charged with neglect in this matter.

One person who has been the target of such accusation, sometimes of quite strong nature, is the Swedish Archbishop Anton Niklas Sundberg. However, having studied the relevant dossiers thouroughly, I am personally prepared to 'acquit' him. Much ink has been spilt on the 'blame' attached to him in connection with accounts of the travels of the Dean (later Archbishop of Canterbury), Randall Davidson, in Scandinavia in the summer of 1889. Yet another account of this journey will be given here, in order that the reader may draw his own conclusions. Concerning the situation in Scandinavia, seen with English eyes, it certainly also has some interesting aspects.

At the beginning of August 1889 Randall Davidson, accompanied by his wife and another couple, embarked on a journey to Denmark and Sweden. At the time, Davidson

213

was the Dean of Windsor, a prominent position at the Court of Queen Victoria, and he already had the confidence of the Queen. The previous year he had made a noted contribution as one of the Secretaries to the Lambeth Conference. He was also much respected by Archbishop Benson, as he had been by the previous Archbishop, A.C. Tait, whom he had served as Chaplain. His wife was the daughter of Archbishop Tait. As a Dean of just over 40, he already held a central position in both the nation and the Church. The journey he was now making was, however, a holiday trip without any official duty attached to it. He had made no contacts in advance, and there was no network of customary inter-church relations. The people he met in the Scandinavian countries therefore represented a fairly haphazard selection.

On arrival in Copenhagen, Davidson sought out the Bishop, B. J. Fog, as well as the senior Court Chaplin (*Kongl. Konfessionarius*) Paulli, but neither was at home when he rang their respective doorbells. Davidson's party decided to continue to Skåne (the southernmost county of Sweden) and Lund, where they visited the cathedral and wandered around for a good look – while a service was in progress.

From Lund they travelled northwards, stopping off here and there. The beauty of Stockholm made a great impression, but the visit to Uppsala was rather a disappointment. The cathedral was in the process of being restored and the Archbishop, whom Davidson had hoped to meet, was away. As with the Bishop of Copenhagen, Davidson had not advised him of his visit in advance.

Back in Stockholm he was able to meet a colourful personality, who provided him with information on the ecclesiastical situation in Sweden – Ernst Beckman, the editor of *Aftonbladet*, a liberal politician from a Free Church background, who spoke English. He nursed a glowing hatred of the Church of Sweden and of Archbishop Sundberg in particular. Davidson visited Beckman. The diary gives no reason why Beckman was chosen. The effect of his unreasonable criticism was, however, quite against Beckman's intentions, to make Davidson even more determined to meet Sundberg. A swearing Archbishop, who would reportedly never use devotional language, and who was a prominent and respected statesman and politician was something to arouse Davidson's curiosity. Here was apparently, according to his diary, a statesman and bishop of a medieval kind. Only at this stage did he write a letter to Sundberg and announced the date on which he proposed to visit.

Then the most incredible thing in Davidson's eyes happened. The Swedish Archbishop replied that he was unable to receive him. This letter (dated 25 August, in The Davidson Papers, in Lambeth Palace Library) has been neglected by most scholars. In a second letter (dated 3 September) he regretted that it was not possible on a second occasion either. This second letter is very short. It is reprinted in G.K.A. Bell's great biography on Davidson and in other accounts of his Nordic travels. From this letter, all those who have described the Church of Sweden at this time have concluded that Sundberg either did not wish to, or did not have the courage to meet the Archbishop of Canterbury to be. Consequently, Sundberg has been blamed for the lack of follow-up of the hopes of the 1888 Lambeth Conference for closer links with the Church of Sweden.

Sundberg's first answer to Davidson however gives a very different impression. There is certainly no indication of any lack of willingness. It begins with the words 'Thank you with all my heart for your kind letter, but I am sorry that I cannot give you a favourable answer . . .' Sundberg continues that he had to go away the following day, and was obliged to travel around in his diocese on official business during the following weeks. It would be extremely difficult to fit in the visit in the week after, when he was due in Uppsala on only one day, and on that day he already had a meeting with his Cathedral Chapter (*Domkapitel*) fixed in the morning and a conference of orientalists at the University in the afternoon. He suggested that he would try to fix a date for a meeting later in September. In the second letter he had to inform Davidson with regret that this second attempt to find a suitable date had also proved impossible.

Davidson had apparently not indicated any particular reason for his visit. Consequently, Sundberg replied in general terms that, if Davidson wanted information about the Church in Sweden, he would be very happy to provide that by letter in the future. He finally expressed his regret, yet again, that circumstances had prevented him from giving a more positive reply, and he sent his respectful regards to the Archbishop of Canterbury before signing himself 'Your servant and brother in Christ, A.N. Sundberg, Archbishop of Upsala'.

It is strange that the first letter has been by-passed in Bell's biography of Davidson. From the hand of Davidson, a reply to Sundberg's second letter is preserved. It is a polite, but quite sarcastic letter, in which Davidson does explain – but not until now! – that what he wanted was to report on the deliberations of the Lambeth Conference the previous year. He promised to report to the Archbishop of Canterbury that Archbishop Sundberg had been so busy with various ministerial duties that he had not found time for a meeting.

Davidson never forgot his annoyance. It is obvious that his pride was deeply hurt. There he was, practically straight from the Queen of England. With her he was like a member of the family, but in Sweden, in this little country close to the North Pole, some Archbishop did not even have time to receive him!

The possibility that Sundberg might have had genuine reasons that prevented him from receiving Davidson has not won any sympathy. The most common assumption about his negative reply has been that he was ashamed of his poor English. Others have thought that he was afraid of criticism from other Lutherans, particularly from Lutherans in the USA. The fact that Davidson had given no advance indication of any official business, and that he had not even written to Sundberg until only a couple of days beforehand, has gone completely unnoticed. Even Nathan Söderblom wrote in the introduction to the reply in 1922 from the Swedish Bishops to the Lambeth Conference (more on this later) that Davidson had 'visited Sweden in order to achieve some follow-up to the initiative of the Lambeth Conference', and he reported, on various occasions, how the visit went, as evidence that his predecessors, Sundberg and then J.A. Ekman, neither knew English nor had any interest in other churches.

The most extensive account of Davidson's visit to Scandinavia is given in an essay by Söderblom's son-in-law, Yngve Brilioth, entitled *Ärkebiskop Davidsons Svenska Resa* (Archbishop Davidson's Swedish Journey). The title itself is misleading; it was not as Archbishop that Davidson travelled in Sweden. He was only made Archbishop fourteen years later. Yngve Brilioth summarized his account with the following comment 'One gets a very sad view of provincial isolation from Archbishop Sundberg's obvious unwillingness to meet Davidson, an unwillingness which might have had no deeper cause than a lack of knowledge of the English language'. He finished with the words 'This gives us a view of the background, against which, historically speaking, we must evaluate developments in the last few decades.' The reply by Sundberg to Davidson is starkly contrasted with the ecumenical breakthroughs which were achieved under Söderblom and Brilioth himself.

Anton Niklas Sundberg was in actual fact not ignorant, either about England or of the English language. In his younger days he had studied in England, and he had published an essay in an academic periodical on English church life. As we have already seen, he took part together with his predecessor, Archbishop Reuterdahl, and the Bishop of Illinois, in the consecration of the English Church in Stockholm and made his communion at the Anglican Eucharist that followed. Is it likely that after he had himself become Archbishop he would suddenly have been afraid of meeting an English Dean? What is otherwise known of

217

A.N. Sundberg – the most confident, outspoken and pompous church leader on the Swedish Archbishop's throne since the Middle Ages – is that he was most certainly not shy and fearful. Is it likely that out of fear of receiving an English priest he had conjured up a whole row of excuses, that he had run away from Uppsala and was sneaking around in the countryside until the danger had passed?

Luckily, Davidson's Scandinavian holdiday ended rather better than it had begun. He went with his companions to Leksand in Dalecarlia, where he found a highly educated Rector Dr Lorents Petersson to talk to and he experienced the Swedish high mass in the best possible form. The worshippers, dressed in national costumes, arrived by 'church boats'. Davidson, as the entry in his diary shows, was most intrigued by this colourful display. Of the seven hundred or so people present, about a hundred received communion. Davidson noted a number of liturgical practices, like the use of vestments, which were controversial in his own church but had quite naturally been preserved in traditional form in the Church of Sweden.

It was, however, particularly in Denmark, on the way back, that everything fell into place in quite a different way than before. It is hard to avoid the reflection that this time Davidson had announced his visit in advance, and therefore he was expected. He certainly was, both by the royal family and by the Bishop of Copenhagen. Christian IX and his Queen, the royal couple who have often been called 'Europe's parents-in-law', invited Davidson to join the happy company at the Palace of Fredensborg together with the large family, including the Prince and Princess of Wales, the Tsar of Russia and his family, the King of Greece and all the royal grandchildren. In the capital he was able to have a long conversation with the Bishop, the staunchly conservative but learned and delightful B.J. Fog. Davidson liked him – 'a really good old man of deep and earnest personal piety', in some ways not unlike his own father-in-law, Archbishop Tait. Fog spoke English, although slowly and with some difficulty. With him Davidson would have been able to discuss Plato, the ecclesiology of Augustine or the philosophy of Descartes, but such subjects were not on his agenda. The discussion centered instead on Grundtvig's ecclesiology and following – which Fog abhorred – and on John Henry Newman, on priestly and episcopal ordinations and on the apostolic succession. On this subject, Fog became both serious and enthusiastic. He made it clear to Davidson that the Danish Church had no desire whatsoever to adapt, either to the Swedish or to the Anglican Church, in this matter, and he seemed almost proud of the fact that the succession had been broken in Denmark during the Reformation.

Davidson's journey in Denmark and Sweden lasted for about four weeks in the late summer of 1889. As Archbishop of Canterbury, he was the first to have seen and made up his own mind about these countries and churches. The journey was not particularly well prepared, and his impressions were consequently rather disparate and odd. But the journey had certainly left its mark. Several of his experiences had been negative. A few years after Davidson's enthronement in Canterbury, official talks started between the Anglican and the Nordic churches (to begin with only with the Church of Sweden) and they continued right through his long primacy. His interest in furthering these talks is obvious. At the same time it is noticeable that he quite frequently held back on what, in his view, seemed to be too much enthuiasm.

NORDIC LUTHERANISM AT THE TURN
OF THE CENTURY

Much literature suggests that church life and theology in the Nordic countries around the turn of the century was marked by isolation and stagnation. That is not true. They were certainly not isolated, but it is remarkable how unilateral the contacts were; they went almost exclusively southwards, to Germany.

219

German theology was widely influential especially on the Continent and in Scandinavia but also in England, and it had followed the emigrating Europeans to the USA. In the inheritance from Kant, Schleiermacher and Hegel, German theologians had a magnificent tradition from the nineteenth century to hand on. It is therefore quite natural that Nordic theologians were dependent on influences from the German universities, and that German theological literature also dominated the theological faculties in Scandinavia. It was a solidly academic philosophy and theology that came from Germany, and the opportunities provided were well used. A review of how the leaders of the faculties and the churches in the Nordic countries at the turn of the century had been trained shows that almost all of them had been educated, in most cases for considerable periods – of two or three years – at the universities on the Continent: Leipzig, Erlangen, Tübingen, Basel. A few had, of course, also visited England, but any direct theological influences from there are hard to prove in the period before 1900.

A general mustering of the entire European Lutheran community took place at a conference in Lund in 1901. (It was the Allgemeine Evangelisch-Lutherische Konferenz, a predecessor to the Lutheran World Federation.) At this conference, which had gathered no less than 1,500 Lutheran theologians, it was obvious that most of them were educated with the same theological approach. This was true also of almost all the delegates from the Nordic churches. The prevailing theology was that of the Universities of Erlangen and Leipzig. Modern biblical criticism was widely acclaimed. With it went a deep concern not to undermine the traditional faith of the Church. This synthesis could be made by a strong emphasis on religious 'experience'. In this way the devotional approach of Pietism was simultaneously satisfied, but it meant a radical break with biblical fundamentalism.

The reason why so much attention was focused on this conference was the fact that yet another theological approach, also of German origin, emerged: liberal theology, whose extremely influential advocate was Adolf von Harnack, the author of *Das Wesen des Christenthums,* which had been published the previous year. The majority of the conference delegates were very critical of this book. Harnack's startingpoint seemed to be not the traditional Creed of the Church, but the imaginations of the so called 'modern man'. The conflict between the old theological school and this new 'liberal' theology reached a climax at the conference in Lund. Thus a primarily German theological debate was implanted in Scandinavia.

The new interpretation had only a few followers at Lund, among them the Norwegian priest, Thorvald Klaveness, who lectured on 'The Increasing Indifference among Educated People'. Klaveness argued that Christian preaching must take greater notice of contemporary conceptions and modes of experience. That was enough to set the debate among these 1,500 theologians aflame. The repercussions in the speaker's own country, Norway, were also considerable. Replies were made, among others by Bishop J.C. Heuch, who wrote a book entitled *Mod Strømmen* (Against the Tide), published 1902. To go 'against the tide' meant to stand up against contemporary rationalist tendencies and to confess clearly that Christ was true God and true man. But there were further consequences. A few years later an independent theological faculty, the *Menighedsfakultet,* was founded, quite separate from the University. This Faculty, which throughout the twentieth century has been by far the largest in the country, attracted students from the various, numerically large, Evangelical groups in Norway.

Otherwise, the theological controversies in Norway were no worse than in many other parts of Christendom. The liberal or, as it was commonly called in the Roman Catholic Church, 'modernist' theology took the lead in many places for quite a long period. The same conflicts between church life and theology raged in Anglicanism.

The prevalence of German influences on Nordic theology was quite in accordance with the cultural climate in general. It is almost impossible for us today, after the two world wars, to imagine how very limited the cultural impulses from England and the USA were in previous generations. It is significant that the English lay preacher Lord Radstock, who was active among the aristocracy in Scandinavia in the 1870s and 1880s, first in Helsinki and later, for quite a long period, in Stockholm, had to either use an interpreter or converse in French. French was the contemporary conversational language among the educated, thereafter German, which gradually gained more and more terrain. Besides, culture and foreign policy were closely united, and relations with Germany were politically most expedient. This was the line taken by Sweden-Norway, particularly in the reign of Oscar II.

Even so, considerable spiritual influence found its way from the West, from Great Britain and the USA, but along other routes than via academic theology and church leaders. The revivalists had frequent personal contacts with spiritual leaders in the English-speaking part of the world, from where they received formative influences. This, however, did not change the one-sided dependence of Nordic theology on Germany. The spiritual movements in the west were felt to be a threat, and this resulted in a defensive attitude. Experience had shown that no support for the national churches was usually forthcoming from those quarters, but instead destructive elements, emanating from their individualistic spirituality and sectarianism.

However, a turning point in contacts with the West came during the decades immediately before the turn of the century. During the 1880s and 1890s young theologians and priests began to receive strong incentives from England in particular and from the USA, impressions which might be put into practice in their work at home, as parish priests and leaders of the national Church. New worldwide Christian organizations began to gather the young: first YMCA and later the Student Christian Movement in its various branches.

YMCA and YWCA embraced both a revivalist ethos and a social passion, which could be channelled through the work of the parishes in the larger cities. The urban population had grown at an explosive rate, and the social misery was often very great. Two young Danish priests, Henry Ussing and Olfert Ricard, both exerting great influence on the young generation in all the Nordic countries, had found the inspiration for their work in Copenhagen in England. The Christian student organizations became a nursery for the pioneers of the Ecumenical Movement, among them the young Nathan Söderblom, who in the 1890s received his formative impression at a Christian students' meeting in the USA. Soon afterwards he took part in an international conference of the YMCA in Amsterdam.

In the general cultural debate in Scandinavia during the last decades of the nineteenth century, Christianity played a fairly limited part. Prominent philosophers and writers had departed from the Christian faith. This was, for example, the case of the Danish philosopher Harald Høffding (1843–1931) and the literary critic Georg Brandes (1842–1927), both of whom exerted great influence also in the other Nordic countries. They both found support in the German philosopher Feuerbach and the school of 'Positivism', in which religion was regarded as exclusively a product of human emotions and instincts. Otherwise their main orientation was towards the West, to French and English philosophers, for example to John Stuart Mill and Herbert Spencer in England. Høffding and Brandes in their turn influenced Henrik Ibsen in Norway and August Strindberg in Sweden. In that cultural climate, humanist values were certainly appreciated – this is particularly noticeable in the dramatic works of Ibsen – but a wide gap, which was to prove difficult to bridge, emerged between the faith and teaching of the Church and the view of, as it was called, the 'Modernist breakthrough'.

At the same time the tensions grew between the revivalist interpretations of the Christian faith and academic theology. Towards the end of the 19th century, the people of the Revivalist Movements had by and large migrated to urban areas. Large 'mission halls' were built for revivalist preaching as alternative to the services of the National Church. (An example is the large complex named 'Bethesda' in Copenhagen). Here Christian social work was also undertaken, with a new focus in the 'Home Mission'. It was also about this time that diaconal work was begun in the Nordic churches after German models.

The most remarkable aspect of the developments in Denmark, Norway and Finland was that the 'Home Mission' and Evangelical revivalism remained almost entirely within the framework of the national Church. Hence the Free Churches never spread very far in those countries. In Sweden the conflict became much more radical, and large groups of Evangelicals formed their own denominations. This in turn led, particularly in Sweden, as a defence against the pressures from these groups, to the development of a conscious theology of the nature of the Church, and of the specific tradition and responsibility of the national Church. The importance of this was to become apparent when, soon after the beginning of the new century, the dialogue between Anglican and Swedish theologians on the identity of the Church got off the ground.

OFFICIAL TALKS

The declaration of the 1888 Lambeth Conference had not led to any official approach to the Church of Sweden. Nor did any definite proposals arise from the next Conference in 1897. It was not until 1907, the year before the following Lambeth Conference, that the issue was seriously taken up.

This time the initiative came from Sweden, though not from the church leaders, but from the Swedish Ambassador in London, Viscount (*Greve*) Herman Wrangel. In itself,

224

this was not particularly strange, even though it may seem to be so from our modern perspective. At the time, the Church of Sweden had no central government of its own apart from the King, the Government of the State and its various ministries. These circumstances led to considerable hesitation about how to contact another church in another country on behalf of the Church of Sweden. Was even the Archbishop of Uppsala entitled to make such an approach? Nor, of course, was it self-evident that such responsibilities were included in the instructions to the London Ambassador. Viscount Wrangel made the approach on his own initiative. He was a skilful and experienced diplomat, a member of the aristocracy and a European with wide outlooks, known for his independent views and strong determination. It was on a legal point, concerning the rights of Swedish priests to act as official registrars at weddings in the Swedish mission-fields in the English colonies that he approached Archbishop Davidson. But Wrangel went further and asked Davidson if he did not think that the time had come for the Anglican churches and the Church of Sweden to draw closer in a more official capacity. Thus the ball was set in motion.

It is not necessary to report here on every move to and fro before the 1908 Lambeth Conference. (A detailed analysis is available in C.H. Lyttkens' book.) Both sides showed a degree of hesitation, for both formal and strategic reasons. On the Anglican side there was the fear of criticism from the Anglo-Catholics, and the Swedish church leaders felt the pressure from strict confessional groups and from the Swedish Lutherans in the USA. But in the end they plucked up courage to take the first step; an official representative from the Church of Sweden was received at the Lambeth Conference. He expressed greetings to the gathered Anglican bishops and was thereafter made a member of the committee on the issues of 'intercommunion' with the Church of Sweden.

The Archbishop of Uppsala, J.A. Ekman, appointed (or rather, asked the Government to appoint) the Bishop of Kalmar, Henry William Tottie (1856–1913) to this task. This proved a very wise and happy choice. Davidson, who was famous for his political skill as a church leader and statesman, had certainly not made a less successful choice of the men who were appointed to lead the work of this committee at Lambeth, and who were then to take part in the continued talks with the Swedes. They were first of all the learned Bishop of Salisbury, John Wordsworth, and, as chairman of the delegation to Uppsala, the Bishop of Winchester, Herbert E. Ryle. The latter came from the Evangelical wing of the Church of England.

The mutual understanding that emerged during the talks was, of course, to a large extent due to the personalities of these people, but also to their approach to theology and church life in Sweden and in England respectively. It may therefore be appropriate to recall a few biographical details about these men.

First Bishop Tottie. When he gave his greeting before the Lambeth Conference, his excellent, even elegant, command of the English language caused astonishment. This was, however, not very strange at all. He came from a family, which was half English and half Swedish, as his first names, Henry William, suggests. He had strong bonds with England and English culture. As a theologian he was particularly concerned with issues on the nature and structures of the Church. He had begun his career as a church historian. At one time he was the Director of the Church of Sweden Mission. From 1901 to 1913 he was Bishop of Kalmar.

Among Tottie's theological works there are several essays on church matters in Great Britain. He had observed with some unease the potential threat from the growth of the Free Churches against the Church of England, and he reported on the, in his eyes ominous, separation of Church and State in Ireland and later in Wales. Tottie emphasized the indispensable value of a national church, a church which for centuries had close historical bonds with its people. He took the same view, of course, with regard to his own Church of Sweden, which was also under serious threat from various Free Church movements. He had expressed these concerns for example in 1893, when speaking to a national conference for the entire priesthood in Sweden on the subject of 'The Importance for a People of a National Church'. A national church is invested with historically binding obligations, Tottie argued, and it has a responsibility for the whole nation, for every individual and for the religious and moral nurture of the whole people. As a church historian, he, like many of his contemporaries, wrote several monographs on famous Swedish bishops from the 'Great Power' period (the seventeenth century), bishops who had sustained both culture and church life in the country, and who had been great examples to and leaders of their people. There was clearly a nationalist streak in these writings, and at the same time a patriotic, even heroic, view of the Church and its obligations. It is easy to see that a mutual understanding, built on shared ideals, would emerge between Tottie and the English bishops. Tottie and Wordsworth became close friends.

The Bishop of Salisbury, John Wordsworth (1843–1911) came from a well-known family, made famous above all by the poet William Wordsworth. Both his father and his uncle were bishops. He himself was known for his great learning, with an academic reputation as the man behind *The Oxford Critical Edition of the Vulgate New Testament*. His *magnum opus* was his edition of Origen's *Contra Celsum*. In the 1890s he published two works in Latin on episcopacy in the Church of England. Both of these were of course caused by the Papal decree that Anglican orders were 'absolutely null and utterly void', e.g. lacking apostolic authority (*Apostolicae Curae*, 1896).

Wordsworth's ecumenical work should be seen against that background. As the gap between the Anglicans and Rome became ever wider, the need to establish unity among other branches of Christendom, notably between Churches which had kept the 'historic episcopate', became ever more urgent. Those churches were, besides the Anglicans, the Old Catholics, the Eastern Orthodox and the Church of Sweden. His efforts to reach these churches were inexhaustible. He sympathizied deeply with the Old Catholics over their break with Rome after the First Vatican Council, and he took part in numerous conferences with the Old Catholics in many countries on the Continent. During the 1890s he visited various Orthodox churches in the Middle East, in Alexandria and Cairo, in Cyprus, in Beirut, Damascus etc., and he reported on his impressions in the work *The Church of England and the Eastern Patriarchates*. After that the Church of Sweden became the main focus for his attention and concern. He understood his own responsibility as a bishop in terms very similar to what we have seen in Bishop Tottie, as a national task. His biography (E.W. Watson, *Life of Bishop John Wordsworth*, 1915) recalls that he approached episcopacy from three aspects: historically, pastorally and ecumenically, and that he showed enormous ambitions personally to supervise the morality of the people within his diocese.

Bishop Herbert Ryle (1856–1925) had been a Fellow of King's College, Cambridge for a long time, teaching biblical exegesis, when he was appointed as Bishop first of Exeter and later of Winchester. During that time he had moved gradually away from the often narrow biblicism of the Evangelicals, and he is regarded as the Cambridge founder of historical criticism of the Old Testament. With this background and approach he made a perfect match for most of the leading theologians in contemporary Sweden. In liturgical matters he was, however, much more of a puritan. He had aroused great attention when, soon after his appointment as bishop, he issued strict prohibitions against all those rites which the younger high church priests had begun to introduce.

It should be noted that on biblical issues there was no great discrepancy between the various participants in the

228

Anglo-Swedish talks. Already the Lambeth Quadrilateral provided an important opening through the phrase, quoted above, that Holy Scripture *contains* everything necessary for salvation (p.211 above). This does not imply any limitation to a doctrine of verbal inspiration. Nor were there any advocates of this rather conservative view in the Swedish delegation from Uppsala. The Swedish group included, besides Herman Lundström, an outstanding professor of church history, also two other professors from the Theological Faculty of the University of Uppsala, who both represented a new and, at least in its day, fairly radical approach: Einar Billing and Nathan Söderblom. They had both, independently of each other, signalled new thoughts on the theme of 'revelation and history' Söderblom in his work entitled *Uppenbarelsereligion* (Revealed Religion) in 1903, and Billing a few years later (1907) in a book called *De Etiska Tankarna i Urkristendomen* (Ethical Thinking in the Early Church). This book became a turning point, even though it was only a 'torso' which did not go far beyond the content of the Old Testament. They both understood the Bible as a *narrative* about God's dramatic actions in history; the book as such could be subjected to the scientific, critical method.

Of equal importance for the ecumenical talks was the interpretation of confessional tradition. Around the turn of the century an attitude towards the Confession emerged in Sweden which was largely different from that of the rest of the Lutheran world. A much more distinctive line began to be drawn between Luther and subsequent Lutheranism. At this time there was in Sweden a renewed interest in research on Luther, which was undertaken with new vigour by scholars like Billing, Söderblom and Gustaf Aulén. They attempted to point to Luther as a religious genius, whose work was inspirational for the *whole* of Christendom. It was, however, prudent to keep a critical distance from the Lutheranism that followed, that of Lutheran Orthodoxy and of Pietism. A certain distance was also to be kept from the Lutheran confession. These formularies ought to be seen primarily as historical documents, and as commentaries on the Evangelical-Lutheran tradition, rather than as normative interpretations thereof. Given this laid-back position on the meaning of belonging to a Lutheran church, the Swedish theologians, at least those whom the Anglicans met, were able to show great openness in the ecumenical talks.

This did of course not mean that the Swedes were prepared to give up their Lutheran identity or to betray their loyalty to their Lutheran sister-churches. They were pressed hard on this point during the talks with the Anglicans in 1908 and 1909. The keenest of the Anglican delegates was the Bishop of Marquette (in Michigan, USA), George Mott Williams. He was determined to convince the church of the Swedish immigrants in the USA, the so-called Augustana Synod, to accept affiliation to the American Episcopal Church, and he wanted to gain support for this plan from their mother-church in Sweden. As we have seen, the question had been raised before, in the days of Archbishop Reuterdahl. It had already been a very sensitive issue in those days and it was no less so now, fifty years later. And it was certainly not a marginal issue: the number of Swedish-speaking Lutherans in the American Mid-West at this time has been estimated at two million, while the population in Sweden was about five million. Bishop Tottie made it quite clear at Lambeth 1908 that the Church of Sweden had every respect for its daughter-church in the USA, and firmly supported its intention to remain an independent Evangelical-Lutheran denomination. The move towards the Anglicans by the Church of Sweden should not be understood as a betrayal of the Lutheran family.

THE MEETING AT UPPSALA IN 1909

The collection of letters in Lambeth Palace Library shows how Archbishop Davidson kept a firm hold on the talks with the Church of Sweden. He kept in frequent contact with Bishop Ryle, who was the Anglican chairman of the commission. Ryle was a man in whom Davidson had complete confidence, and together they staked out the course which they wanted to follow: official links should be established with the Church of Sweden, but agreements on particular issues should be kept within a very limited framework.

On the way to Sweden the English delegates made a stop-over in Copenhagen. Here extra-ordinary diplomatic cautiousness was called for in view of ecclesiastical regularity as Ryle put it in one of his letters to Davidson. Ryle asked whether he ought to decline an invitation to preach in a Danish church, and Davidson replied that he thought so, since an acceptance would lead to problems back in England. (Davidson alluded to the tension between the high church Bishop of Birmingham, Charles Gore, and his antagonist, Bishop Hensley Henson.) Bishop John Wordsworth, however, took greater liberties. He met a number of theologians and church leaders in Copenhagen (Valdemar Ammundsen, Henry Ussing, J. Oskar Andersen and others) and he spoke at Bethesda, the meeting point in Copenhagen for the young low-church groups who sought contacts with the West, in Great Britain and the USA.

But it was not only apprehension about criticism from the high church wing in England which made Ryle rather cautious. He also considered the political consequences to which closer relations with the Nordic national churches might lead. It is obvious that both sides understood their church to be so fully integrated into the political establishment that it was not possible to act in a completely independent manner during these talks, nor to disregard the potential political consequences. Ryle mentioned in one of his letters to Davidson that he understood the Nordic churches as 'more truly departments of state' than the Church of England. Cautiousness was therefore called for, so that the conference in Uppsala might not be interpreted as a step towards 'a closer entente' between Great Britain and Scandinavia, directed against Russia or Germany.

231

This might have been an over-interpretation, but the visit certainly had an air of official state business. This can be seen from the solemn reception of the Anglican delegation in the Swedish capital on their way to Uppsala. For later generations this reception seems rather amazing. It was, after all, only a matter of receiving a couple of bishops and a few other theologians for a minor conference. On arrival in Stockholm they were received in audience by King Gustaf V. The delegation was driven by royal carriage from the Palace to Riddarholmskyrkan (the burial church for the majority of Swedish monarchs) in order to lay wreaths (as was customary on state visits) on the tombs of Gustav II Adolf and Oscar II. Later they had lunch with the Crown Prince and Princess. Ryle had carefully considered the various points on the programme with the British Ambassador in Stockholm in advance, and he wrote to his Archbishop that they had put up with all this in order to sustain good relations between Sweden and Great Britain. And he made the reflection that the Swedes were strong nationalists and 'the loss, first of Finland and then of Norway, tends to make the people sensitive and touchy'.

Ryle approached the meeting with the Swedish delegation at Uppsala with great determination, but he also assured Davidson that they would only move forward with great caution. Bishop Wordsworth was keener and more enthusiastic. Ryle tried to keep the reins on him: 'There will be difficulties in restraining John Sarum' he wrote in one of his letters (Sarum is the old Latin name for Salisbury, Wordsworth's episcopal see). Ryle wanted to limit the agenda at Uppsala to three points: If we can a. mutually recognize succession, b. interchange criticism and suggestions. c. discuss a *modus vivendi* 'for the United States difficulty', (i.e. the integration of the Swedes in the American Episcopal Church).

Precisely this became the agenda for the meeting. To summarize, it can be said that the purpose was fully achieved regarding the first point; thereafter a number of questions were discussed, on which the parties differed but where the disagreements were not sufficiently strong to become a hindrance to further fellowship, and on the third point it was noted that the Church of Sweden was in no way prepared to support the intentions of the American Episcopal Church.

The Swedish Archbishop, J.A. Ekman, won the sympathy, even the admiration, of the Anglicans. He was very friendly and hospitable towards his guests, but he also showed great diplomacy and caution in the talks. He had delegated to Bishop Tottie, who had the greatest command of the English language among the Swedes and who also had the greatest knowledge of the Anglican Church, the task of leading the discussions. From the minutes of the meeting (the manuscript of which is kept in Lambeth Palace Library) it is obvious that the two leaders at the Conference in Uppsala were Bishop Ryle on the one hand and Bishop Tottie on the other. (There are frequent references in the literature to the singular importance of Nathan Söderblom's contribution. This may be an anticipation of the role Söderblom was to play *after* the conference and later, as Archbishop from 1914. During the 1909 conference he was certainly active as one of the Swedish hosts, and he won the friendship of the Anglicans by his enthusiasm and radiant personality, but he did not take the lead in the discussions.)

Bishop Tottie started the deliberations by referring to the declaration on the Scandinavian churches by the 1888 Lambeth Conference. In his view, the 'final goal' ought to be the establishment of 'permanent intercommunion', which would mean the interchangeability of priests and the right of the laity to receive communion in each other's Churches. But he did not want to move forward too fast. The main business of this meeting was to analyse the historic succession in both Churches, and the professor of church history and Dean of Uppsala Cathedral, Herman Lundström, expounded the subject thouroughly from the perspective of the Church of Sweden. With that, the first point on Ryle's agenda had been dealt with. The discussion

233

on the discrepancies between the churches focused particularly on the diaconate and on confirmation. It was on the matter of the Swedes in America and the Episcopal Church that Nathan Söderblom made his contribution. (He was the only member of the Swedish delegation who had visited America.) He spoke warmly of these American Swedes, 'blood of our blood', and of their church, but argued that the expectations of the Episcopal Church and their hope of a union with them was completely without prospect; this Swedish Church in the USA was 'extremely low-church with a harsh Lutheran Orthodoxy'.

The meeting in Uppsala went well, to the satisfaction of the Swedish and the English party; it was only the American hopes which had been dashed. In the history of the Ecumenical Movement this meeting broke new ground as a pioneering contribution. It is the first example in modern times of a searching dialogue between two churches. It marks a milestone in Anglican-Swedish relations. Bishop Ryle reported to his Archbishop: 'I think good has really been done; we have visited Sweden at a time when the encouragement will give stimulus to a church movement already begun. The Archbishop's consent to appoint a Standing Committee to work with us carries us forward without committing us', Ryle ended with characteristic caution.

The official report of the Anglicans was available two years later and was presented to the 1920 Lambeth Conference. It was declared that the Swedish episcopal succession was unbroken, and that the Church of Sweden held the 'right' view on episcopacy and priesthood. A recommendation followed that allowed members of the Church of Sweden to receive Holy Communion and priests of the Church of Sweden to preach in Anglican churches. (The celebration of the Eucharist was not mentioned, and the term 'intercommunion' was avoided.) It was also recommended that mutual invitations to participate in episcopal consecrations should be extended.

Even though the Lambeth Conference is only empowered to make recommendations and not to make binding decisions for any of the Anglican Churches, this declaration has become very important indeed. It was a direct follow-up of the discussions in Uppsala in 1909. For the Church of Sweden this meant, just as Bishop Ryle had reported to Davidson, a stimulus to increased self-respect, and in some ways to a deeper understanding of its own unique tradition, which was gradually brought more and more into focus, and also of its particular ecumenical responsibility. It was this development, following the Uppsala Conference, which in everything essential bore the marks of Nathan Söderblom.

AFTER THE MEETING IN UPPSALA

The history of the Ecumenical Movement is, particularly at the pioneering stage, the history of enthusiastic personalities – a story of the dedication and friendships of the people involved. This is true not least of the new relationship between the Church of Sweden and the Church of England at the beginning of the twentieth century.

To begin with, it is good to recall the work of John Wordsworth. Although it was short, he laid the foundation. His enthusiasm at the deliberations in Uppsala, which rather worried the Anglican chairman, has already been mentioned. Wordsworth died in 1911, only a year and a half after the meeting in Uppsala, but during these short months he managed to make a remarkable contribution towards bringing the Church of Sweden and the Anglicans closer together. He cultivated his friendship with the Swedes, in particular with Bishop Tottie. Even more remarkable is his great achievement of writing a major work on Swedish church history, entitled *The National Church of Sweden*, a tome of 450 pages, in a very short time. In order to do this, he learned to read Swedish and made use of almost all the available academic literature on the subject. His new Swedish friends provided material. The book was created out of a series of lectures which Wordsworth gave in Chicago and which he later extended and published in England (Mowbray, 1911). It was quickly translated into Swedish, on the initiative of Söderblom, and for many years it was the mainstay of church history literature at the universities.

In the context of the talks with the Anglicans, the interest in travelling to England to study Anglican church life was aroused among young theologians and priests in Sweden. Nathan Söderblom, while still a professor at Uppsala, encouraged them, and in England they were well received by, among others, Bishop John Wordsworth. Some of these youngsters were ambitious enough to publish the accounts of their travels, and interest in Anglicanism spread among their contemporaries. They were particularly drawn to the Anglo-Catholic wing and to the religious communities in the Church of England, like the Cowley Fathers in London and the communities at Kelham and Mirfield. There was a certain irony in this priority, as it was these circles who were the least enthusiastic about contacts with a Protestant church such as the Church of Sweden, and it was the fear of criticism from that direction that had made Davidson and Ryle so cautious about the discussions with Sweden.

There was certainly much to admire among the Anglo-Catholics: enthusiasm for mission, social passion, a deep appreciation of liturgy. The young Swedes were mostly impressed by the liturgical aspects, which, by the way, were hotly debated in England at this time. Back in Sweden they attracted attention by dressing in cassocks and by the frequent use of genuflections and the sign of the cross. Of deeper significance was the love they had learnt for the Daily Office and the incentive to more frequent celebrations of the Eucharist. The so called high church movement in Sweden received much inspiration from England during this period. Attempts to form religious communities were also made: first *Sankt Sigfrids Brödraskap* (the Brotherhood of St Sigfrid) and later *Societas Sanctae Birgittae* (the

Society of St Birgitta) and *Den Apostoliska Bekännelsens Brödraskap* (the Brotherhood of the Apostolic Confession).

A more official visit to England was made for a whole month in the summer of 1914 by three Swedish professors of theology accompanied by their wives. One of them was Gustaf Aulén, who, in his autobiography *Från Mina 96 År* (From My 96 Years), states that the trip could be seen 'as a direct consequence of the discussions in Uppsala in 1909'. The other two were Einar Billing and Edward Rodhe. All three of them were working on subjects which might also be relevant for the talks with the Church of England. In 1912 Aulén had published an analysis on *Den Lutherska Kyrkoidén* (The Lutheran Concept of the Church). Billing was working on his interpretation of the 'religious motive' of the national Church, and Rodhe investigated Swedish liturgical manuscripts (Breviaries) from the Reformation period. All three of them eventually became extremely influential bishops of the Church of Sweden, and they all in various ways made important contributions to Swedish-English church relations.

Davidson invited them to Lambeth Palace, and they were also received in Canterbury. Aulén says that, just as they left Canterbury Cathedral, the news broke of the murder of the Austrian heir to the throne and his wife in Sarajevo. That was the prelude to the First World War, which among other things meant that inter-church contacts had to be postponed for the future. The visit of these three professors from Sweden to England in 1914 does however show that it was not only the high church youngsters who established contacts in England at this time.

The person who became most deeply involved in this matter was, however, Nathan Söderblom. The new relationship with the Church of England and other Anglican churches which was established at the meeting in Uppsala in 1909 contributed greatly to Söderblom's interpretation of the identity of the Church of Sweden and its responsibility within the whole of Christendom. This was made quite clear in his writings after 1909 and in the

237

context of his consecration as Archbishop in 1914. He gradually became more and more convinced of the totally unique position of the Church of Sweden within Christendom. More than any other Protestant church, it had preserved the continuity with the past, which was evident from its rich liturgical tradition and not least from the fact that it had kept the 'historic episcopate' intact. Therefore the Church of Sweden, like no other church, would be able to act as a mediator, primarily between Anglicans and Lutherans but also within Christendom as a whole. There was no small measure of a grandiose Swedish nationalism in this conception. Nationalistic tones prevailed in the culture of the day, and Söderblom played happily on its strings. At the same time, a remarkable ecumenical programme emerged.

The Swedish episcopate with its apostolic succession might play a key role in worldwide ecumenism, and it was therefore all the more urgent to make the most of the links with the Anglican partner, which had a corresponding episcopal tradition.

After the end of World War I, Söderblom was able to make the most of that possibility. He did so by inviting one of the English bishops, Hensley Henson, to assist at the consecration of two bishops in Uppsala Cathedral in 1920. Henson was a personal friend of Söderblom, and at the same time he was, on Söderblom's initiative, to give a series of lectures in Uppsala. The choice of Henson must otherwise be considered a somewhat daring, or even careless, move, since he was an extremely controversial person and, because of his liberal views, involved in a spectacular doctrinal dispute in the Church of England at this very time. When Archbishop Davidson was informed of Söderblom's initiative, he made haste to suggest to Söderblom that another English bishop, one from the Evangelical wing, namely the Bishop of Winchester, Theodore Woods, might also be invited. Bishop Woods was to become Söderblom's faithful collaborator in the ecumenical efforts of the 1920s. Both Söderblom's invitation to Henson and the involvement by Davidson are characteristic of these two church leaders: one was an impulsive enthusiast, the other a cautious diplomat with a longer perspective. Together they achieved the important breakthrough in Swedish-Anglican relations in 1920, namely the beginning of mutual participation in episcopal ordinations.

LAMBETH 1920 AND UPPSALA 1922

The 1920 Lambeth Conference, held soon after the ending of the War, has been remembered particularly for its strong determination to overcome all ecclesiastical divisions, both in British Christianity and around the world. There were many areas in which people were striving for unity and reconciliation after the Great War; the decision to found the League of Nations had been instigated in January 1920. The will of the Lambeth Conference to work for church unity took the form of an appeal, *The Appeal to All Christian People*, which has been called 'probably the most memorable statement of any Lambeth Conference' (Adrian Hastings, *A History of English Christianity 1920–1985*). The proposal to make this great statement came from the then Archbishop of York, later Davidson's successor in Canterbury, Cosmo Gordon Lang. Lang was sympathetic to the Anglo-Catholic wing which, in many ways thanks to him, gained more and more support in the 1920s. The support for the ecumenical appeal at the Lambeth Conference was general and honest, and it was immediately received with good will among the British Free Churches. The tone of the appeal was appreciated and the seriousness behind it understood: sorrow over the divisions among Christians and a deep longing for reconciliation. There was a desire to break away from all the bitter controversies of the past and generously to acknowledge everything essential that was held in common.

In principle, the Appeal of the Lambeth Conference, however, in spite of its good will, meant nothing beyond

239

its old 'Quadrilateral', and for the Free Churches, this Anglican 'offer' of 'historic episcopacy' as a basis for unity became, yet again, a stumbling-block. The Bishop of Durham, Hensley Henson, always on the ball with his sharp and fearless criticism, argued that this Appeal in fact offered nothing to other churches, like, for example, the Church of Scotland, except an invitation to 'unconditional surrender'. At the end of day, nothing very much came from this, at least not for 'ecumenism at home'. It can, nevertheless, be seen as an important starting-point for many seminal contributions which were to be made by Anglican church leaders within the international ecumenical organizations 'Life and Work' and 'Faith and Order' during the following decades. For the Church of Sweden came the confirmation of what had already been achieved at the conference in Uppsala in 1909, the formal recommendation to allow members of the Church of Sweden to receive Holy Communion, and to allow priests of the Church of Sweden to preach in Anglican churches, and the proposal that the bishops of the two churches might mutually assist as episcopal ordinations. During the following years, new efforts were made to include the other Nordic and Baltic churches in this communion.

The person who had made most of the preparations for the 'Lambeth Appeal' was the Oxford Professor, later Bishop of Gloucester, Arthur Cayley Headlam (1862–1947). From the mid-1920s he was deeply involved in the ecumenical talks with churches in Northern Europe. In his younger days Headlam had a great deal in common with John Wordsworth, and like him, he was very knowledgeable about the Orthodox churches in the Middle East and in Egypt. As a theologian he became well-known, particularly through his book, entitled *The Doctrine of the Church and Reunion*. It was published just before the 1920 Lambeth Conference, and it became a kind of Reference Book for the issuing of this Conference's Ecumenical Appeal. Headlam's book was a thorough and learned thesis of systematic theology on the nature of the Church and the basis for church unity. At the same time it must be said that it has a very simple message: to present the Anglican position as obviously the best and most suitable for the achievement of church unity.

Headlam's own ecumenical programme was directly adapted to the Lambeth Quadrilateral. In order to begin the process towards reunification, it was not, he argued, necessary to go deeper into the first three points than what was stated in the formula. Instead the starting point was the issue of the historic episcopate. He also argued that what had been lacking in 'succession' in the past need not block its reinstatement. Nor should the 'validity' of all ecclesiastical acts be condemned, for instance in the British Free Churches. It was future unity, with bishops in historic succession, that mattered. This was a clear, unambiguous approach, which Headlam was to employ in his contacts with the Nordic and Baltic churches. 'For him it was all perfectly clear and simple' is a remark made about Headlam's ecumenical view (Ronald Jasper, *A.C. Headlam*, 1960). One could say that both the strength and the weakness of his programme lay precisely in this simplicity.

Nathan Söderblom organized the official reply from the Swedish bishops to the letter to the Church of Sweden from the Lambeth Conference. The House of Bishops had, for a couple of decades earlier, become the recognized highest ecclesiastical authority, even though this position was not enshrined in law. The letter that was sent to the Anglican bishops' conference was described by Söderblom as a 'Document on the Question of Intercommunion with the Church of England'. (It was published in *Kyrkohistorisk årsskrift*, The Annual Year Book of Church History, 1923). Strictly speaking, the question concerned not just the Church of England, but all the Anglican churches, and the Lambeth Conference was no more a body with juridical authority than the Swedish Bishops' Conference was.

Binding decisions for the Church of England had therefore, long afterwards, to be taken in the Convocations of the Provinces of Canterbury and York.

The official Swedish reply to the question of 'intercommunion' with the Anglicans is rightly famous and has been regarded as a statement of almost equal status to the confessional documents. The main author was Bishop Einar Billing. In addition to him, Söderblom had made a contribution, and the church historian Professor Knut B. Westman was the third contributor. As an immediate reply to the recommendation on 'intercommunion' by the Lambeth Conference, the Swedish statement is very positive. There could be no hindrance for members admitted to Holy Communion in the Anglican Church to receive communion also in the Church of Sweden. They were also prepared to give permission, 'on suitable occasions', to Anglican priests to preach and administer the sacraments in the Church of Sweden's churches. The particular questions which were debated in Uppsala in 1909 on the diaconate and on confirmation are touched on again, this time as an explanation and a defence of the legitimacy of the tradition of the Church of Sweden.

The main interest is, however, in presenting what were, for a Lutheran Church, the central points, the decisive importance of Scripture and the utterly crucial point about the grace of God: 'God's preventing and unconditional unmerited grace, preceding all human work and independent thereof'. It is this grace of God that Scripture proclaims, and to which the Creeds and confessions of the Church, throughout time, testify. What has previously been observed about the leading Swedish theologians at this time is here clearly expressed, their free stance with regard both to the Bible as a book and to the Lutheran confessional documents. The pivotal point is the emphasis on God's grace. Taking that as the starting-point, the letter from the Swedish bishops also rejects certain aspects of various ecclesiastical traditions, by implication including the

Anglican tradition, namely the tendency to such a stress on moral living as might obscure the unmerited grace (probably against puritanism), and also the tendency to make absolute certain institutional elements, for example a particular form of the ordained ministry of the Church; this was an expression of the greater freedom which had always prevailed in Lutheranism: every shape of the ministry of the Church must be acceptable, as long as it proved itself able to 'serve the Gospel and to bring God's revelation to the people'. At the same time they were anxious to state their high appreciation of the tradition of episcopacy and priesthood which had been kept in the Church of Sweden as well as in the Anglican churches. (Without, however, necessarily making the distinction between episcopacy and priesthood which was customary among the Anglicans.)

Remembering the critical judgements made throughout many centuries on the Church of England by, among others the Swedish Lutherans, it is quite remarkable that nothing was said on this occasion about the continuation of Calvinism in Anglicanism. The only indication of a reference to Calvinism is the point made that there are different interpretations of the Eucharist current within Anglicanism. The writers seem to be satisfied by the fact that the faith in the real presence of Christ is also represented. This interpretation had of course, with the advance of the new high church movement in Anglicanism, become more and more prevalent.

In summary, it may be said that the answer by the Swedish Bishops' Conference to the Lambeth Conference was marked, not only by openness, but also by a significant independent stance. Great joy and delight was expressed about the closer relations and deeper communion between the Church of Sweden and the Anglicans, as well as a grateful awareness of the special tradition of the Church of Sweden in its unbroken continuity with the common tradition of Christendom as a whole. At the same time there was nothing in this reply that implied a rejection of other

Lutherans, neither with regard to the emphasis on Scripture and on God's unmerited grace, nor to the question of 'apostolic succession' in the ordained ministry of the Church.

The chancel of Stavanger Cathedral, Norway. Built towards the end of the 13th century, its architecture clearly expresses an influence from England. *Photograph: The Archaeological Museum, Stavanger.*

CHAPTER 11

The Nordic Perspective

The various peace treaties at the end of the First World War were of considerable importance for the Nordic nations. Denmark was given back from Germany that part of Schleswig where the majority of the population were Danish-speaking. The sovereignty of Iceland as an independent state was recognized in 1918, although it remained in union with Denmark right up until 1944. Finland gained independence from Russia, and – after a short but bloody civil war – an independent republic was formed. This was to have two official languages, Finnish and Swedish, and two established 'state' churches, the Lutheran and the Orthodox. Finland's participation in the Nordic community was taken for granted. Its cultural and religious history of belonging together with Sweden for thousands of years was, of course, impelling. Norway was an independent state from the early years of the twentieth century, its union with Sweden having been dissolved in 1905.

In addition, the Baltic states regained their freedom from Russia and the Soviet Union. Estonia and Latvia especially were, for many reasons, soon to be counted among the community of the Nordic peoples. Lithuania as well, even though its geography and culture are rather different, bordering as it does the former East-Prussia (now part of Poland) and having a primarily Roman Catholic religious tradition, may be considered part of the Nordic-Baltic area. In the period between the wars, the Nordic national churches, particularly those of Sweden and Finland, made contacts with the protestant Churches in the Baltic States. The Church of England too, soon showed an interest in extending to the Lutheran Churches in the Baltic

States the move towards greater unity which had begun so well in relation to the Church of Sweden.

Nordic co-operation intensified soon after the end of the First World War. *Föreningen Norden* (The Nordic Association), which was formed in 1919, was an expression of the greater sense of belonging together which was soon to become evident in the Nordic churches as well. Nathan Söderblom wrote an article on this in 1920, for the first Year Book of the Nordic Association. Interest in Nordic ecclesiastical co-operation came from Denmark as well, where the initiative was taken by Bishop Harald Ostenfeld (1864–1934), first Bishop of Zealand and then, from 1923, Bishop of Copenhagen. Besides Ostenfeld, the Bishop of Haderslev in the recently regained South of Jutland, Valdemar Ammundsen, was also a keen supporter of Nordic co-operation. Theologically, they both held a position similar to that of Söderblom, with whom they collaborated on ecumenical issues. Nathan Söderblom was, however, the obvious leader, right from the beginning.

THE NORDIC BISHOPS' CONFERENCE

The Nordic Bishops' Conference, initiated by Söderblom in 1919, became the most important body for co-operation between the Nordic national churches. Reactions in the various Nordic countries were mainly positive, except in Finland where the Church rejected the idea. The reason for this was the strong antipathy of the Archbishop of the Finnish Church, Gustav Johansson (1844–1930), towards his Swedish counterpart. Johansson was a conservative church leader, steeped in orthodox-pietistic conservatism and with a theological outlook determined by German biblicism. In his eyes, Söderblom, with his openness and a position halfway towards liberal theology, was a real danger to Nordic Lutheranism. Right through the 1920s, Johansson blocked, as far as he was able, every attempt at collabor-

246

ation with the Church of Sweden. He even went as far as to 'forbid' Söderblom to visit Finland. Nevertheless, Söderblom had a friend amongst the Finnish episcopate in the ecumenically minded Jakko Gummerus (1870—1933), church historian and Bishop first of Porvoo and later of Tampere.

Söderblom took it for granted that it was the bishops who should lead the Nordic communion of churches. For him, it was precisely from the Nordic Bishops' Conference that a wide and far-reaching ecumenical vision emerged. Through it, the Nordic churches would make a strategically important unit in Christendom. Right from the beginning, there were plans to invite bishops from Estonia and Latvia as well. When the Bishop of Oslo, Johan Lunde, wondered whether the President of the Norwegian–American Synod might also be invited, Söderblom immediately wanted to extend that idea to include also the other Nordic churches in the USA.

Nothing came of this, but their ambitions were great; already in conjunction with the first Nordic Bishops' Conference, the press made comparisons between this Nordic meeting and the Lambeth Conference. Söderblom clearly had something like that in mind. He even spoke of the three great centres of Christianity besides Rome, namely Constantinople, Canterbury and Uppsala. Uppsala should lead the North European block, which he called *corpus evangelicorum*, a terminology used in Swedish history in the context of Gustav II Adolf's plans following his victory over the Emperor at the battle of Breitenfeld. Quite apart from such global perspectives, the Nordic Bishops' Conference was a useful and much-needed institution. It's meetings provided a forum for discussion, not only of theological developments, but also of many other issues in Church and society which were common to all the Nordic countries.

247

Nathan Söderblom's 'ecumenical' cope, Uppsala Cathedral, Sweden. This cope of violet silk was made at the Licium studio, Stockholm, in accordance with Söderblom's detailed instructions. In a letter to the textile artist Agnes Branting (26th September 1924) he expressed his wish for 'a symbol of our endeavours towards unity – so that at the top, there will be some form of the Orb of St Erik with its Cross; and underneath, across the chest, the Luther Rose, flanked on the one side by the Canterbury Cross, and on the other, by the Constantinople Image of our Saviour'. The Orb of St Erik symbolizes Uppsala as the North-European centre of the Church. 'On each side are placed the two other centres of the Church, Constantinople and Canterbury', reads another letter to Agnes Branting. 'On a broad middle line lie Rome (Geneva), Wittenberg and Upsala.' The key of St Peter, symbolizing Rome, can be seen furthest down, below the symbols of Uppsala and Wittenberg. (Quotations from Inger Estham in *Uppsala Domkyrka*, ed. Öyvind Sjöholm, 1982.) *Photograph: ATA.*
after 'Budstikken'.

248

TOWARDS A WIDER EPISCOPAL COMMUNION

Against the background of the Anglican–Swedish agreements on inter-communion on the basis of the historic espicopate, it was easy to conceive of a corresponding relationship with several other Nordic churches as well. The letter from the 1920 Lambeth Conference to the Church of Sweden made it clear that the Anglicans were no less sympathetic towards the other Scandinavian churches, but that, due to 'different problems' (e.g. the loss of succession), the time was not yet right to enter into dialogue with them. Even so, they were already part of the longterm plans.

Was it possible that anything could be done about these 'different problems' in the other Nordic churches? The thought arose in view of an episcopal consecration in Copenhagen Cathedral in 1921, at which Ostenfeld was due to officiate. Ostenfeld suggested that, as a manifestation of Nordic collaboration, both Söderblom and the Bishop of Oslo might be invited to participate. This suggestion immediately met fierce criticism: the Swedish Archbishop ought not to be allowed to participate; it might cause a split in the Danish Church if one of its bishops were drawn into the Swedish succession. Among the keenest opponents was the professor of church history, J. Oskar Andersen. Many arguments were proffered: the doctrine of apostolic succession was 'un-evangelical', the Danes might be forced into the re-unification efforts of the Anglicans, etc. Ostenfeld thought it wisest to withdraw his suggestion, and he never repeated it at subsequent episcopal consecrations in Copenhagen.

But Nathan Söderblom was to make an important contribution to episcopal consecrations in the Lutheran churches in Estonia and Latvia instead. Even before Estonia's independence, in the period of the freedom fighters, Söderblom was actively engaged in making contacts, although the German occupation put a stop to that. In 1921 he was invited to officiate at the consecration of

249

the first Lutheran Bishop of Tallin/Reval, J. Kukk. Both parties, the Estonians as well as Söderblom, were well aware of the historical bonds which made the invitation to the Swedish Archbishop appropriate on this occasion. For centuries, Estonia had been an integral part of the Swedish dominion around the Baltic Sea, and the character of the Estonian national church had been formed in the sixteenth and seventeenth centuries, during the Swedish 'Great Power' period. Söderblom's grand vision of church unity always included historical memories as an important component. As a Swedish nationalist, he found such remembrances inspirational, even a binding obligation. During his visits to Estonia and Latvia, the memories of Swedish history from the period of Sweden's *Dominium maris Baltici* were always alive in his mind. He did not come as a foreigner, he used to say; he did not report these trips as 'official foreign visits', because he went as the Archbishop in the old Swedish ecclesial provinces. In this way he provided a very great service to the Lutheran churches in these newly created states. They were grateful for the support of their western neighbour. The past came alive and was made relevant. They were included in an ecclesial community wider than just their own nation. At the episcopal consecration in Reval, Söderblom was assisted by Bishop Gummerus of the Finnish Church. This was of no less importance, as the Estonians acknowledged both cultural and linguistic kinship with the Finns.

In the following year, 1922, Söderblom also officiated at the consecration of a bishop in Riga, the capital of Latvia. Here the historical memories were no less tangible, centered mainly around the Swedish hero, King Gustav II Adolf. Söderblom had brought with him a picture of Gustav Adolf, which he presented to the Latvian Lutheran Church. In other aspects, the situation was more complicated in Latvia. The population was to a greater extent German, and consequently there was a large German Lutheran Church alongside the Latvian one. A prominent church leader, Karlis Irbe, had been appointed as Bishop of the Latvian Lutheran Church, and Söderblom included him in his great plans for a Lutheran–Episcopal block under Swedish leadership. To mark the special position of the Latvian Lutheran Church, and to stress that this, and not the church of the Germans, was the 'national church', Söderblom – during the consecration-service – gave the title 'Archbishop' to Bishop Irbe. The indigenous church itself had made no decision about this; Söderblom acted on his own initiative, inspired by the historical moment. This intervention, in a church other than his own, has been called 'unconventional' even by an author otherwise completely congenial with Söderblom's ecumenism. (Bengt Sundkler, *Nathan Söderblom. His life and work*, 1968).

The Baltic episcopal sees are today, as they were in the 1920s and 1930s, an important basis for ecumenical fellowship, with both the Nordic and the Anglican churches. For Söderblom himself, it was of great important that he was able to hand on the historic episcopate to the churches of Estonia and Latvia. In his view, the apostolic succession of the Swedish episcopate was an important instrument in furthering communion – in the long term between *all* the Lutheran and Anglican Churches throughout the world.

Without a doubt Söderblom, with a deep sense of vocation, made use of every opportunity to move further towards this goal. He felt that, given his position and all his useful contacts, he had unique opportunities to build bridges between these two church families. Even so, his actions on episcopal consecrations outside the Church of Sweden were, on some occasions, not very considerate, and in some cases this gave the apostolic succession a 'bad name'. An example of this was Söderblom's initiative to force – as one must acknowledge that, in fact, he did – episcopacy with Swedish succession on the Lutheran Church of South India. He was unstoppable, in spite of both the extended opposition on the part of the church itself and of the repeated protests from the German missionary society, which for generations had built up this Indian church. Equally strange was his sudden idea during the consecration of a bishop in Uppsala Cathedral, when in the sacristy immediately beforehand he asked the visiting leader of the Lutheran Church of Slovakia if he would be prepared to kneel beside the new Swedish bishop to receive 'a blessing'. The guest from Slovakia was rather surprised, but gratefully accepted, without an inkling that, in a few moments, he would find himself consecrated a bishop within the apostolic succession. Not only he himself, but also his church, was caught completely unawares. There were, of course, many who wondered about the meaning of such an ordination without any foundation or intention whatsoever in the receiving church itself. One might also ask if this action was not the complete opposite of what the Swedish College of Bishops had written in its reply to Lambeth in 1922, in which they said that they wanted to respect every form of ministry, as long as it served the Gospel.

A STRATEGIC PLAN FOR THE NORDIC CHURCHES: HEADLAM AND SÖDERBLOM

In spite of Söderblom's often impulsive enthusiasm, his numerous and fearless initiatives certainly contributed greatly towards bringing many churches out of their national and confessional isolation. There is no need here to describe his greatest and most famous work, his appeals for peace and reconciliation during and after the First World War, and the 'Meeting of Christendom' in Stockholm in 1925. His many efforts to bring Anglicanism and Lutheranism in Europe closer together ran parallel with all this work. Much of it was never put into practice during his life-time, but he nevertheless continued tirelessly. One example is his attempt to encourage observers from the Church of England to attend the various conferences of the Lutheran World Convention held in Germany. Another attempt was to gather Anglican and Lutheran theologians

252

for a conference in the Wartburg; it took place, but it was not very successful. Bitter memories of the war proved to be great obstacles.

The continued work of bridge-building between the Church of England and the Nordic and Baltic parts of Europe's Lutheran churches seemed all the more important. And for this, there was just as much interest among church leaders in England as on the part of Söderblom and other ecumenically-minded bishops and theologians in the Nordic churches.

Arthur Cayley Headlam now accepted the main responsibility for this work on behalf of the English bishops, and he continued with it for many years. In 1927 he travelled extensively in Denmark, Sweden and Finland. He lectured at the University of Copenhagen, and he engaged in many conversations with old and new friends. Not formal talks with the purpose of bringing the Church of England and the Danish National Church closer together, which was at the moment without prospect, but personal conversations. These contacts were deep and lasting, especially with Bishop Harald Ostenfeld and Bishop Valdemar Ammundsen, and also with a 'sognepraest' (parish priest), who later became the Bishop of Aarhus, Skat Hoffmeyer, and who was a keen anglophile. Headlam felt very much at home in Denmark, and his impression was that interest in England was greater there than in any of the other Nordic countries.

Nathan Söderblom was his host in Sweden, and he had also arranged for Headlam to give a series of lectures at the University of Uppsala. Hospitality in the Archbishop's Palace was, as usual, a splendid affair. Headlam sent a detailed report to Davidson, including the seating-plan at the great dinner party which Söderblom gave in his honour. On that occasion Headlam met the English Ambassador, ecclesiastical dignitaries, Nobel prizewinners and other scientists. At the bottom of the table was a young man, Dag Hammarskjöld, the son of the Crown Constable (*Landshövding*) of Uppsala.

On the occasion of the restoration in 1925 of the diocese of Stavanger, Norway, the local newspaper imagined what an episcopal procession might have looked like 800 years earlier. This was the result, featuring the first bishop of Stavanger, Swithun of Winchester. *Photograph: The Archaeological Museum, Stavanger; after 'Budstikken'*.

An important aspect of Headlam's conversations with Söderblom touched on the plans for the incorporation of the Lutheran Church of Finland into the Anglo-Scandinavian community. Preparations for Headlam's visits to Finland were made by Söderblom's son-in-law, Yngve Brilioth, who was Professor of Church History at the Swedish-speaking Academy of Turku at the time. The purpose was to reinstate the historic episcopate in the Lutheran Church of Finland. For almost a millenium, the Church of Finland had been an integral part of the Church of Sweden with bishops in the Swedish succession, but, at the time that Finland was conquered and made a duchy under the Tsar of Russia, contacts with the Church of Sweden were broken off. Very strangely, in 1884 it so happened that all the bishops of Finland died in the same year, and those who were appointed to replace them were consecrated not by a bishop, but by a professor of theology. Many of them had hoped for an officiating bishop from Sweden, but due to political circumstances this proved impossible. Suddenly, the Church of Finland had lost its succession. Even so, the situation was unlike the circumstances which had emerged in the Churches of Denmark, Norway and Iceland at the Reformation. The Church of Finland had kept its episcopal succession for centuries, and the break in tradition had come completely unprovoked, due to very special circumstances. In the 1920s, since the country had regained its independence, there was increasing interest in many areas in restoring contacts with the West. Headlam therefore met a positive interest in his plans for what he, using English terminology, called a 'reunion'. He had useful conversations with Söderblom's friend and supporter Bishop Gummerus in Tampere, and with him two younger men, who were soon to become well known, Erki Kaila, Bishop of Viipuri (and Archbishop from 1935) and Aleksi Lehtonen, who succeeded Gummerus as Bishop of Tampere and became Archbishop in 1945. Continued specific talks on ecumenical issues had to be postponed, however. The Archbishop of the Finnish Church was still the old man Gustav Johansson,

255

the staunch opponent of anything to do with Söderblom and his ecumenical endeavours.

All in all, Headlam's Nordic trip was very successful, and he gained much experience which proved useful in future relations with the churches in the Nordic countries. The same year, 1927, saw another success in Anglo–Scandinavian ecumenism. For the first time, a bishop of the Church of Sweden, Ernst Lönegren, who was Bishop of Härnösand, was invited to participate in the consecration of a bishop in Canterbury Cathedral. The appointment of Lönegren was made by Söderblom, following an invitation from Davidson. The agreement at Lambeth in 1920 and the letter from the Swedish Bishops in 1922 had thereby been mutually and fully adopted in practice. It ought to be said that, without Söderblom's perseverance and, it should also be stressed, the courage and decisiveness of Davidson, this would probably not have been achieved. Among the Davidson Papers at Lambeth Palace Library, under the heading 'Sweden', there is a large collection of fierce protests which were sent to him because of the Swedish participation in the consecration in Canterbury. Much of it consists of cuttings from the *Church Times*, which, at this time, was dominated by the Anglo–Catholic wing of the Church. No invectives were spared on the Church of Sweden; this 'Lutheran sect', with its 'crude doctrine of justification by faith'. Appeals were made to the Archbishop to stop this 'catastrophe' and not have anything to do with this 'betrayal' of the Anglican churches.

HEADLAM, RODHE AND BELL

At the 1930 Lambeth Conference, the issue of the Nordic churches and the Anglicans was taken a step further. The Church of Sweden had been invited to send a representative, whose task was primarily to take part in a committee on reunion. Söderblom, who was unable to go himself because of ill-health, sent instead the Bishop of Lund,

Edward Rodhe, who five years previously had succeeded his father-in-law, Gottfrid Billing, on the ancient and venerable episcopal throne of Lund. Rodhe had visited England on several occasions, including as a member of the 1914 delegation to Lambeth and Canterbury. Headlam was the chairman of the Committee on Reunion, and among the Anglican participants the Bishop of Chichester, George Bell (1883–1953), was particularly noticeable. His knowledge of ecumenical issues was outstanding, not least due to his work as editor of *Documents on Christian Unity*, a series of several volumes of ecumenical documents from various conferences. He had great admiration and affection for Söderblom, whom he had met at an ecumenical conference in Holland just after the War. Rodhe visited Bell at Chichester before the Lambeth Conference, and together they made plans for the work in the committee. Söderblom had sent his suggestion that the Finnish Church should be high on the agenda.

Bishop Rodhe made a strong contribution to this Lambeth Conference; looked at from the perspective of present ecumenical thinking, his statements seem remarkably luminous and forward-looking. (Minutes of the discussions are in the Bell Papers in Lambeth Palace Library.) Rodhe argued that the privileged position according to the Church of Sweden ought to apply to all the Nordic churches. He wanted the Anglicans to understand how strong this desire was on the part of the Church of Sweden. Because of the close and deep community among the Nordic churches themselves, this difference in relation to the Anglicans was very embarrassing. The Church of Sweden had most certainly valued its historic succession, but in its view, there was no great difference on this point between the Church of Sweden and the Church of Denmark. Rodhe wanted the Anglicans to know that the Danish Church was indeed 'established', also in terms of episcopacy. The Danish Church had always been able to show its ministerial succession very clearly, a 'succession of office'. That had never been broken, the Danish Church had always had bishops, and it had in fact been very strict with regard to its organisation.

Rodhe argued that it was highly desirable to incorporate the Danish Church (and the Norwegian and Icelandic Churches as well) in the same tradition of succession as that of the Anglican and Swedish Churches. He knew, for instance, that Bishop Ostenfeld was in support of this, even though his suggestion of Swedish participation in a consecration of a Bishop in Copenhagen had been opposed. Rodhe could well understand why this suggestion had met such strong opposition. It was regarded as a disqualification of the Danish Church and its way of life for the last four hundred years. If only the Anglicans would not press the issue of episcopal consecration quite so hard, it would be much easier to reach an agreement. The Danes found it both hurtful and paradoxical that the Anglicans, who had such high appreciation of the continuity in the history of the Church, wanted to discredit the 'holy history' of the Danish Church.

The situation in the Finnish Church was different. A common history with Sweden, including the same episcopal tradition, had prevailed for hundreds of years. It would therefore probably be reasonably easy to re-establish the historic episcopate, as it was so much a part of the history of the country. It would therefore be expedient to begin with Finland. Rodhe and Bell were in full agreement: Finland was the key to the situation. Then the discussion with the Danes and the other Nordic churches could begin. It was however necessary to wait for a change of Archbishop in Turku.

Headlam agreed with this plan, and on that basis the Committee took its decision. Headlam wrote a letter to Rodhe after the Conference, in which he thanked him and also told him of the remarkable coincidence, that the same day that this decision was taken at Lambeth, the old Archbishop of Turku had died. (The Rodhe Papers, Lund University Library). Headlam could therefore proceed with the Nordic issue without any obstacles.

258

For many years in the early 1930s deep discussions were held between an Anglican and a Finnish delegation, with on the one hand Headlam as chairman and, on the other, first Gummerus and then, after his death, Aleksi Lehtonen. Any real difficulties to overcome did not emerge. Relations with the Finnish Church were regulated in a roughly similar way to relations with the Church of Sweden. Succession was restored again when Lehtonen was consecrated bishop in Tampere in 1934, where the Swedish Archbishop Erling Eidem, Söderblom's successor, assisted in the laying on of hands. From both the Finnish and the Swedish side, it was emphasized that his participation was motivated by the fact that these two sister churches, after centuries of unity, must quite obviously be allowed to manifest their unity again. From the Nordic point of view, this did not imply any change in status or authority of the Finnish episcopal ministry. An undertaking was also made that from now on, without exception, priests in the Church of Finland would be ordained by a bishop. (The practice at priestly ordinations had varied from the nineteenth century onwards.)

Difficulties only emerged when the subject was discussed in the Church of England. This time the strict legal course was followed from the start, which meant that any decisions on the matter must be taken in the Convocations. The Anglo-Catholic wing had grown stronger in the last decade. Headlam had some difficulty in gaining support for the form of ministerial and sacramental fellowship that had been agreed in the Anglican–Finnish talks, but he was able to refer to the recommendations of the last two Lambeth Conferences, and so the motion was passed. It was followed by strong criticism in the *Church Times*.

No official talks with the remaining three Nordic churches were entered into during the 1930s. Headlam continued his ecumenical project by contacting the Lutheran churches in Estonia and Latvia. His trip to those countries provided a personal satisfaction, as he had Estonian blood in his ancestry. (Headlam belonged to an ancient family, and he was the owner of an inherited mansion in the north of England. He counted Tsar Peter, who had had an affair with an Estonian lady, among his ancestors.) His conversations in Tallinn and Riga were however, not as successful as those with the Finnish Church. Both these Baltic churches certainly possessed the historic episcopate, which Nathan Söderblom had made sure of, but they did not fully draw the consequences of ensuring that all priests were ordained by bishops. However, friendly relations had begun between the Baltic and the Anglican churches, and new discussions could be held very successfully in the new situation in the 1990s.

INCREASED FELLOWSHIP IN THEOLOGY AND CHURCH LIFE

Both English and Swedish church leaders had continued to work energetically on their plans towards the integration of yet more churches in the Nordic–Baltic area into their respective ecclesial communion. Strangely enough, these efforts had not, to begin with, been accompanied by any theological exchange of any depth. Those who led the discussions were certainly theologically well qualified, but they knew little about each other's theological positions. Lutheran and Anglican theology had developed along different lines for quite a long time. With a risk of oversimplification, one could say that Lutheran theology had concentrated on 'soteriological' issues (i.e. on issues about reconciliation and the salvation of the individual) while Anglicans had focused on social-ethical problems and on issues of ecclesiology, ministry and sacraments. The only area which was immediately accessible to mutual collaboration was the subject of biblical exegesis.

It is also remarkable that two such eminent men as Headlam and Bell, who were to expend so much work on ecumenical contacts with the Lutheran churches (in Bell's case also on Continental Lutheranism) were in fact not very interested at all in Lutheran theology. In the same way,

260

there were exceptionally few among the Nordic church leaders whose knowledge of Anglican theology was more than elementary; their theological contacts were still, during the period between the wars, mainly with Germany. Yngve Brilioth was one of a few shining exceptions. His work on the Oxford Movement, *The Anglican Revival*, (published in Swedish in 1921–23, and in English in 1925) has attracted much attention, and is still considered as authoritative. In 1925 he published his great work on the Eucharist, a review of eucharistic theology and the shape of the Mass from the early Church onwards, with a detailed analysis of the variance between the major ecclesial traditions, including that of Anglicanism. This work won international acclaim. It was widely read and has influenced liturgical developments in a number of different churches (English edition: *Eucharistic Faith and Practice*, 1930).

In order to bridge the gap between Anglican and Lutheran theology, an institution was created in 1929 which has proved to be surprisingly able to survive: the Anglo–Scandinavian Theological Conference. A limited number of about twenty members, chosen from among theologians and church leaders from the Church of England and the four Scandinavian countries (in the 1930s, and again in the present, also including delegates from Estonia and Latvia, though seldom from Iceland) have met regularly ever since, usually every second year, for about a week. The initiator of the first of these continuing conferences was the then Professor of Systematic Theology in Lund, Gustaf Aulén. He, together with G. E. Newsom, Master of Selwyn College, Cambridge, arranged for the first conference to be held there in 1929. (In 1967 the conference was again held in a Cambridge College, this time with Aulén, at the age of almost 90 but still very active and productive, as one of the lecturers. On that occasion he was greeted by Archbishop Michael Ramsey as 'our young and promising theologian from Sweden'!). Among the Anglican theologians present at this first conference, Canon Oliver Quick deserves a mention. Besides Aulén, those present included

Brilioth, Professor Arvid Runestam from Uppsala and the Bishop of Viipuri, Erkki Kaila. At the following conference (1931) Professor Anders Nygren from Lund presented a first draft of his famous work *Den kristna kärlekstanken genom tiderna. Eros and Agape*, (The Christian Concept of Love. Eros and Agape).

As it happened, Nordic Lutheran theology had developed in a way that made it easier for the Anglicans to understand than the older Lutheranism. Aulén regarded the doctrine of redemption as the early Church did – more as a drama of salvation than as a legal process. Modern Lutheran research had gone behind the pietistic, individualistic interpretations of salvation and of the Church. It had also been discovered that Luther was close to patristic theology, particularly to the thought of the Greek Fathers. This aroused great interest among the Anglicans.

The Nordic theologians were introduced to the emphasis, characteristic for English theology, on the Incarnation. The tradition of the 'Christian Socialists' united the inheritance from Tractarianism with the social 'revival'. The Anglo-Catholic Bishop of Oxford, Charles Gore (editor of a collection of essays entitled *Lux Mundi, A series of Studies in the Religion of the Incarnation*), was the leading light behind this theological line. Gore did not take part himself in the conference with the Lutherans. Anglo-Catholics were seldom represented. But incarnational theology was conceived by the Nordic delegates as a useful challenge to Lutheran theology. The roots of English theology among the Eastern Fathers was also more and more appreciated by the Nordic theologians. Both Danish and Norwegian theologians were working on the Fathers: in Denmark Hal Koch and in Norway Einar Molland, the latter a very active participant in several Anglo–Scandinavian Conferences. (Hal Koch produced a doctoral thesis in 1932 on Origen, while Einar Molland's doctoral thesis in 1938 was entitled *The Conception of the Gospel in Alexandrian theology*).

The Anglo–Scandinavian Conferences have, in principle, chosen to lie low on publicity, and they have never worked on the basis of any common statements. The advantage was that the conversations could be both relaxed and honest. In a small group of limited numbers it was also possible to get to know each other better. Gradually, these conferences have built mutual understanding and many deep friendships. Tangible results have been shown, particularly in reviews and sometimes in translations of each other's books. A tremendous contribution as a translator was made by Arthur Gabriel Hebert, who began to participate in these conferences in 1931. Fr Gabriel Hebert was a member of the Anglican religious order of the Society of the Sacred Mission (Kelham), and he was one of the few Anglo-Catholics in the group. (A biography of Hebert's life and work was published by Christopher Irvine in 1993). These translations were such an important work of bridge-building between Nordic and English theology that they deserve a listing: Brilioth's book on the Eucharist (1930); the English edition of Aulén's book on Redemption, entitled *Christus Victor* (1931) was spread throughout the world; Nygren's *Eros and Agape*, vol I, 1932, and Söderblom's sermons on the Passion, under the English title *The Mystery of the Cross* (1933). For Hebert himself, the most important was Brilioth's book on the Eucharist, which bore fruit in his own works on liturgical issues. These works were mutually inspirational, encouraging a eucharistic revival in both Swedish and English church life, – but more on this further on.

At this time English theology was considered fairly insular, even by the English themselves. The fact that at least some of the Nordic theological literature was translated into English was certainly not without importance, even though the influence of these works could never be compared to those which, ever since the 1920s, began to appear from the Continent and from the USA, works by Barth, Bultmann, Brunner, Tillich, Bonhoeffer and Reinhold Neibuhr.

The 1931 Anglo–Scandinavian Conference was held in Sweden, at the country manor of Sparreholm. Nathan Söderblom, who had prepared a large part of the programme for the English guests, also made a visit to the Conference. He was very ill, and his condition worsened during the Conference; he died while the English guests were still in the country. Thus his concern for the Anglo–Scandinavian Conference became his last ecumenical contribution, and this made a deep and lasting impression on the delegates. Gabriel Hebert is one of those who have described the experience. The Conference delegates were all present at Söderblom's funeral service.

The Church of England participants in these conferences were mostly from the large 'middle-of-the-road' persuasion in theology and churchmanship. It was only occasionally that the high church and the evangelical wings were represented. Oliver Quick (1885–1944), a considerable theological writer, has already been mentioned. His book *The Christian Sacraments* (1927) had made an impression on the Nordic Lutherans at the first Theological Conference. That book cleared up a number of old misconceptions about Anglican theology and stimulated discussion on the Church and the sacraments, which, not least for the Swedes, were current issues at this time. Besides Quick, the Bishop of Southwark, R. G. Parsons (1882–1948), well-known for his doctrinal works but also for his deep interest in contemporary social issues, was a faithful attender. There was a deliberate continuity in the group on both sides, and in time, mutual understanding of each other's tradition and ways of thinking was greatly increased.

Luther was not well known in England, nor particularly appreciated. Especially with the Tractarians, Lutheranism had always had a low profile. Political allusions also played a part. In the 1930s and during the Second World War, there were English theologians who drew a malicious parallel between Luther and Hitler. It was consequently all the more important that these serious theological conferences took place, at which the most prominent experts in theological research on Luther were represented, and that they came not from Germany but from Scandinavia. And there were certainly eminent Lutheran scholars available. Arvid

Runestam and Anders Nygren took part from the beginning, and following them, Professor Ragnar Bring from Lund and Professor Regin Prenter from Aarhus became regular members.

There was perhaps a risk of too much concentration on Luther, of his becoming an absolute authority. The eventual move away from using the lectures as presentations of the respective traditions to considerations of common themes was therefore a helpful development, which also represents both an academic and an ecumenical achievement. It was no longer necessary to introduce oneself, nor to make mutual comparisons, but it was possible instead to discuss common issues. It should also be stressed that throughout all this period, from the 1920s onwards, the Nordic participation has if possible always been drawn from all the Nordic churches together, and also from the Baltic churches. No distinction within this Lutheran group has ever been made in respect of the doctrine on ministry and succession. It has always been taken for granted that the celebrations of the Eucharist during the Conference were open to everybody. And there has been a consistent view towards the Nordic churches as a whole. In this way a fount of knowledge and mutual confidence has been built up as a useful preparation for the official ecumenical dialogues between the Anglican, Nordic and Baltic churches.

COMMON PROBLEMS

The national churches have met ever greater challenges. This was particularly evident in the 1920s for both the Church of England and the Nordic churches, not least for the Church of Sweden. Active interest in the national Church declined more and more among large groups of the population. In the Nordic countries, the Workers' Movement took a negative attitude towards the Church; but in England the Labour Movement and the churches, both the Church of England and the Free Churches, had better relations. Nathan Söderblom tried, sometimes successfully, to win sympathy among the leaders of the Workers' Movement. A clever move was to make a socialist writer, Fabian Månsson, a member of the Committee which was working on a new hymnal for the Church of Sweden.

Otherwise, the matter of the hymnal proved problematic for Söderblom. He had expended great efforts on getting a new hymnal to replace the official hymnal of 1819. The Government, however, rejected the proposal. (As a compromise, an addition to the old hymnal was agreed instead.) This raised the issue of the authority of the State over the internal church matters, and thus the whole issue of Church–State relations was again on the table. The Church of Sweden did of course have its own representation in the form of the Church Assembly, but the authority of this body was much more limited than its present equivalent, and did not include the final decision on the Church's official liturgical books. The Church of England experienced a similar set-back in 1928. In that year Parliament rejected a motion for a new version of the Book of Common Prayer. Davidson moved the proposal in the House of Lords, where it was accepted, but the House of Commons rejected it. For Davidson this was a keenly felt disappointment, and it raised the question of Church and State in England as well.

One aspect of this problem, the matter of membership, has proved more difficult to solve in the Church of Sweden that in the other Nordic countries and in England. Swedish law admitted no withdrawal from membership of the Church of Sweden, except for immediate admittance into membership of another recognized faith-community. Voices within the Church itself found this an unjustified compulsion. The 1929 Bishops' Conference therefore proposed a revision of the law to allow free withdrawal from Church membership; the purpose was to indicate that membership of the Church was not the same as citizenship of the State, but required a 'religious motivation'. Extended religious freedom was however not legalized until 1951.

266

The issue of membership of the Church of Sweden is still a matter of debate, since formal membership can still apply even for the unbaptized, which is of course an anomaly. In England, membership is considered in a different way, but the issues concerning the legal relationship between the national Church and civic society are otherwise fairly similar.

Traditionally, social problems have been the concern of Anglican theologians and Church leaders to a greater extent than of their counterparts in most Protestant denominations. This has proved an interesting experience during the Anglo–Scandinavian Theological Conferences. For several years (until 1963) these Conferences were led by the Bishop of Sheffield, Leslie Hunter, who was well-known as the initiator of the 'industrial mission' in his diocese. Many subjects on the borderline between theology and social ethics were debated in that period, as well as issues like 'A Christian view of Man' and 'The Church and the People'. The application of classic theological themes to these up-to-date issues has been a useful challenge. Biblical exegesis as well as the interpretation of the Fathers, of Luther and of Hooker have stood side by side with contemporary issues. This tradition has continued under the leadership of Bishop Hunter's successors, first Professor Geoffrey Lampe, and after him the present Bishop of Ely, Stephen Sykes, (formerly Regius Professor at Cambridge).

THE ISSUE OF WOMEN PRIESTS

A major issue for the Church, pressing for many and painful for others, depending on their perspective, has been the issue of women priests. It will only be discussed here in so far as it affects the Church of England and the Nordic national churches, and only from one perspective, namely as an aspect of the tension between Church and Society. For years there have been several connections, probably

267

unknown to most people, between this issue and the Anglo
–Scandinavian Theological Conferences.

The timetable for women's ordination to the priesthood
has been very different in the Nordic national churches and
the Church of England. The Danish Church was first, and
the event was fairly undramatic. In the Church of Norway
this reform was based on the change in the law of the land
in 1938, which read: 'Women can, on the same conditions
as men, be appointed to the offices of State' (Kvinner kan
under de samme betingelser som menn ansettes i Statens
embeder). A right of reservation clause (reservasjonsrett)
was however also included in this legal paragraph, which
indicated that those parishes should be respected who for
reasons of principle state their opposition (av principielle
grunner uttaler sig emot). It was not until 1961 that the
first woman was ordained as a priest in the Church of Norway. (In 1993 the first woman bishop was consecrated in
Norway, and in 1995 in Denmark). In Iceland, as in Norway, it was the application of the regulations enshrined in
the law of the land on equal employment opportunities that
led to the same reform in the National Church. The first
woman was ordained as a priest in 1974.

In the Church of Sweden a decision on the matter was
taken in the 1958 Church Assembly (a supportive opinion
in favour of women priests had prevailed in the *Riksdag*
for quite some time), and the first ordinations took place
in 1960. The Church of Finland had a widespread system
of women 'lectors' in the parishes, and even in Finland the
next step of ordaining women to the priesthood was taken,
but not until the 1980s. By that time, the position in the
Church of England had changed. Anglicanism was clearly
divided on this issue. Women were ordained as priests in
several Anglican churches throughout the world, and in
some of them also as bishops. In the Church of England
the first women priests were ordained in 1994.

When the first women priests had been ordained in Denmark, this was noted in an official comment by the Church
of England as a circumstance which added to the difficulties

of making closer contacts between this church and the Anglican churches. A real crisis in mutual relations emerged when the Church of Sweden took its decision. The Church of Sweden was close to being 'in communion' with the Church of England, and because this relationship included ministry and ordinations, i.e. precisely those areas where the new situation might cause complications, the matter was very serious.

In November 1958 the Archbishop of Canterbury, Geoffrey Fisher, wrote a letter to Archbishop Hultgren of Uppsala, in which he in a most diplomatic manner and in a very friendly tone clarified the view of the Church of England on the decision which the Swedish Church Assembly had just taken. He had marked the letter 'Personal and Private' and the content of his letter was therefore not made public either in England or in Sweden. He reported on it to the Convocation of Canterbury, though only in general terms. Fisher expressed his understanding that, for a church so closely bound up with the State, it was only natural that the view of equality in the secular law should also infiltrate into the structures of church order. He was also aware that demands for the ordination of women priests were frequently voiced in the debates of the World Council of Churches. He emphasized that he had no intention of getting involved in the internal affairs of the Church of Sweden, but that he had to express his view in the light of the theological and psychological situation in the Church of England. He was worried that the decision in the Church of Sweden might affect groups in his own country who were anxious to have women priests in the Church of England too; even though he felt that interest in this was not very great in England at that moment. Nor did he think that any move towards the deregulation of the existing 'eucharistic hospitality' between the two churches would be made. He thought that, from now on, in the light of what had happened, it would be best to avoid sending any Church of England bishops to participate in episcopal consecrations in the Church of

Sweden, since this could cause conflicts. He finished with a few lines of assurance that it was because of his brotherly affection for the Archbishop of Uppsala and for the Church of Sweden that he had written this letter in a spirit of total honesty and open discussion. In November the following year an English bishop took part in the consecration of a bishop in Uppsala, but after the first ordination of a woman priest in the Church of Sweden, in the spring of 1960, there was a long gap, right until 1979, before an English bishop again assisted at a Swedish episcopal ordination. (The custom was reinstated on the initiative of Archbishop Olof Sundby and Archbishop Donald Coggan after the statement by the General Synod of the Church of England that, from a theological point of view, there were no 'fundamental objections' to the ordination of women as priests.)

The calm and friendly tone in which Archbishop Fisher communicated with Archbishop Hultgren on this matter contrasts sharply with the strong, sometimes almost hateful, attacks against the Church of Sweden which appeared over these years in the *Church Times* and other English ecclesiastical publications. Strangely enough, most of these contributions do not discuss the matter itself: the conclusion by the Church of Sweden that there was no theological objection to a woman holding office in the Church. It was instead the Church of Sweden as such that was stigmatized as following the lead of the State and as lacking spirituality and life. Against the fact that it was the highest authority of the Church itself, the Church Assembly, that had taken the decision, it was argued that the previous Church Assembly, in 1957, had rejected the decision following a weighty contribution from, among others, Bishop Anders Nygren, the world-famous theologian. In the intervening period widespread propaganda had appeared in the media, and it was, it was argued, under this pressure that the Church of Sweden had changed its view. Such pressure had certainly been exerted, but it did not come from 'the State', unless that term is used for what has sometimes been called 'the third state-power', i.e. the press or

270

the 'public opinion'. Here the dilemma behind the action of the Swedish Church emerged, a dilemma which might be applicable to every national Church in the present time.

It is no less interesting to find, on closer investigation, that the majority of the contributions to English periodicals in fact originated from, or at least were inspired by, Swedish sources. The anger and disappointment of the inner circle of the Swedish opponents of the decision in their own Church was expressed to English readers. There were people in the Church of England who were well informed about the Church of Sweden, and who replied, pointing out that a very black picture was being painted. (Among them was John Toy, nowadays Canon of York Minster, who had studied in Sweden and who was the Secretary to the Anglo–Scandinavian Conferences, and among the bishops, Leslie Hunter, the Bishop of Sheffield.)

It was, of course, the intention of those who published these fierce attacks on the Church of Sweden to prevent every possibility that the step taken in the Swedish Church might encourage the Church of England to follow. But the Swedish writers also had another purpose. In something that looks like total desperation, they wanted to persuade the Church of England to revoke the agreement on intercommunion with the Church of Sweden, which had come about after many years, in order to force the Swedish Church to recognize its 'mistake'. To this end, a Swedish high church priest, Rune Klingert, sent a circular to his English friends, in which he painted a dark picture of the situation in the Church of Sweden, and in which he made this appeal: 'Personally, I think it would be good if the Church of England officially dissociated itself from this decision by withdrawing intercommunion ... The more powerful the reaction in England is, the more help it will be to us'.

The nevertheless fairly harmonious relations between the Church of England and the Church of Sweden after the step which the Church of Sweden took in 1960, were highly dependent on the personal initiative of the leaders of these two churches. Fisher and Hultgren were on very good terms. In his letters to Hultgren, Fisher was able to assure him that he had calmed the opinion in England, and, among other things, had dissuaded an attempt by the clergy in the Convocations to make a negative statement. He also reported that his colleague, the Archbishop of York, Michael Ramsey, shared the same desire that the good relations with the Church of Sweden should continue. The correspondence between Fisher and Hultgren which has been preserved shows that they kept in touch over the decisive period. Hultgren also kept himself informed via the very experienced Rector of the Swedish Church in London, Sven Evander. In the summer of 1959 Hultgren was Fisher's guest in Lambeth before taking part in the Anglo–Scandinavian Conference at Ripon Hall, Oxford. During the Conference a close friendship was started between him and the Chairman of the Conference, Bishop Hunter. This was to prove very useful in the years to follow. Altogether, Gunnar Hultgren was the one person among the Swedish Archbishops in this century who fitted in particularly well among the Church of England episcopate. His friendship with Fisher's successor, Michael Ramsey, was very deep and warm and their differences over ecclesiology took second place.

Ambassador Gunnar Hägglöf, who was the Swedish Ambassador in London for many years, reflects in his book, *Engelska År*, (The English Years, 1974) on the Swedish Archbishops he had met during their visits to England. Having heard Erling Eidem preach in the Swedish Church in London, he commented: 'This was probably the most eloquent and moving address I have ever heard in the Swedish language'. But then he added: 'He (Eidem) was never able to make any real contacts with the English episcopate. Brilioth was, he says, very well known and respected in England, particularly because of his book on the Oxford Movement, but he was 'so introvert and absorbed in his own thoughts and musings that there were

272

Archbishop Gunnar Hultgren and the Archbishop of Canterbury, Michael
Ramsay, in Uppsala Cathedral at the Jubilee in 1964 of the foundation of the
archdiocese. *Photograph: Rein Välme, Stockholm.*

273

too many and too long pauses in the conversation'. Then comes his judgement on Hultgren: 'Brilioth's successor, Gunnar Hultgren, was the man who really found his way to the heart of the English episcopate.' The following comment is also interesting: 'It is a rather special world of its own, this leading group in the Church of England, a church rich in tradition and very self-aware, with branches all around the British Empire and elsewhere as well. Hultgren became a close friend of Dr Michael Ramsay...' Hägglöf finished the paragraph by recalling the splendid dinner conversations he had experienced at Lambeth Palace – 'quite in accordance with what can be heard at the high table in the best colleges in Cambridge or Oxford'.

During the years that the English bishops stayed away from the episcopal consecrations in Uppsala, there were several people who deliberately made frequent use of every opportunity to show their solidarity with the Church of Sweden. At one of the first ordinations of women priests (Margit Sahlin's ordination in Österskär) Geoffrey Lampe, Regius Professor in Cambridge and previously mentioned here in the context of the Anglo–Scandinavian Conferences, was present. Leslie Hunter came to Sweden on almost every possible occasion, church jubilees and various similar occasions, when he was able to represent the Church of England. In 1964 Michael Ramsay himself came to the great celebration of the eight hundredth anniversary of the consecration of the first Archbishop of Uppsala in 1164. The following year Leslie Hunter published *The Scandinavian Churches,* a collection of essays on the Nordic national churches with a review of the Anglo–Scandinavian Conferences, written by Professor Ragnar Bring (Faber, 1965).

In actual fact, the contacts between the Church of England and the Swedish Church deepened during these years. Besides the Anglo–Scandinavian Conferences, new avenues of contacts were created. Groups of ordinands from English theological colleges made annual visits to the Nordic churches in the 1960s, usually including a longer stay in

Sweden. A little later these trips were replaced by the Anglo
–Scandinavian Pastoral Conferences.

TOWARDS THE FUTURE

One similarity between the Anglican and the Lutheran tradition is the emphasis on the liturgical life of the Church.
There has, of course, always been awareness of this, to a
greater or lesser extent at various periods and in various
ecclesiastical traditions. In the twentieth century there has
been a liturgical renaissance, which has brought a new sense
of the importance of the liturgy, both for the worshipping
congregation and as a whole and for the spiritual growth
of the individual in prayer and praise. The liturgy has been
rediscovered as an important 'language' of symbols, which
often speak better than words. In worship, many have rediscovered their spiritual roots, both in the tradition of their
own church, and in the universal tradition of Christianity
throughout time. First and foremost: the importance of the
Eucharist, as the central act of the regular, common worship of the parish has been recovered.

Much of this 'rediscovery' has made its mark on theology
and church life in many churches at the present time,
including the Roman Catholic Church, and there have been
mutual influences – conscious and unconscious – or perhaps
it might rather be called 'parallel developments' in the same
direction. For mutual understanding between the churches,
these similar experiences are vitally important. It is not
least along this path that the Anglican and Lutheran
churches have drawn closer to each other. We have been
able to understand our own traditions in a new way, and
at the same time to emphasize how much these two traditions have in common, as a shared, rich inheritance.

Liturgical renewal began back in the nineteenth century. This was particularly the case in the Anglican
churches under the influence of Tractarianism. But in
Lutheranism as well, a new interest in liturgical matters

275

was already noticeable towards the end of the nineteenth century. Here the discussion will focus on the importance of contacts between the Church of England and the Nordic churches for liturgical developments. The impressions made on a number of young Swedish priests by the worship of Anglo–Catholic groups in England in the first decades of the twentieth century and its influence on them have already been mentioned. The great work on the Eucharist by Yngve Brilioth, published in 1925, was another, possibly even more, important factor. Both Brilioth and his father-in-law, Nathan Söderblom, worked for the renewal of the celebration of the Eucharist and it is not known who was first and who influenced the other. Here Gabriel Hebert from the Church of England came in; as already mentioned, he translated Brilioth's book, and he himself advocated the same thoughts in a new programme for the Church of England called Parish Communion. This programme was both about the restoration of the pattern of the early Church, and of ways in which the Eucharist might gain a central position in the life and witness of the local parish. The continuation came in England in the work of Dom Gregory Dix and in Sweden in Gustaf Aulén's contribution to the Church's liturgical books in the 1930s and 1940s. Using the rites which were introduced in both England and Sweden in the 1980s, it is possible today to celebrate the main Sunday services in both these Churches in almost exactly the same way. Among the other Nordic churches, the Finnish Church is closest to the Church of Sweden, in this aspect as in so many others.

This has been the main line. Alongside it, an often patient, sometimes very courageous work of renewal was undertaken at the local level by priests from the high church wing in the Nordic churches. Gabriel Hebert kept in touch with them, and in 1927 he joined some of them for the first time for 'Quiet Days'. In 1928 he visited the liturgically very aware and much respected Rural Dean of St Peter's, Malmö, Albert Lysander. In the mid-1930s he visited Gunnar Rosendal in his parish in Osby. Father Gabriel's impressions of Rosendal's work was, according to Christopher Irvine's biography, more mixed. In a letter, reprinted by Irvine, Hebert warned Rosendal against making the Swedish high church movement too unilaterally 'ritualistic' or into a 'party' in the Church. He argued that the high church persuasion in Sweden ought to take hold of the rich inheritance of their own Lutheran church.

The Swedish church leader whom Hebert admired most was Gustaf Aulén. It was Aulén's book on redemption, *Christus Victor*, which Hebert translated. Their personal friendship lasted for many years. After a visit to Aulén in Lund in 1961 he wrote admiringly about the then 82 year old Bishop: 'He is a musician, expert in church music, and a hymn writer, a dogmatic theologian, a theologian of the eucharistic liturgy, and ecumenist; for it is always with the catholic, or universal Christian faith he is concerned and not with the tenets of some school of thought or party.' These words also characterize Hebert himself, and they express something of what he found in the common traditions of Anglicanism and Lutheranism.

But it was not only in the Church of Sweden that Hebert had made close friends. In Denmark he made contact at an early stage with a group of theologians who had founded *Theologisk Oratorium*, an organization which among other things published a Danish version of the Breviary. The man to whom he was closest in the Danish Church was the Professor in Systematic Theology at the University of Aarhus, Regin Prenter. In his young days, Prenter had been a student at the Lincoln Theological College, made friends with Michael Ramsay and visited the Society of the Sacred Mission at Kelham. His disappointment at not being able to receive Holy Communion in the Church of England as a member of the Danish Church did not in any way diminish his love for English church life, but ever since those student days the desire to be able to do so was an inner, driving force behind his many ecumenical contributions. He was a frequent member of the Anglo–Scandinavian Conferences and also of the official talks between

277

the Church of England and the Danish, Norwegian and Icelandic Churches (R. Prenter, *Erindringer*, Memories, 1985).

The question of communion between the Anglican churches and the Lutheran churches in Denmark, Norway and Iceland was still unresolved. The committee on 'reunion' in the 1930 Lambeth Conference had discussed it in the absence of representatives from these churches. Bishop Rodhe had pinpointed the question (see above). After the ending of the Second World War, at the 1948 Lambeth Conference, the matter was taken up again. A special committee was set up, which included members from the churches in question. A special preparatory conference had been held previously in Chichester in 1947, and it was followed by yet another conference in Oslo in 1951.

The driving force behind this was all the time the Bishop of Chichester, George Bell. From the English side, this whole matter was put forward with great energy. The countries were closer to each other now, after the War, than they had perhaps ever been before. Denmark, Norway and Iceland all were allied with England in the great power-struggle with Nazi Germany. In relation to the other Nordic countries, feelings were much cooler at this time. In Sweden there were too many reminders, the English thought, of 'Finland's special case' and warnings against the Soviet Union. (This was prior to the Cold War between the West and the Soviet Union.) Anyway, there was keen interest in an agreement on closer ecclesial relationships with Denmark, Norway and Iceland. On doctrinal matters, this was achievable without too many problems, but on the issue of the 'historic episcopate' it was impossible to go much further than before. The Oslo Conference was important in itself, as Michael Ramsay was one of the Anglican representatives. It would be interesting to reprint his contribution, but space does not permit this. (The minutes of the meeting are preserved in Lambeth Palace Library.)

The only one of these three Nordic churches to show any openness on the crucial issue was the Church of Iceland, which was represented at the 1948 Lambeth Conference by Bishop Sigurgeir Sigurdsson. As early as 1866, the then newly appointed Bishop of Iceland, Dr Pjeter Pjetersson, had wanted to be consecrated by an English bishop in order to establish closer contacts with the Church of England. This was however prevented by the Danish Bishop Martensen of Zealand. The Church of Iceland was now able to show a mind of its own, since the nation had gained independence from Denmark in 1944. In Iceland, a structure of special 'ordaining bishops' (*vigbiskopar*) had already been introduced for various reasons, alongside the Bishop of Iceland. One of the reasons was that a 'vigbiskop' would be able to officiate precisely at episcopal consecrations and in case of a vacancy in see. These 'ordaining bishops' occupy the two medieval episcopal sees in Iceland, Skálholt and Hólar, and can be considered the equivalent of the Anglican suffragan bishops.

No desire to turn away from earlier positions on succession could be discerned among either the Danish or the Norwegian delegates. The Bishop of Oslo, Eivind Berggrav, who had become particularly famous in the Church's struggle during the German occupation, spoke for Norway. The Professor of Church History at the University of Oslo, Einar Molland, also defended the Norwegian claim that succession in terms of 'succession of office', had been preserved unbroken. The most prominent theological expert in the Danish delegation at the Oslo Conference was Regin Prenter. He too was unwilling to accept that the ministry in these churches had lost the critical aspect of continuity, and on this issue he had to argue against his old friend, Michael Ramsay.

It could be said that at both the conferences in Chichester 1947 and in Oslo 1951, as in the committee work at Lambeth in 1948, the positions seemed to be fairly closed. A degree of progress was however achieved shortly afterwards, when Danes, Norwegians and Icelanders were

279

admitted to communion in Anglican churches if they were abroad and without access to their own services. In the long run, these intensive conversations were important from another aspect. It was clarified beyond doubt that, if progress was to be made at all, the question of the apostolic continuity of the Church must be approached from a perspective which was not exclusively focused on episcopal consecration. It was to emerge that it was only in the context of new thoughts on this issue that a breakthrough could be achieved.

Chapter 12

A Breakthrough

THE PORVOO COMMON STATEMENT

On 13 October 1992, a common statement was issued on the concrete and visible unity of the Anglican Churches of England, Scotland, Wales and Ireland and all the Nordic and Baltic Lutheran Churches. This was the result of a long series of official conversations and negotiations. The most recent have been conducted over the period of 1989–1992 and concluded in Finland. The document is entitled *The Porvoo Common Statement* after the Finnish diocese in whose cathedral the delegates had celebrated the Eucharist together on the previous Sunday.

The signatories of the Porvoo Common Statement represent twelve churches in different countries. Independent though these churches are, each with its own distinctive character, they also display enough such similarities, now to make it possible, after thorough examination, to acknowledge one another without reservation as sister churches with a common mission.

In the previous chapters we have, with the Church of Sweden as our starting-point, followed the history of the churches in this part of Europe over more than a thousand years. We have seen their beginnings and much of their shared tradition. We have also been able to observe how, over long stretches of time, they came to glide away from one another. Now and again, it was possible to rediscover and retrieve that which was held in common. But, due to what were variously perceived as serious differences, there were always barriers which, more often than not, proved unsurmountable. This concerned either doctrinal issues of the Christian faith, the understanding of the mystery of the

281

sacrament, or the view of the 'continuity' in church and ministry. It is against this background in its entirety that we should view the Porvoo Declaration and the importance of making it known and implemented. Its purpose is greater than those of previous conversations. As clearly stated in the Introduction to the Porvoo Common Statement. 'The aim of these Conversations was to move forward from our existing piecemeal agreements towards the goal of visible unity'.

The Common Statement provides a detailed justification for the Declaration itself, which consists of acknowledgements and commitments. It is the Declaration which will be placed before the appropriate decision-making bodies of the twelve churches. The time has come, at last, for substantial, concrete decisions.

There are six acknowledgements:

1. we acknowledge one another's churches as churches belonging to the One, Holy, Catholic and Apostolic Church of Jesus Christ and truly participating in the apostolic mission of the whole people of God;

2. we acknowledge that in all our churches the Word of God is authentically preached, and the sacraments of baptism and the eucharist are duly administered;

3. we acknowledge that all our churches share in the common confession of the apostolic faith;

4. we acknowledge that one another's ordained ministries are given by God as instruments of his grace and as possessing not only the inward call of the Spirit, but also Christ's commission through his body, the Church;

5. we acknowledge that personal, collegial and communal oversight (*episcope*) is embodied and exercised in all our churches in a variety of forms, in continuity of apostolic life, mission and ministry;

6. we acknowledge that the episcopal office is valued and maintained in all our churches as a visible sign expressing and serving the Church's unity and continuity in apostolic life, mission and ministry.

Porvoo Cathedral, from which the Porvoo Common Statement takes its name.
Photograph: Maj-Britt Höglund, 'Kuriren', Vasa.

In effect, these paragraphs represent a total and mutual acknowledgement of one another with regard to the Scriptures, Doctrinal Confession, Baptism, the Eucharist and Ministry. I shall return to the matter of how, gradually and after a long sequence of conversations, such complete accord came to be reached. But perhaps even more notable are what the Porvoo Common Statement refers to as 'commitments'. This term conveys their firm and binding nature – a great deal more, then, than the devout hopes and wishes so often expressed in ecumenical documents under the heading of 'recommendations'. Maximum conviction is expressed in the wording of the first three commitments

1. to share a common life in mission and service, to pray for and with one another, and to share resources;
2. to welcome one another's members to receive sacramental and other pastoral ministrations;
3. to regard baptized members of all our churches as members of our own.

As there are no fewer than ten commitments, I would refer the reader to the document itself for the full text.

Some comments are of special interest, given our historical context. Commitment 4 commits us to 'welcome diaspora congregations into the life of the indigenous churches, to their mutual enrichment'. During the 18th century this was in fact a practice common to the Danish –Norwegian and Swedish congregations in London: they enjoyed a strong relationship with the Bishop of London, and the Swedish rector in London fulfilled the function of Swedish Lutheran 'ambassador' in England. He still does to today, and certainly this fact could be formally recognized.

Commitments 5 and 6 refer to the orders of ministry, i.e. to the offices of bishop, priest and deacon. It is stated that the holders of these offices, each ordained according to the rite of their own church, may be invited to exercise their ministry in the other churches. This is a concrete consequence of these offices having been mutually and fully acknowledged (see above, acknowledgements 4, 5 and 6).

Of special importance is the wording of commitment 6: 'to invite one another's bishops normally to participate in the laying on of hands at the ordination of bishops as a sign of the unity and continuity of the Church'. Notable here is, first that the acknowledgement of the episcopal ministry of all these churches comes before any further ordination in the apostolic succession has taken place in those churches where it was previously in doubt, and secondly, the choice of the word 'sign' and not 'guarantee' or any similar word with that implication. As frequently noted in previous chapters, the bone of contention of earlier Conversations between Anglicans and Lutherans was that the Anglicans were not willing to enter into an interchangeability of ministries with churches which had not retained the sign of unbroken succession in the laying on of hands in episcopal consecrations until those churches' ministries had been incorporated into the historic succession as traditionally understood. The Porvoo Common Statement makes it quite clear that these churches – all of them – *already* participate in 'apostolic succession'. Indeed, we find this explicitly stated in the very first acknowledgement: 'we acknowledge one another's churches as churches belonging to the One, Holy, Catholic and *Apostolic* (my italics) Church of Jesus Christ . . .'.

Another point of special interest concerns the office of deacon. During earlier ecumenical discussions between, primarily, the Church of England and the Church of Sweden, views on this office had been divided. In the Anglican churches, the office of deacon customarily preceeds ordination to the priesthood; in the Lutheran churches, it is a distinct office with, above all, what are nowadays frequently called 'social and caring' duties. The Porvoo Common Statement expresses the intention 'to work towards a common understanding of diaconal ministry'. This wording bears witness to a convergence over the twentieth century. Anglicans came to absorb their experience of churches with a distinct office for, among other things, 'social' duties; Lutherans were learning to appreciate the value of integrating the diaconal office with the liturgical life of the Church. We had, then, already achieved some agreement – but the expressed intention now to expand and deepen diaconal ministry is an important part of the Porvoo Agreement.

Clearly, the several 'commitments' point to an advance. The idea is to 'establish appropriate forms of collegial and conciliar consultation' between the churches concerned. Conferences, on both a large and a smaller scale, have of course been frequent, but formal consultations of official representatives of the churches do not at present take place, either on the subject of 'faith and order, life and work', or on that of another area brought into the Porvoo Agreement: 'theological and pastoral matters'.

The Porvoo Declaration will, once it has been presented, accepted and signed, have significance in law. Much is of course required in order to make it possible in practice to translate this special Anglican–Lutheran relationship in Northern Europe into a concrete communion: first and foremost we need effective information, and then imaginative powers and stamina. For this will be a task, both of creating quite new forms of collaboration, to be incorporated into the existing structures of the various churches concerned, and of encouraging openness to fresh stimuli.

In the light of all this, the last of the ten commitments appear relatively modest: 'to establish a contact group to nurture our growth in communion and to co-ordinate the implementation of this agreement'. The word 'contact-group' does not sound very empowering or authoritative. But of course, only time will tell what will be needed in the future.

HISTORY BROUGHT TO LIFE

Attached to the Porvoo Common Statement is a map of Europe, on which the countries with the twelve churches – Anglican and Lutheran – have been marked out. They

286

cover the same area of Northern Europe as that in which the first chapter of this book takes place, illustrating the same unity between the churches. This had been the world of the Vikings, and it was along their highways and in their new dwelling-places in the West that the Christian faith was gradually introduced – by Irish and Anglo-Saxon Christians – to the peoples of the North Atlantic Islands, to the Nordic peoples and to their neighbours along the coasts to the east of the Baltic sea. The map used in order to make visible the religious unity between the peoples of Northern Europe one thousand years ago showed exactly the same picture as does the one put before us now, as we discuss the development of a 'visible unity' between the churches of those same peoples.

This observation touches on a fundamental relationship. We have noted the great depth and duration of the Christian influence in the early Middle Ages – from the Atlantic in the west, to the coasts and rivers by the Baltic Sea in the east. Although these events took place a long time ago, they have never completely sunk into oblivion. The peoples of Great Britain and Ireland have not forgotten the Nordic immigrants, and neither have the Nordic peoples forgotten the missionaries who came to them from neighbouring countries in the West. Our own century has seen the addition to the west front of Trondheim Cathedral of a statue of the Irish missionary and noble abbess, St Sunniva, seated beside St Olav, the patron saint of Norway. In the 1960s a statue of St Swithun of Winchester was raised in Stavanger, on the front of the Cathedral which bears his name; and in Sweden, the priests of the Diocese of Västerås make a pilgrimage to the church and spring of St David, the English missionary, at Munktorp during their Clergy Conference (*Prästmöte*). Archaeologists and art-historians in the Nordic countries find traces of Anglo-Saxon and Norman styles in the earliest church buildings, and researchers at the various State archives piece together fragments from liturgical books, to remind us of the many missionaries and saints who came to us from churches in the West.

The possession of a common history is no modest asset, and these churches are aware of themselves as 'historic'. They do not see themselves as new ecclesiastical organisations, created during the great schism of the 16th century. No, they had already in the Middle Ages been considered as national church provinces: *Ecclesia Anglicana, Danica*, etc. These were the very same churches that, after the break with Rome, lived on in their respective countries among their peoples. In principle, the ecclesial parishes remained the same; so too did the medieval dioceses; not to mention the Scriptures, the common confession, the liturgical year and traditional forms of worship. These historically developed and preserved churches, conscious of their abiding relationship with their respective nations and peoples, are rediscovering each other by talking together and seeking mutual support and inspiration for their similar tasks. The common history of these churches, which has sometimes developed along parallel lines, has been traced in the previous chapters of this book. The reason why so much attention has been paid to their shared history is that this is part of the incentive for these particular churches to seek a visible unity which can be given practical expression.

One might wonder whether other areas of ecumenism might not be of equal urgency, for example relations with the Free Churches in their own countries, or with the Roman Catholic Church, with whom all the twelve Churches of the Porvoo-conversations share their historical origin. According to the Porvoo Common Statement, such ecumenical efforts are of the greatest importance: the affinity between the twelve sister churches must not merely be an end in itself. It should also be seen as a step along the road to a further, extended unity. It must also be the intention and hope that the deeper union between these churches in Northern Europe will enrich the life of the wider Anglican Communion and that of the Lutheran World Federation,

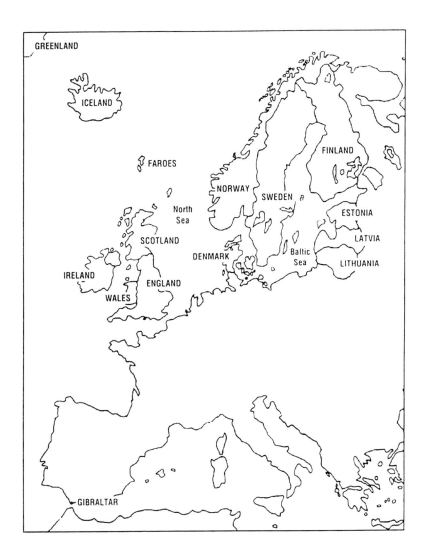

Map of Europe attached to the Porvoo Common Statement, showing the countries whose Anglican and Lutheran churches participated in the Conversations. (Gibraltar is marked due to the fact that the Church of England congregations in mainland Europe form the Diocese of Gibraltar in Europe.) The map is reproduced by permission of the Church of England Council for Christian Unity.

both of which (of course) lay the greatest emphasis on relationships within their own membership.

To the twelve Anglican and Lutheran churches, signs of their close relationship are found, not only in the tradition from the missionaries and the Medieval Church, but also in the similarity of their experiences in the 16th century, with all the ups and downs of the Reformation period. They have all broken with the late medieval 'Roman' Church, and they have all also, through the Reformation, deepened and rediscovered their connections with the apostles and the faith of the Church Fathers. In this twofold relationship both Anglicans and Lutherans find their true identity.

The Puritan wing of the Anglican Church wanted, to a great extent, to sever the links with the medieval inheritance of the National Church. From the perspective of the Nordic Churches, it often looked as if this puritan strand dominated the entire Anglican Church. This was the main reason why Lutherans for a long time kept a distance from English church life. The most likely explanation for the relative ease with which it has now been possible to renew contacts, seems to be that the 'Calvinist' strand of Anglican church life is nowadays less apparent. Also, current divisions often split the various confessional traditions right down the middle. There are 'Evangelical' and 'High Church' wings in the Lutheran just as much as in the Anglican Churches.

Those who participate in ecumenical Conversations may not be able to speak for all groups within their churches, but they must be assumed to represent the main lines, and it is along that route that an unreserved, mutual acknowledgement of the various positions of these different churches has been reached.

The main body of the twelve churches consists of the large National Churches in England and in the five Nordic countries of Iceland, Norway, Denmark, Sweden and Finland. Ecumenical dialogues between these churches have been going on for a long time, and they have a variety of mutual contacts at different levels. They are all National

Churches, an original characteristic, which they have all brought with them throughout their history, and they have all experienced the difficulties of continuing to impress the peoples and nations in this region in the present situation of secularisation and religious pluralism. Even so, their task remains the same: to extend an invitation without limits to every individual and to the entire nation, within which they have received their calling. It is not least because of this, that it is highly appropriate to co-operate in the future towards meeting the challenges and opportunities of such a monumental task.

The other churches, whose representatives also signed the Porvoo Common Statement, took part in the deliberations because of their close relationship with one or more of the six larger churches, and they also share a common tradition. This applies, on the one hand, to the Anglican Churches in Scotland, Wales and Ireland, and on the other to the Lutheran Churches in the Baltic States. And their participation brings further enrichment. Their situation is otherwise quite unlike those of the major national Churches. Their contribution makes the full picture of the issues of church and society far more complex and tense, but in the long run probably also much more realistic.

THE PATH TO PORVOO

The direct background to the Porvoo Common Statement was a series of so-called bilateral conversations between Anglicans and Lutherans, which began over twenty years ago. These in turn form part of a very large number of similar discussions in the 1970s and 1980s between various churches all over the world. A general openness to closer understanding between the churches prevailed. It was the period immediately following the Second Vatican Council that 'broke the ice' in ecumenism. The Roman Catholic Church was the most frequent participant in such dialogues, closely followed by the Anglicans and the

Lutherans. The various dialogues were also largely characterized by the fact that it was these three major confessions that took the lead – all of which have a strong sense of continuity with regard to confessional doctrine, sacramental theology and ministry. The fruits of many years' work in the Faith and Order Commissions of the World Council of Churches were also harvested.

In this favourable ecumenical climate one Anglican-Lutheran dialogue followed another. This is not the place to give an account of them all. They have been described in a well documented essay by Christopher Hill, now Canon of St Paul's Cathedral, London, in a collection of essays published together with the Porvoo Common Statement (*Together in Mission and Ministry*, Church House Publishing, London, 1993). Another more general essay on the pre-history of Porvoo was recently written by Bishop Tore Furberg, himself the Lutheran Co-Chairman of the Conversations (in the series Tro och Tanke, Supplement 2/1994: *Svenska Kyrkan i det nya Europa*, The Church of Sweden in the new Europe).

The Nordic Churches have taken part both in Conversations with a wide international perspective and in those focusing on the European situation. The talks that led to the Porvoo Common Statement were the first to concentrate solely on the British/Irish and Nordic/Baltic region. Concurrently there have been specially successful dialogues between Lutherans and the Episcopal Churches of the USA and Canada, from which the European dialogues have gained much by way of important inspiration and experience.

Looked at purely from the Swedish point of view, it would seem that much of what emerged during the successive dialogues in the 1970s and 1980s had already been established by the contacts between Sweden and England at the beginning of the century. The vital issue now was however to bring the other Lutheran Churches as well into fellowship, and it was in relation to them that great difficulties remained to be overcome. One good thing is of course that

292

a number of issues affecting the mutual understanding between Anglicans and Lutherans, for example the interpretation of the Bible, the doctrine of Justification etc., have been thoroughly penetrated by a number of theologians on both sides in the course of these repeated discussion. This has given a breadth to the conversation and a wider network for the respective churches.

The first international Anglican–Lutheran Conference was co-chaired by Archbishop Gunnar Hultgren, and the Bishop of Leicester, R. R. Williams. Among the Lutheran theologians, the Nordic Churches were represented by Professor Prenter of the University of Aarhus, who had long experience of several earlier Anglican–Lutheran conferences and dialogues. The Lutheran delegation also included Bishop J. Kibira of Bukoba, Tanzania. He was well-known in the Nordic countries through his contacts with Scandinavian Missions. The Report of this Conference (signed in 1973 in Pullach, Bavaria) shows that the closeness of these two families of churches was already appreciated. The issues of episcopal ministry and succession was of course a stumbling block. As a possible way forward, it was pointed out that all the churches in question did at least have ecclesiastical offices with episcopal functions, which could be called *episcope*. This was an opening. The term *episcope* came to be used in all subsequent dialogues. In the 1980s an international Anglican–Lutheran consultation was held on the subject of *episcope* alone (Niagara Falls, 1987).

In order to relate the dialogues more closely to the respective churches, it was decided to arrange regional meetings. A European round of talks held during 1979–1982 (Report: Helsinki 1982) particularly paved the way for the Porvoo Agreement ten years later. In the European talks, the Nordic Churches contributed the largest delegation. It was now possible fully to understand that the Danish, and therefore also the Norwegian and Icelandic, Churches had been forced at the Reformation to break the tradition of episcopal succession, and to agree that this break did not imply a rejection of episcopal Church Order.

Full respect for the Danish–Norwegian–Icelandic episcopal tradition by the Anglicans has proved an absolute condition for closer relations between the Anglicans and this part of Lutheranism.

New trust was created between Continental Lutheranism and Anglicans through the personal friendship between John Gibbs, the Bishop of Coventry, and Johannes Hempel, the Bishop of Dresden. Their two cities had been reduced to ruins by the relentless bombing raids of World War II, and now the two Bishops wanted to rebuild church unity and mutual friendship. The main contributions to the dialogue which resulted in the Helsinki-document 1982 were made by Professor Günter Gassmann, from Germany, and Canon Christopher Hill among the Anglicans, the same two who have borne much of the work on the Porvoo document. Professor Gassman is the only person who has participated in all the Anglican–Lutheran conversations in the 1970s and 1980s, and the growth in mutual understanding is to a large extent due to him.

Anglican interest in continental Lutheranism has increased steadily. This has of course been linked to the reunification of Germany and the increased activity on European issues. Stephen Sykes, Bishop of Ely and chairman of the Anglo–Nordic–Baltic (previously Anglo–Scandinavian) Theological Conferences, and John Hind, Bishop of Gibraltar in Europe, who is responsible for the Anglican congregations in mainland Europe, show a clearly increasing interest in the Lutheran Churches, both Nordic and in mainland Europe. Negotiations between Anglicans and the Evangelical Church in Germany have been especially successful. They resulted in an official agreement, the Meissen Common Statement, to which the Porvoo Agreement provides the counterpart. The Anglican Co-Chairman of both the Meissen and the Porvoo Conversations, David Tustin, Bishop of Grimsby, speaks German fluently, as does another member of the Anglican delegation the Dean of Durham, John Arnold. (Knowledge of this language being, perhaps, an unusual accomplishment among the British).

294

The present focus is, however, first and foremost on the Nordic/Baltic churches, i.e. on the region closest to Great Britain and Ireland, both geographically and ecclesiastically, and where therefore similarities with the Anglican churches in Europe are most marked. It is as evident in the Helsinki Report as it is in the Porvoo Common Statement – the two texts focusing on Europe – that the aim is not some form of abstract internationalism. On the contrary, there is a very clear intention to link in with the ordinary life of these separate churches, as they have developed historically, each within its own separate geographical location.

Nor does the analysis come to a close with the century of the Reformation, i.e. the concern is not merely with the sixteenthth century confessional documents, but also with efforts to understand one another's interpretation of faith, sacramental life and ministry, in the light of currently accepted liturgical texts and current church practice. At the same time, attempts are being made to sound out and analyse the position of these national churches in today's society. These, then, are seen as the routes to a better understanding of one another's distinctive characteristics – while revealing existing similarities in the process.

The unreservedly extended understanding of apostolic succession expressed in the Porvoo Text constitutes a clearer breakthrough than any achieved by previous agreements. As the various dialogues have continued over the years, so it has been possible to observe the changes in attitude, step by step. The Lutheran side now recognizes the momentous importance of continuity in apostolic character and catholicity. It is on this level that the very identity of the Church can be recognized. This continuity, this identification of its origin, in the Church founded by Jesus Christ, must be rendered visible in its totality: in faith and doctrinal confession, in sacramental life and ministry. The one is no less important than the other, and here, the Anglicans have expressed a fundamental acknowledgement: traditional episcopal consecration, by a bishop, including the laying of on hands, is certainly an important sign, but it is not the primary basis of continuity.

It is recognized that all churches connected with the Porvoo Common Statement have kept continuity on all these levels, but that none has done so completely. All have, however, preserved the episcopal office. Those who, on the invitation of a sister church will take part in its consecrations of bishops and priests, will do so in order to display the already existing continuity and unity – and *not* out of any need to augment the purity and identity of sister churches.

The path to this breakthrough appears not to have been altogether smooth. According to a report by Professor Ola Tjørhom of Stavanger, half way through the negotiations, it actually looked as if agreement in this vital matter would not be reached. The Anglican delegation comprised noticeably differing views. And he also points to the occasional show of disrespect from the Lutheran quarters for the deeper meaning of ministry, adding that such a stance could make unity between the two traditions more difficult to achieve. His report states: 'In my view, we Lutherans ought to do rather more to show that we have accepted the personal practice of *episcope* as something far more important than the work of a kind of branch manager, i.e. we look upon it instead as an office which substantially contributes to the mission, apostolic continuity and unity of the church'. This honest comment reflects Ola Tjørhom's deep commitment to the dialogues. He published several important contributions to the ecumenical debate of the time. The Bishop of Oslo, Andreas Aarflot, became a delegate in the final round, and the Norwegian contribution in general did much to secure the positive outcome.

Pope John Paul II with the Bishop of Iceland, Pétur Sigurgeirsson. The Pope's visit to the Nordic countries in 1989 had a marked ecumenical purpose. It was not only a visit to the Roman Catholic dioceses, but in a major way also to all the Lutheran national churches. *Pressfoto, Reykjavik.*

THE COMMON PROFILE

If one wants a long perspective on the Porvoo Common Statement one might try to step back in time, by about a hundred years – to 1888 and to Lambeth, where the Anglican bishops expressed their desire for closer relations with 'the Scandinavian churches', by which they meant the Nordic churches. (The Baltic and Finnish churches being at that time beyond reach, for political reasons.) As we have seen, the fact that initial negotiations were held with the Church of Sweden only, did not at all imply the indefinite exclusion of the other churches. The vision at that time covered the whole of the region concerning us today, and was based on concrete ground. The Nordic churches were perceived to have clear correspondences with the Anglican churches: they were national churches, they were established churches, and they were of manifest continuity with their origin in the common medieval Church in Europe and as part of 'the One, Holy, Catholic and Apostolic Church'.

Nor should we disregard the fundamental importance of the four elements of 'The Lambeth Quadrilateral' (see above 211). The six acknowledgements of the Porvoo Declaration, in which complete recognition of sister churches across the Northern European region is expressed, has a great deal in common with the Lambeth Quadrilateral. Both documents contain theses on the Scriptures as foundation, on the Apostolic Creed, on Baptism and the Eucharist and finally on the episcopal office. Anyone who thinks that the Porvoo Common Statement by-passes the requirements of the Lambeth Quadrilateral's fourth thesis, regarding historic episcopacy, must be assumed to have misunderstood the meaning of the Porvoo Common Statement. Indeed, it is the fourth element which has now – at long last – been both deepened and extended. The office of bishop – rather than merely their consecration – has been allowed its rightful significance as carrying the continuity and unity of the Church.

In this vital respect, the path to mutual understanding

between Anglicans and Lutherans has been long. It has been travelled with the help, above all, of the patient work of many decades by the Faith and Order Commission. The fact that Anglicans and Lutherans from the Nordic churches have taken a prominent part in that work provides one explanation for the increasing Anglican—Lutheran understanding with regard to what ought to be contained in the articles on the identity of the Church. In this regard, it has become less and less difficult for the two sides to interpret their respective traditions. A milestone was reached in 1882, with the Faith and Order conference in Lima, Peru, and the text *Baptism, Eucharist, Ministry* (BEM), which has greatly inspired and influenced subsequent Anglican–Lutheran negotiations. (In the Lima document, for example, can be found one of the earliest examples of the enlarged interpretation of *episcope*.)

By far, the main cause of current successes is the great and good experience of ecclesiastical and theological unity within the region covered by the Porvoo Agreement. Much has been said about this in previous chapters of this book. The longest sequence of meetings between representatives of both the Church of England and the Nordic – and at times the Baltic – churches is the unbroken series of Anglo-Scandinavian, now Anglo–Nordic–Baltic Theological Conferences, begun in 1929. This perseverance is a symptom of mutual understanding and ease in each other's company, while our differences afford fresh experiences – and contribute to the charm of the meetings!

Since 1978, and in order to extend the common frame of reference for representatives of these churches, similar meetings, the 'Anglo–Scandinavian Pastoral Conferences', have been held. These are more practical in approach, with wider participation. (Pioneers were Geoffrey Brown of the Church of England and Anders Bäckström of the Church of Sweden.) Experiences here have been similar to those gained from the theological conferences, and amount to a strong sense of having found enough agreement, and enough disagreement to render mutual appraisal interesting. Language no longer presents much of a barrier, the younger generation being quite capable of making its views understood in English.

Further examples are easy to find. A large and unwieldy all-European association with the aim of concord and debate between the great cathedrals was, after some years, found to require reorganisation into smaller, regional connections. Whereupon were born, in 1992, the 'British/Nordic Cathedral Conferences'.

Another, very recent, example is to be found in the 'London Conferences' held in the first few months of 1994, organized by the Central Board of the Church of Sweden. The participants were leaders of local church councils from across the whole of Sweden. The conferences were held in England, in continuous contact and negotiation with representatives from various dioceses and parishes of the sister church. It was discovered that one's own church is not alone in having certain problems and possible shortcomings, and that there is, in the parishes of another church, a wealth of positive and inspiring observations to be made, to take home and implement.

One consequence of the gradual acceptance of Porvoo Declaration will be that its several Commitments, too, must figure as a common starting point for far greater cooperation between the Churches – including unity on matters of education and within the decision-making bodies at national and local level. We can look forward to a hitherto probably undreamed-of wealth of inter-church connections, incorporating not only the Nordic churches' relationship with the Anglican churches, but also – and this too, will obviously broaden the horizon – close and concrete relations between the Nordic and Baltic churches themselves.

It is hard to predict the extent to which the Porvoo Common Statement will be realized on a practical level. The various churches whose representatives will have signed this document have hitherto not, to any great extent, shown their wish to 'share resources', nor are they very open to advice from one another. It is to be hoped that

A living and active National Church: The Cathedral of Trondheim is the national shrine of Norway. The picture shows the present King and Queen during the Ceremony of Blessing, i.e. the equivalent of Crowning. *Photograph: 'Pressens Bild', Oslo and Stockholm.*

the process of mutual agreements, to which the Porvoo Common Statement points, will awaken renewed interest in communion and exchange. It may also be that the challenges facing the national churches in the forseeable future will bring them closer to one another in consultation and mutual support.

The national churches intend to retain their character of, as the Nordic churches have often preferred to say, 'folk churches' (The term 'folk' is hard to convey in English, where one might easily be led to thoughts of 'folk-singers' etc.) All are at the same time conscious of the need to achieve greater independence from the decision-making bodies of secular society, together with a greater clarity of definition when it comes to membership and structure at parish level. If these churches wish to protect their historically given profile, they can also surely stand to gain much future help from continued mutual consultation.

To the Church of Sweden, the Porvoo Common Statement points to a clear choice with regard to ecumenical relations without, of course, implying a halt to the strengthening of other connections. It is with the sister churches in the British/Nordic/Baltic regions that the Church of Sweden experiences its closest links. This is the conclusion, explicitly expressed in the important essay on the Swedish Church and the tendencies towards denominational coalitions in Europe (*Tro och Tanke*, Supplement 2/1994), by Dr Ragnar Persenius, Director of the Church of Sweden Central Board Secretariat for Theology and Ecumenism. His conclusions are explicitly based on the Porvoo Agreement.

According to the Porvoo Common Statement, full equality exists between the churches of this region. No one Lutheran church is more of a sister church to the Anglican churches than are any of the others. This equality has been much longed for – not least by the Church of Sweden, which has frequently felt embarrassed by certain tensions in its relations with the Danish, Norwegian and Icelandic Churches. The Church of Sweden can no longer consider

302

The consecration of Bishops of the Church of Sweden nowadays always takes place in the Cathedral of Uppsala. The picture shows the consecration of Dr K. G. Hammar as Bishop of Lund on 23rd August 1992 by the Archbishop of Uppsala. Bertil Werkström, assisted by two Bishops (inside the altar-rail): the immediate predecessor in the See of Lund, Bishop P. O. Ahrén (hidden from view) and the senior member of the College of Bishops, Martin Lönnebo, Bishop of Linköping. Outside the altar-rails are representatives from the Diocese of Lund, from the other Nordic Churches and from the Eastern German 'twin-Church' of the Diocese of Lund. *Photograph: Lennart Jonson, Lund.*

its own closeness to the Anglican churches to be greater than that enjoyed by the other Nordic churches.

At the same time *all* the Nordic churches need fully to recognize that their respective profiles in actual fact very closely resemble the features that characterize their Anglican brothers and sisters. This is part of our common, historically given and inherited tradition. However, the increasing light of recognition must not be made to focus solely on extended and strengthened family connections. The affinity between all these sister churches ought to lead also to a deepening self-knowledge, each of our own church.

Acknowledgements

This book, originally published in Swedish (Verbum 1994), is now, with a few minor changes, coming out in English, in order to make it available to readers in England and all the Nordic countries.

With regard to the content, I have made an attempt to write it with readers from all these churches in mind, and this explains why some factual information has been included: even though it may seem axiomatic to some readers concerning their own church, but it might not be so well known to readers from the other churches.

It would be a great joy to me personally, if my presentation can contribute to a continued and deepened communion between the Anglican and the Lutheran Churches in this part of the world. This book is primarily an expression of my great gratitude for what I have received over the years of so much inspiring companionship with colleagues and friends, not only in our neighbouring Nordic countries, but also in the Church of England; friends of many generations, all with a generous openness towards extended ecclesial relations.

I would like to mention particularly the companionship that has been available to me through the Anglo-Scandinavian Theological Conferences, ever since the Meeting at Ripon Hall, Oxford, in 1959, first under the leadership of the Bishop of Sheffield, Leslie Hunter. Then I had the privilege for many years of participating in these Conferences under the chairmanship of Professor Geoffrey Lampe, and to work closely with his eminent Conference Secretary, Canon David Isitt.

Dr Lampe's successor, Dr Stephen Sykes, now Bishop of Ely, has particularly encouraged me to write this book.

He has greatly honoured me by indicating its ecumenical significance in his Foreword.

I have also experienced an inspiring working relationship through the Anglican–Lutheran Dialogues in the 1970s and early 1980s. From those years stems my friendship with Canon Christopher Hill, at the time the Ecumenical Assistant to the Archbishop of Canterbury, now Precentor of St Paul's Cathedral, London, who has followed this book with keen interest. Among my other Anglican friends, who have been involved in the Porvoo talks, I would like to mention John Hind, the Bishop of Gibraltar in Europe. I have also been able to count on the tireless support of Dr Mary Tanner and Dr Colin Podmore of the Council for Christian Unity of the General Synod of the Church of England.

Both for the Swedish edition, and for the perhaps even more adventurous enterprise of producing an English version, I have been generously and warmly encouraged by the Archbishop of Uppsala, Gunnar Weman, and also by the Lutheran Co-Chairman of the Porvoo Commission, Bishop Tore Furberg. The Dean Lennart Sjöström, Rector of the Swedish Church in London, has given great and friendly help throughout this project.

The financial support for this edition has been given by the Thora Ohlsson Trust in Lund, represented by its Chairman, The Bishop of Lund, Dr K. G. Hammar and Thora Ohlsson's two nephews, Per-Håkan Ohlsson and Sven Håkan Ohlsson with his wife Birgit Bram Ohlsson, Trustees, and for many years Directors of the Håkan Ohlsson Printing and Publishing Family Firm. I am very grateful indeed to them, and I hope that the publication of this book will be a worthy memorial to their aunt, Miss Thora Ohlsson, who was for many years a faithful member of the Swedish Church in London.

Thanks are also due to The Canterbury Press Norwich for including my book among their publications, and for their friendly and efficient co-operation.

The English translation has been done partly by Mrs Elizabeth Kondahl, M.A. and partly by The Revd Sr Gerd Swensson, Teol. and Fil. Kand, M.Phil. Dr Colin Podmore has made an important contribution particularly as adviser on English theological terminology. Two of my friends from the Anglo–Scandinavian Theological Conferences, Canon John Toy and Canon David Isitt have also contributed greatly. Technical help and advice has come from my friends at the Secretariat for Theology and Ecumenism of the Church of Sweden Central Board: the Director, Dr Ragnar Persenius, Dr Johan F. Dalman and Fil Mag. Gunborg Blomstrand, who have all offered much helpful support. My grateful thanks for our happy collaboration is due to them all.

Sources and Literature

Limited references to the principal sources and main works of church history behind this presentation are included in the text itself. I have however deemed it neither possible nor necessary to list all the vast number of overviews, monographs etc. which are available on the history of these peoples and churches.

The use of research undertaken by other scholars is obvious and, in my view, quite natural in a work like this, which provides a general overview in a very long perspective. My ambition has been to enable readers to familiarize themselves with current research, Nordic and British, in this area. At crucial points I have consulted the published and unpublished primary sources myself.

Among the archives I have used, I would mention particularly the Lambeth Palace Library, London. There I have found a very rich source of material on the late 19th century and the whole of the 20th, particularly in the collections of *Randall Davidson's Papers* and *George Bell's Papers*, and also the entire documentation of the Anglican–Nordic ecumenical conversations.

It is a joy to know that currently quite a large number of scholars, both in Great Britain and in the Nordic countries, are undertaking historical research on subjects which concern the collaboration between the churches in this North European region. As recently as in April 1995, about 40 of these scholars, half from Great Britain and half from the Nordic countries, met at Vanbrugh College, University of York, in order to confer on their work under the theme of *Church and People in Britain and Scandinavia*.

Some of these works home in on the period of the Vikings and on the Middle Ages. On that period a major project, based at the University of Uppsala and entitled *Sveriges kristnande* (The conversion of Sweden), is currently taking place.

Among recently published works on later periods, I would mention *The Scandinavian Reformation from evangelical movements to institutionalisation of reform,* edited by Ole Peter Grell, Cambridge University Press, 1995, and *German and Scandinavian Protestantism, 1700–1918,* by Nicholas Hope, Oxford University Press, 1995.

The document on Porvoo: *The Porvoo Common Statement. Conversations between the British and Irish Anglican Churches and the Nordic and Baltic Lutheran Churches* is published by The Council for Christian Unity of the General Synod of the Church of England, Occasional Paper No.3, 1993, together with a collection of essays: *Essays on Church and Ministry in Northern Europe,* published by Church House Publishing, London, 1993.

The origin of each picture included is given in the appended text. The letters 'ATA' stands for 'The Antiquarian-Topographical Archive' in Stockholm. I would like to thank all those institutions and photographers who have made their material available for inclusion in this book.

Index of Names

J

Jablonski, Daniel Ernst, 127, 128, 139, 130, 131
James I, 96, 97
James Edward Stuart, 132
Jasper, Ronald, 241
Jensen-Klint, 175
Jewell, John, 92
Johan III, 67, 68, 69, 81, 82, 91
Johannes Botvidi, 100
Johansson, Gustav, 246, 255
Johansson, Hilding, 24
John Paul II, 31, 46, 297
Johnson, Gisle, 160
Jon Arason, 74
Juusten, Paul, 82
Jørgen (George), 144
Jørgensen, Ellen, 51

K

Kaila, Erkki, 255, 262
Kant, Immanuel, 220
Katarina of Sachen-Lauenburg, 65, 78
Katarina Jagellonica, 66
Keble, John, 180, 181
Kekkonen, Urho, 161
Kibira, J, 293
Kierkegaard, Søren, 169, 173, 177, 178
Kingsley, Charles, 28
Kjöllerström, Sven, 79, 82
Klaveness, Thorvald, 221
Klingert, Rune, 271
Knud, St, 38, 39, 51
Knud Lavard, 33
Koch, Hal, 262
Koch, Jørgen, 73
Konstantinos VIII, 15
Kukk, J, 250

L

Lagerfelt, Israel, 102
Lamberg, Erik, 150, 151
Lampe, Geoffrey, 267, 274, 305
Lang, C G, 239
Laud, William, 101
Laurentius Andreae, 62
Laurentius Petri, 63, 65, 66, 67, 68, 78, 80, 81, 96, 142
Lee, Robert, 207
Lehtonen, Aleksi, 255, 259
von Leibniz, G W, 129
Lidén, Johan Hinric, 151, 152
Lindhart, P G, 59
Longley, Charles Thomas, 206
Lönnebo, Martin, 303
Louis the Pious, 8
Lund, David, 132, 170, 171
Lunde, Johan, 247
Lundström, Herman, 229, 233
Luther, Martin, 61, 62, 71, 73, 94, 95, 104, 110, 118, 134, 158, 162, 188
Lysander, Albert, 276
Lyttkens, Carl Henrik, 200, 225
Lönegren, Ernst, 255

M

Margareta, Crown Princess, 232
Margrethe I, 47
Marlborough, John Churchill, Duke of Marlborough, 125
Martensen, H L, 177
Mary Tudor, 65
Mary II Stuart, 113, 143
May, F S, 202, 203, 208
Melanchton, Philip, 94
Mikael Agricola, 82
Mill, John Stuart, 223
Molland, Einar, 159, 262, 279
Mundy, Peter, 97
Mynster, J P, 177, 178
Månsson, Fabian, 260

316